高等学校"十二五"规划教材

给排水科学与工程专业应用与实践丛书

给排水科学与工程专业英语

蓝 梅 ■ 主编

陈 新　苏馈足 ■ 副主编

化学工业出版社

·北京·

丛书编委会名单

主　　　任：蒋展鹏
副　主　任：彭永臻　章北平
编委会成员（按姓氏汉语拼音排列）：
　　　　　　　崔玉川　蓝　梅　李　军　刘俊良　唐朝春　王　宏　王亚军
　　　　　　　徐得潜　鄢恒珍　杨开明　张崇淼　张林军　张　伟　赵　远

内容提要

本书涵盖了给水排水科学与工程专业给排水管网、水和废水处理技术、污泥的处理处置以及建筑给排水系统，知识结构全面合理。具体包括六个部分。第一部分是水系统循环概述，第二部分为供水及输配水系统和污水（雨水）收集与排水系统，第三部分为水的物理化学处理法，第四部分为污水的生物处理法，第五部分为污泥的处理利用与处置，第六部分为建筑给水排水系统。

全书 23 个单元，每个单元包括一篇课文，两篇阅读材料，并附有难点注释、词汇表、练习题。希望能使读者掌握阅读翻译专业文献资料的基本技能和技巧，获取国外与本专业有关的科技信息。

本书可供给排水科学与工程专业、市政工程专业和环境工程专业的师生使用，也可作为相关行业人员的阅读参考资料。

图书在版编目（CIP）数据

给排水科学与工程专业英语/蓝梅主编.—北京：
化学工业出版社，2013.1（2025.1重印）
高等学校"十二五"规划教材
（给排水科学与工程专业应用与实践丛书）
ISBN 978-7-122-16263-2

Ⅰ.①给… Ⅱ.①蓝… Ⅲ.①给排水系统-英语
Ⅳ.①H31

中国版本图书馆 CIP 数据核字（2013）第 003733 号

责任编辑：徐　娟　　　　　　　　　　　　　　装帧设计：关　飞
责任校对：宋　夏

出版发行：化学工业出版社（北京市东城区青年湖南街 13 号　邮政编码 100011）
印　　装：北京虎彩文化传播有限公司
787mm×1092mm　1/16　印张 13　字数 328 千字　2025 年 1 月北京第 1 版第 19 次印刷

购书咨询：010-64518888　　　售后服务：010-64518899
网　　址：http://www.cip.com.cn
凡购买本书，如有缺损质量问题，本社销售中心负责调换。

定　　价：32.00 元　　　　　　　　　　　　　　　　　　　版权所有　违者必究

丛 书 序

在国家现代化建设的进程中,生态文明建设与经济建设、政治建设、文化建设和社会建设相并列,形成五位一体的全面建设发展道路。建设生态文明是关系人民福祉,关乎民族未来的长远大计。而在生态文明建设的诸多专业任务中,给排水工程是一个不可缺少的重要组成部分。培养给排水工程专业的各类优秀人才也就成为当前一项刻不容缓的重要任务。

21世纪我国的工程教育改革趋势是"回归工程",工程教育将更加重视工程思维训练,强调工程实践能力。针对工科院校给排水工程专业的特点和发展趋势,为了培养和提高学生综合运用各门课程基本理论、基本知识来分析解决实际工程问题的能力,总结近年来给排水工程发展的实践经验,我非常高兴化学工业出版社能组织全国几十所高校的一线教师编写这套丛书。

本套丛书突出"回归工程"的指导思想,为适应培养高等技术应用型人才的需要,立足教学和工程实际,在讲解基本理论、基础知识的前提下,重点介绍近年来出现的新工艺、新技术与新方法。丛书中编入了更多的工程实际案例或例题、习题,内容更简明易懂,实用性更强,使学生能更好地应对未来的工作。

本套丛书于"十二五"期间出版,对各高校给排水科学与工程专业和市政工程专业、环境工程专业的师生而言,会是非常实用的系列教学用书。

蒋展鹏

2013年1月

前　言

　　为了提高高等学校给排水科学与工程、环境工程和环境科学专业学生阅读和翻译英文专业文献的能力，扩大专业词汇量、掌握学科发展的动态、参加国际交流以及今后在工作学习中获取专业知识，我们感到非常有必要编写一本专业性较强并结合当今水处理新技术的专业英语教材。因此我们根据大学专业英语教学大纲的要求，结合给排水科学与工程专业英语教学实践的经验和体会，根据给水排水行业的发展状况编写了本书。

　　本书英文文献选材针对性强，兼顾专业性和学术性，题材范围广泛、难度适中，紧密结合学生学习的专业知识和当今给排水科学与工程的新理论、新技术。考虑到专业技术的发展、课堂教学的时间以及学生知识结构能方面的因素，本书主要包括六个部分。第一部分是水系统循环概述，第二部分为供水及输配水系统和污水（雨水）收集与排水系统，第三部分为水的物理化学处理法，第四部分为污水的生物处理法，第五部分为污泥的处理利用与处置，第六部分为建筑给水排水系统。涵盖了给水排水科学与工程专业给排水管网、水和废水处理技术、污泥的处理处置以及建筑给排水系统，知识结构全面合理。建筑给水排水是给排水科学与工程专业一个非常重要的组成部分，针对目前面市的给水排水专业英语教材中基本没有或很少涉及建筑给水排水内容的情况，本书特增加该部分课文和阅读材料。希望通过学习和练习使学生掌握阅读翻译专业文献资料的基本技能和技巧，获取国外与本专业有关的科技信息。

　　本书由河北工程大学蓝梅主编，苏州科技学院陈新、合肥工业大学苏馈足副主编，合肥工业大学王玉兰，常州大学赵玲萍，北京建筑工程学院冯利利，河北建筑工程学院王淑娜，东北石油大学林红岩，内蒙古农业大学杨红，徐州工程学院万蕾，黑龙江建筑职业技术学院李丽参加编写。全书由蓝梅统稿。本书在编写过程中，得到河北工程大学李清雪教授的大力支持，在此表示由衷的谢意！

　　鉴于编者水平所限，书中难免有疏漏和不足之处，恳请广大读者和同行专家给予批评指正。

编者
2013 年 1 月

目 录

Part One　Introduction ·· 1
　Unit 1　Hydrologic Cycle ··· 1
　　Important Words and Expressions ··· 3
　　Exercises ·· 4
　　Reading Material A ·· 4
　　Reading Material B ·· 7
　Unit 2　Water Legislation and Regulation ·· 8
　　Important Words and Expressions ··· 10
　　Exercises ·· 11
　　Reading Material A ·· 12
　　Reading Material B ·· 14
　Unit 3　Analytical Technique and Methodology ·· 16
　　Important Words and Expressions ··· 18
　　Exercises ·· 19
　　Reading Material A ·· 20
　　Reading Material B ·· 22

Part Two　Water Supply and Sewerage System ··· 24
　Unit 4　Water Supply System ··· 24
　　Important Words and Expressions ··· 25
　　Exercises ·· 26
　　Reading Material A ·· 27
　　Reading Material B ·· 29
　Unit 5　Wastewater Collection and Sewerage System Design ··· 31
　　Important Words and Expressions ··· 34
　　Exercises ·· 35
　　Reading Material A ·· 36
　　Reading Material B ·· 39
　Unit 6　Stormwater Collection and Sewer Design ··· 41
　　Important Words and Expressions ··· 43
　　Exercises ·· 44
　　Reading Material A ·· 45
　　Reading Material B ·· 47
　Unit 7　Pumps and Pumping Stations ··· 50

Important Words and Expressions ··· 53
Exercises ··· 54
Reading Material A ··· 55
Reading Material B ··· 57

Part Three Physical-Chemical Treatment Process ··· 60
Unit 8   Coagulation and Flocculation ··· 60
Important Words and Expressions ··· 62
Exercises ··· 63
Reading Material A ··· 64
Reading Material B ··· 67
Unit 9   Sedimentation ··· 69
Important Words and Expressions ··· 72
Exercises ··· 73
Reading Material A ··· 74
Reading Material B ··· 76
Unit 10   Filtration ··· 79
Important Words and Expressions ··· 81
Exercises ··· 81
Reading Material A ··· 82
Reading Material B ··· 86
Unit 11   Chemical Oxidation ··· 88
Important Words and Expressions ··· 91
Exercises ··· 92
Reading Material A ··· 93
Reading Material B ··· 96
Unit 12   Adsorption ··· 99
Important Words and Expressions ··· 102
Exercises ··· 103
Reading Material A ··· 104
Reading Material B ··· 107
Unit 13   Membrane Filtration Processes ··· 110
Important Words and Expressions ··· 112
Exercises ··· 113
Reading Material A ··· 114
Reading Material B ··· 116

Part Four Biological Treatment Process ··· 118
Unit 14   Activated Sludge Process ··· 118
Important Words and Expressions ··· 120
Exercises ··· 120

  Reading Material A ··· 121
  Reading Material B ··· 123
 Unit 15 Attached Growth Biological Treatment Process ··············· 125
  Important Words and Expressions ··· 127
  Exercises ··· 128
  Reading Material A ··· 129
  Reading Material B ··· 131
 Unit 16 Anaerobic Biological Treatment ··· 134
  Important Words and Expressions ··· 136
  Exercises ··· 137
  Reading Material A ··· 138
  Reading Material B ··· 139

Part Five Sludge Treatment, Reuse and Disposal ··············· 142
 Unit 17 Thickening ··· 142
  Important Words and Expressions ··· 144
  Exercises ··· 144
  Reading Material A ··· 145
  Reading Material B ··· 148
 Unit 18 Anaerobic Digestion ··· 150
  Important Words and Expressions ··· 152
  Exercises ··· 153
  Reading Material A ··· 154
  Reading Material B ··· 157
 Unit 19 Dewatering ··· 160
  Important Words and Expressions ··· 163
  Exercises ··· 164
  Reading Material A ··· 164
  Reading Material B ··· 167
 Unit 20 Sludge Utilization and Disposal ··· 170
  Important Words and Expressions ··· 171
  Exercises ··· 172
  Reading Material A ··· 173
  Reading Material B ··· 175

Part Six Building Water Supply and Drainage ······················ 178
 Unit 21 Cold Water Supply ··· 178
  Important Words and Expressions ··· 180
  Exercises ··· 180
  Reading Material A ··· 181
  Reading Material B ··· 183

Unit 22　Building-Drainage System ·· 185
　　Important Words and Expressions ·· 187
　　Exercises ·· 187
　　Reading Material A ··· 188
　　Reading Material B ··· 189
Unit 23　Fire-Fighting Systems ··· 192
　　Important Words and Expressions ·· 194
　　Exercises ·· 195
　　Reading Material A ··· 196
　　Reading Material B ··· 197

References ·· 200

Part One

Introduction

Unit 1 Hydrologic Cycle

The hydrologic cycle (Figure 1.1), also known as the water cycle or H_2O cycle, describes the continuous movement of water on, above and below the surface of the earth. Water can change states among liquid, vapour, and solid at various places in the water cycle. Although the balance of water on Earth remains fairly constant over time, individual water molecules can come and go, in and out of the atmosphere. The water moves from one reservoir to another, such as from river to ocean, or from the ocean to the atmosphere, by the physical processes of evaporation, condensation, precipitation, infiltration, runoff, and subsurface flow. [1] In so doing, the water goes through different phases: liquid, solid, and gas.

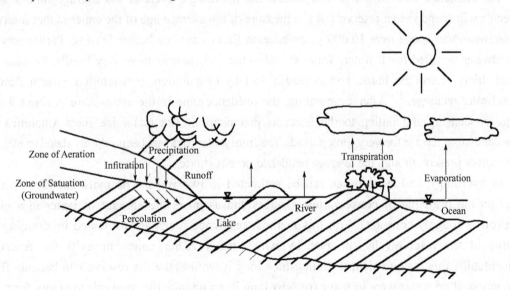

Figure 1.1 The hydrologic cycle

The water cycle involves the exchange of heat energy, which leads to temperature changes. For instance, in the process of evaporation, water takes up energy from the surroundings and cools the environment. Conversely, in the process of condensation, water releases energy to its surroundings, warming the environment. The water cycle figures significantly in the maintenance of life and ecosystems on Earth. Even as water in each reservoir plays an important role, the water cycle brings added significance to the presence of water on our planet. By transferring water from one reservoir to another, the water cycle purifies water, replenishes the land with freshwater, and transports minerals to different parts of the globe. [2] It is also involved in reshaping the geological features of the Earth, through such processes as erosion and sedimentation. In addition, as the water cycle also involves heat exchange, it exerts an influence on climate as well.

The sun, which drives the water cycle, heats water in oceans and seas. Water evaporates as water vapor into the air. Ice and snow can sublimate directly into water vapor. Evapotranspiration is water transpired from plants and evaporated from the soil. Rising air currents take the vapor up into the atmosphere where cooler temperatures cause it to condense into clouds. Air currents move water vapor around the globe, cloud particles collide, grow, and fall out of the sky as precipitation. Some precipitation falls as snow or hail, sleet, and can accumulate as ice caps and glaciers, which can store frozen water for thousands of years. Most water falls back into the oceans or onto land as rain, where the water flows over the ground as surface runoff. A portion of runoff enters rivers in valleys in the landscape, with streamflow moving water towards the oceans. Runoff and groundwater are stored as freshwater in lakes. Not all runoff flows into rivers, much of it soaks into the ground as infiltration. Some water infiltrates deep into the ground and replenishes aquifers, which store freshwater for long periods of time. Some infiltration stays close to the land surface and can seep back into surface-water bodies (and the ocean) as groundwater discharge. Some groundwater finds openings in the land surface and comes out as freshwater springs. Over time, the water returns to the ocean, where our water cycle started.

The residence time of a reservoir within the hydrologic cycle is the average time a water molecule will spend in that reservoir. It is a measure of the average age of the water in that reservoir. Groundwater can spend over 10,000 years beneath Earth's surface before leaving. Particularly old groundwater is called fossil water. Water stored in the soil remains there very briefly, because it is spread thinly across the Earth, and is readily lost by evaporation, transpiration, stream flow, or groundwater recharge. [3] After evaporating, the residence time in the atmosphere is about 9 days before condensing and falling to the Earth as precipitation. The major ice sheet-Antarctica and Greenland-store ice are for very long periods. Ice from Antarctica has been reliably dated to 800,000 years before present, though the average residence time is shorter.

In hydrology, residence times can be estimated in two ways. The more common method relies on the principle of conservation of mass and assumes the amount of water in a given reservoir is roughly constant. With this method, residence times are estimated by dividing the volume of the reservoir by the rate by which water either enters or exits the reservoir. Conceptually, this is equivalent to timing how long it would take the reservoir to become filled from empty if no water were to leave (or how long it would take the reservoir to empty from full if no water were to enter). An alternative method to estimate residence times, which is gaining in popularity for dating groundwater, is the use of isotopic techniques. This is done in the subfield of isotope hydrology.

Human activities that alter the water cycle include:
- Agriculture
- Industry
- Alteration of the chemical composition of the atmosphere

- Construction of dams
- Deforestation and afforestation
- Removal of groundwater from wells
- Water abstraction from rivers
- Urbanization

Effects on climate: The water cycle is powered from solar energy. 86% of the global evaporation occurs from the oceans, reducing their temperature by evaporative cooling. Without the cooling, the effect of evaporation on the greenhouse effect would lead to a much higher surface temperature of 67℃ (153℉), and a warmer planet.

Aquifer drawdown or overdrafting and the pumping of fossil water increases the total amount of water in the hydrosphere that is subject to transpiration and evaporation thereby causing accretion in water vapour and cloud cover which are the primary absorbers of infrared radiation in the Earth's atmosphere. [4] Adding water to the system has a forcing effect on the whole earth system, an accurate estimate of which hydrogeological fact is yet to be quantified.

Important Words and Expressions

hydrology [haiˈdrɔlədʒi]　n. 水文学，水文地理学
reservoir [ˈrezəvwa:]　n. 蓄水池；储液器；储藏；蓄积
evaporation [iˌvæpəˈreiʃən]　n. 蒸发，发散；消失
condensation [ˌkɔndenˈseiʃən]　n. 冷凝；冷凝液；凝结的水珠；节略
precipitation [priˌsipiˈteiʃən]　n. 匆促；沉淀；（雨等）降落；某地区降雨等的量
figure [ˈfigə]　n. 数字；算术；图解；轮廓　vt. 估计；推测；认为
replenish [riˈpleniʃ]　vt. 补充；重新装满；把…装满
sedimentation [ˌsedimenˈteiʃən]　n. 沉淀，沉降
sublimate [ˈsʌblimət]　n. 升华物　vt. (使某物质)升华；使净化；纯化
infiltration [ˌinfilˈtreiʃən]　n. 渗透
residence time　停留时间
deforestation [ˌdiˌfɔriˈsteiʃn]　n. 采伐森林，森林开伐
afforestation [əˌfɔriˈsteiʃən]　n. 造林，造林地区
aquifer [ˈækwifə]　n. 地下蓄水层，砂石含水层

Notes

[1] 由于蒸发、凝结、降水、入渗、径流、潜流等物理过程，水从一个蓄水池到另一个，比如从河流到海洋，从海洋到大气。

[2] 通过水从一个蓄水池到另一个，水循环净化了水，为陆地补充了淡水，把矿物质运送到地球不同的部位。

[3] 土壤中储存的水停留很短暂，因为土壤水薄薄地分布在地表，通过蒸发、蒸腾、河川径流和地下水补给而容易消失。

[4] 地下水位降低或者超采以及化石水的抽取增加了水圈中水的总量，水圈中的水易于蒸腾和蒸发，从而产生水蒸气以及云量的堆积，这些是地球大气中红外辐射最主要的吸收体。

Exercises

1. Answering the following questions in English according to the text:

(1) How many physical processes happened in hydrologic cycle according to the text?

(2) Try to explain the method of estimating the residence time of the water.

2. Using the following each word to make up the sentences, respectively:

(1) Hydrologic cycle

(2) subsurface flow

(3) runoff

(4) residence time

(5) conservation of mass

3. Put the following English into Chinese:

(1) Groundwater is an important direct source of supply that is tapped by wells, as well as a significant indirect source since surface streams are often supplied by subterranean water. Near the surface of the earth, in the zone of aeration, soil pore spaces contain both air and water. This zone, which may have zero thickness in swamplands and be several hundred feet thick in mountainous regions, contains three types of moisture. After a storm, gravity water is in transit through the larger soil pore spaces. Capillary water is drawn small pore spaces by capillary action and is available for plant uptake. Hygroscopic moisture is held in place by molecular forces during all except the driest climatic conditions. Moisture from the zone of aeration cannot be tapped as a water supply source.

(2) In the zone of saturation, located below the zone of aeration, the soil pores are filled with water, and this is what we call groundwater. A stratum that contains a substantial amount of groundwater is called an aquifer. At the surface between the two zones, called the water table or phreatic surface, the hydrostatic pressure in the groundwater is equal to the atmosphere pressure. An aquifer may extend to great depths, but because the weight of overburden material generally closes pore spaces, little water is found at depths greater than 600m (1200ft). The amount of water that will drain freely from an aquifer is known as specific yield.

4. Put the following Chinese into English:

(1) 水循环

(2) 蒸发

(3) 停留时间

(4) 地球上的水不是静止的，而是不断运动变化和相互交换的。

(5) 在太阳辐射和地心吸引力的作用下，地球上各种状态的水从海洋面、江河面、湖沼面、陆地面和动植物表面蒸发、蒸腾变成水汽，上升于空中，或停留在空中，或被气流带到其他地区，在适当条件下凝结，然后以降水形式落到海洋面或陆地表面。

Reading Material A

The Water Balance

In hydrology, a water balance equation can be used to describe the flow of water in and out of a system. A system can be one of several hydrological domains, such as a column of soil or a drainage basin. Water balance can also refer to the ways in which an organism maintains water in dry or hot conditions. It is often discussed in reference to plants or arthropods, which have a variety of water retention mechanisms, including a lipid waxy coating that has limited permeability. [1]

Water balance calculations

Water balance calculations can help to determine if a drainage area is large enough or has the right characteristics to support a permanent pool of water during average or extreme conditions. [2]

When in doubt, a water balance calculation may be advisable for retention pond and wetland design. The details of a rigorous water balance are beyond the scope of this manual. However, a simplified procedure is described herein that will provide an estimate of pool viability and point to the need for more rigorous analysis. Water balance can also be used to help establish planting zones in a wetland design.

Basic equations

Water balance is defined as the change in volume of the permanent pool resulting from the total inflow minus the total outflow (actual or potential). Equation 1-1 presents this calculation.

$$\Delta V = \Sigma I - \Sigma O \qquad (1\text{-}1)$$

where

Δ = delta or change in

V = pond volume (ac-ft)

Σ = the sum of

I = Inflows (ac-ft)

O = Outflows (ac-ft)

The inflows consist of rainfall, runoff and baseflow into the pond. The outflows consist of infiltration, evaporation, evapotranspiration, and surface overflow out of the pond or wetland. Equation 1-1 can be expanded to reflect these factors, as shown in Equation 1-2. Key variables in Equation 1-2 are discussed in detail below the equation.

$$\Delta V = PA + R_0 + B_f - IA - EA - E_t A - O_f \qquad (1\text{-}2)$$

where

P = precipitation (ft)

A = area of pond (ac)

R_0 = runoff (ac-ft)

B_f = baseflow (ac-ft)

I = infiltration (ft)

E = evaporation (ft)

E_t = evapotranspiration (ft)

O_f = overflow (ac-ft)

Rainfall (P) Monthly rainfall values can be obtained from the National Weather Service climatology at http://www.srh.noaa.gov/mrx/climat.htm. Monthly values are commonly used for calculations of values over a season. Rainfall is then the direct amount that falls on the pond surface for the period in question. When multiplied by the pond surface area (in acres) it becomes acre-feet of volume.

Runoff (R_0) Runoff is equivalent to the rainfall for the period times the efficiency of the watershed, which is equal to the ratio of runoff to rainfall (Q/P). In lieu of gage information, Q/P can be estimated one of several ways. The best method would be to perform long-term simulation modeling using rainfall records and a watershed model.

Baseflow (B) Most stormwater ponds and wetlands have little, if any, baseflow, as they are rarely placed across perennial streams. If so placed, baseflow must be estimated from observation or through theoretical estimates. Methods of estimation and baseflow separation can be found in most hydrology textbooks.

Infiltration (I) Infiltration is a very complex subject and cannot be covered in detail here. The amount of infiltration depends on soils, water table depth, rock layers, surface disturbance, the presence or absence of a liner in the pond, and other factors.

Evaporation (E) Evaporation is from an open lake water surface. Evaporation rates are dependent on differences in vapor pressure, which, in turn, depend on temperature, wind, atmospheric pressure, water purity, and shape and depth of the pond.[3] It is estimated or measured in a number of ways, which can be found in most hydrology textbooks. Pan evaporation methods are also used, though there are no longer pan evaporation sites active in Knox County. Formerly pan evaporation methods were utilized at the Knoxville Experiment Station.

Evapotranspiration (E_t) Evapotranspiration consists of the combination of evaporation and transpiration by plants. The estimation of E_t for crops is well documented and has become standard practice. However, the estimating methods for wetlands are not documented, nor are there consistent studies to assist the designer in estimating the wetland plant demand on water volumes. Literature values for various places in the United States vary around the free water surface lake evaporation values. Estimating E_t only becomes important when wetlands are being designed and emergent vegetation covers a significant portion of the pond surface. In these cases conservative estimates of lake evaporation should be compared to crop-based E_t estimates and a decision made. Crop-based E_t estimates can be obtained from typical hydrology textbooks or from the web sites mentioned above. A value of zero shall be assumed for E_t unless the wetland design dictates otherwise.

Overflow (O_f) Overflow is considered as excess runoff, and in water balance design is either not considered since the concern is for average precipitation values, or is considered lost for all volumes above the maximum pond storage.[4] Obviously, for long-term simulations of rainfall-runoff, large storms would play an important part in pond design.

Notes

[1] 关于植物或者节肢动物的水平衡也经常被论及，有多种水保持机制，包括有限渗透性的脂蜡质覆盖层。

[2] 水平衡的计算可以帮助确定一个排水区域是否足够大或者是否能够在平常或极端条件下支撑一个永久的水池。

[3] 蒸发速率取决于蒸汽压的不同，而蒸汽压依次取决于温度、风、大气压力、水的纯度、水池的形状和深度。

[4] 溢流被认为是多余的径流，在水平衡设计中，要么因为关心的是平均降水量，不被考虑，要么是作为超出最大池容量的所有容积损失。

Reading Material B
Water Resources Protection

Water resources involve surface water, water below ground and water that falls from the sky. Protecting groundwater resources will be a major challenge in coming years because of increased development pressures and water demands, climate change, and the uncertainty of surface water availability.

Groundwater is a hidden resource, and to learn more about this resource we have to rely on more than our five senses. Fortunately, we do not have to resort to dowsing to gain a better understanding of groundwater. Groundwater mapping and modeling helps us make decisions about how to manage water resources in terms of both water quality and water quantity. [1]

Groundwater is one of the nation's most critical natural resources. It is the largest source of usable water storage in the United States, containing more water than all reservoirs and lakes combined, excluding the Great Lakes. According to scientists, an estimated 1 million cubic miles of groundwater is located within one-half mile of the land surface. Only a very small percentage of groundwater is accessible and can be used for human activities. Most cities meet their needs for water by withdrawing it from the nearest river, lake, reservoir, but many depend on groundwater as well. [2]

Water is already in short supply in many parts of the United States, and the situation is only going to get worse. According to a 1999 United States Geological Survey. Groundwater is the source of about 40% of the water used for public supply and provides drinking water for more than 97% of the rural population in the United States. [3] Between 30% and 40% of the water used for the agricultural industry comes from groundwater. We need to understand groundwater if we are going to continue to make good decisions about sustainable water resources.

In recent years, people have begun to understand that groundwater and surface water are fundamentally interconnected and are integral components of the hydrologic cycle. Nevertheless, most laws governing groundwater issues are based on this notion that groundwater and surface water have nothing to do with each other. In most parts of the country, surface water is governed by doctrines of riparian law or prior appropriation.Groundwater traditionally has been treated as a common resource, with virtually no restrictions on accessing the water. If you can afford to pay someone to drill a well and you happen to hit water, you can do whatever you want with it.

The unregulated pumping of groundwater is no longer a viable option. In many parts of the country, groundwater is being withdrawn at rates that are no sustainable, and the result is a degradation of water quality and quantity. [4] The water level in aquifers is being lowered, and because we keep digging deeper and deeper wells to access the water, the water quantity is further depleted. In coastal areas, intensive pumping of fresh groundwater has caused saltwater to seep into freshwater aquifers.

Groundwater is also critical for the environmental health of rivers, wetlands and estuaries throughout the country. Groundwater withdrawals can result in reduced flows to streams and alter wetland hydrology. Changes in stream flow have important implications for water and flood management, irrigation and planning.

There are hundreds of examples across the country where groundwater is threatened. The California Department of Health Services reported in 2008 that more than 300 public supply sources and an equally large number of private homeowner wells were contaminated and should not be used.[5] In portions of the Southwest, Northwest, and Midwest, arsenic occers naturally in groundwater at levels that exceed drinking water standards and many municipalities are now debating whether to build treatment plants or reservoirs. Either will cost hundreds of millions of dollars.

According to the Arizona Department of Environmental Quality, approximately one-third of Arizona water systems exceed the level set for arsenic poisoning. One long-term impact of the 1988 drought in the Midwest is that many aquifers were overpumped by farmers seeking to save their crops and their way of life. Arkansas residents use groundwater to meet approximately 93% of their water needs.

In many parts of Florida, the existing aquifer is not sufficient to meet the needs of the state's growing population and the needs of the environment, agriculture, and industry. Florida is one of four states in the country that uses more groundwater than surface water.

The Ground Water Protection Council (2007) has defined a broad vision of what it would take to maintain a sustainable source of groundwater. It wrote that the nation needs to: Continue to conduct research and provide information-at a scale that is useful to states and local entities-about such matters as the safe, or sustainable, yield of aquifers (and methods for determining that yield); water-use data; and delineating boundaries and water budgets of three-dimensional watersheds, including scientifically based and cost-effective methods of quantifying interactions between ground water and surface water.

Notes

[1] 地下水的测绘和模型帮助从水质和水量两个方面管理水资源。

[2] 许多城市从最近的河流、湖泊，或者水库中抽水满足他们的需求，但是也有很多是依赖地下水的。

[3] 依据美国1999年的地质调查，公共供水中的40%来自于地下水，地下水为97%的美国农村人口提供饮用水。

[4] 国内许多地方，地下水的抽取速度是不可持续的，结果是导致了水质和水量的下降。

[5] 加利福尼亚卫生服务部门2008年报告：超过300个公共供应来源和同样数量的私人水井被污染了并且不能再使用。

Unit 2   Water Legislation and Regulation

The aim of national drinking-water laws and standards should be to ensure that the consumer enjoys safe potable water, not to shut down deficient water supplies.

Effective control of drinking-water quality is supported ideally by adequate legislation, standards and codes and their enforcement. The precise nature of the legislation in each country will depend on national, constitutional and other considerations. It will generally outline the responsibility and authority of a number of agencies and describe the relationship between them, as well as establish basic policy principles (e.g. water supplied for drinking-water should be safe). The national regulations, adjusted as necessary, should be applicable to all water supplies. This would normally embody different approaches to situations where formal responsibility for drinking water quality is assigned to a defined entity and situations where community management prevails.[1]

Legislation should make provision for the establishment and amendment of drinking-water quality standards and guidelines, as well as for the establishment of regulations for the development and protection of drinking-water sources and the treatment, maintenance and distribution of safe drinking-water.

Legislation should establish the legal functions and responsibilities of the water supplier and would generally specify that the water supplier is legally responsible at all times for the quality of the water sold and/or supplied to the consumer and for the proper supervision, inspection, maintenance and safe operation of the drinking-water system.[2] It is the water supplier that actually provides water to the public-the "consumer"-and that should be legally responsible for its quality and safety. The supplier is responsible for continuous and effective quality assurance and quality control of water supplies, including inspection, supervision, preventive maintenance, routine testing of water quality and remedial actions as required. However, the supplier is normally responsible for the quality of the water only up to a defined point in the distribution system and may not have responsibility for deterioration of water quality as a result of poor plumbing or unsatisfactory storage tanks in households and buildings.

Where consecutive agencies manage water-for example, a drinking-water wholesaler, a municipal water supplier and a local water distribution company-each agency should carry responsibility for the quality of the water arising from its actions.

Legal and organizational arrangements aimed at ensuring compliance with the legislation, standards or codes of practice for drinking-water quality will normally provide for an independent surveillance agency, as outlined in section 1.2.1 and chapter 5. The legislation should define the duties, obligations and powers of the water surveillance agency. The surveillance agency should preferably be represented at the national level and should operate at national, regional and local levels. The surveillance agency should be given the necessary powers to administer and enforce laws, regulations, standards and codes concerned with water quality. It should also be able to delegate those powers to other specified agencies, such as municipal councils, local health departments, regional authorities and qualified, government-authorized private audit or testing services. Its responsibilities should include the surveillance of water quality to ensure that water delivered to the consumer, through either piped or non-piped distribution systems, meets drinking-water supply service standards; approving sources of drinking-water; and surveying the provision of drinking-water to the population as a whole.[3] There needs to be a high level of knowledge, training and understanding in such an agency in order that drinking-water supply does not suffer from inappropriate regulatory action. The surveillance agency should be empowered by law to compel water suppliers to recommend the boiling of water or other measures when microbial contamination that could threaten public health is detected.

Implementation of programmes to provide safe drinking-water should not be delayed because of a lack of appropriate legislation. Even where legally binding guidelines or standards for drinking-water have yet to be promulgated, it may be possible to encourage, and even enforce, the supply of safe drinking-water through educational efforts or commercial, contractual arrangements between consumer and supplier (e.g., based on civil law) or through interim measures, including health, food or welfare legislation, for example.

Drinking-water quality legislation may usefully provide for interim standards, permitted deviations and exemptions as part of a national or regional policy, rather than as a result of local initiatives. [4] This can take the form of temporary exemptions for certain communities or areas for defined periods of time. Short- and medium-term targets should be set so that the most significant risks to human health are controlled first.

The authority to establish and revise drinking-water standards, codes of practice and other technical regulations should be delegated to the appropriate government minister – preferably the minister of health – who is responsible for ensuring the safety of water supplies and the protection of public health. The authority to establish and enforce quality standards and regulations may be vested in a ministry other than the one usually responsible for public and/or environmental health. Consideration should then be given to requiring that regulations and standards are promulgated only after approval by the public health or environmental health authority so as to ensure their conformity with health protection principles.

Drinking-water supply policy should normally outline the requirements for protection of water sources and resources, the need for appropriate treatment, preventive maintenance within distribution systems and requirements to support maintaining water safety after collection from communal sources.

The basic water legislation should not specify sampling frequencies but should give the administration the power to establish a list of parameters to be measured and the frequency and location of such measurements. [5] Standards and codes should normally specify the quality of the water to be supplied to the consumer, the practices to be followed in selecting and developing water sources and in treatment processes and distribution or household storage systems, and procedures for approving water systems in terms of water quality.

Setting national standards should ideally involve consideration of the quality of the water, the quality of service, "target setting" and the quality of infrastructure and systems, as well as enforcement action. For example, national standards should define protection zones around water sources, minimum standard specifications for operating systems, hygiene practice standards in construction and minimum standards for health protection. Some countries include these details in a "sanitary code" or "code of good practice". It is preferable to include in regulations the requirement to consult with drinking-water supply agencies and appropriate professional bodies, since doing so makes it more likely that drinking-water controls will be implemented effectively.

Important Words and Expressions

  legislation [ˌledʒisˈleiʃən] n. 立法，制定法律；法律，法规
  outline [ˈautlain] n. 梗概，大纲 vt. 概述；略述
  provision [prəˈviʒən] n. 规定，条项，条款 vt.& vi. 为…提供所需物品
  supervision [ˌsjuːpəˈviʒən] n. 监督；管理；监督的行为、过程或作用
  inspection [inˈspekʃən] n. 检查；检验；视察；检阅
  deterioration [diˌtiriəˈreiʃən] n. 恶化；变坏；退化；堕落

consecutive [kən'sekjutiv]   adj. 连续的，连贯的
surveillance [sə'veiləns]   n. 盯梢，监督
delegate ['deligit]   n. 代表，代表团成员   vt. 委派代表；授权给
audit ['ɔːdit]   n. 审计，查账   vt. 审计，查账；旁听   vi. 审计
promulgate ['prɔməl,geit]   vt. 宣扬（某事物）；传播；公布；颁布（法令、新法律等）
interim ['intərim]   adj. 暂时的，临时的；期中的   n. 间歇，过渡期间；临时协定
preventive [pri'ventiv]   n. 预防；防止；预防措施；预防药   adj. 预防的；防止的
infrastructure ['infrə,strʌktʃə]   n. 基础设施；基础建设

Notes

[1] 对于社区管理盛行的情况或者饮用水水质规范中的责任被分配给明确的实体的情况，国家规范通常会体现出不同的方法。

[2] 立法应该确立供水商的法律职能和责任，而且应该明确提出供水商在任何时间对于出售或者提供给消费者的水的水质以及对饮用水系统的正确的监督、检验、维护和安全操作负有法律责任。

[3] 监督机构的职责应该包括监测水质，保证通过管道或者非管道分配系统输送到用户的水符合饮用水供应服务标准；核准饮用水来源；把提供给全体居民的饮用水作为整体进行测量。

[4] 饮用水水质立法在规定作为国家或者区域政策一部分的允许偏差和豁免的暂行标准方面可能比作为地区倡议的结果更为有用。

[5] 基本的水法不应该指定取样频率而是应该赋予行政机关权力来制定一系列需要检测的参数以及这些测定的频率和地点。

Exercises

1. Answering the following questions in English according to the text:
　(1) What is the aim of national drinking-water laws and standards?
　(2) Which aspect may be useful for the use of Drinking-water quality legislation?

2. Using the following each word to make up the sentences, respectively:
　(1) water quality
　(2) protection of water sources
　(3) water supply
　(4) drinking-water
　(5) microbial contamination

3. Put the following English into Chinese:
　(1) The costs associated with drinking-water quality surveillance and control should be taken into account in developing national legislation and standards. To ensure that standards are acceptable to consumers, communities served, together with the major water users, should be involved in the standards-setting process. Public health agencies may be closer to the community than those responsible for its drinking-water supply. At a local level, they also interact with other sectors (e.g., education), and their combined action is essential to ensure active community involvement.

　(2) Volatile substances in water may be released to the atmosphere in showering and through a range of other household activities. Under such circumstances, inhalation may become a significant

route of exposure. Some substances may also be absorbed through the skin during bathing, but this is not usually a major source of uptake. In some parts of the world, houses have a low rate of ventilation, and authorities may wish to take inhalation exposure into account in adapting the guidelines to local conditions, although other uncertainty factors used in the quantitative assessments may render this unnecessary. For those substances that are particularly volatile, such as chloroform, the correction factor would be approximately equivalent to a doubling of exposure.

4. Put the following Chinese into English：

(1) 饮用水水质

(2) 暂行标准

(3) 允许偏差

(4) 生活饮用水卫生标准规定了生活饮用水水质卫生要求、生活饮用水水源水质要求、集中式供水单位卫生要求、二次供水卫生要求、涉及生活饮用水卫生安全产品卫生要求、水质监测和水质检验方法。

(5) 生活饮用水卫生标准适用于城乡各类集中式供水的生活饮用水，也适用于分散式供水的生活饮用水。

Reading Material A

The Safe Drinking Water Act

The Safe Drinking Water Act (SDWA) is the principal federal law in the United States intended to ensure safe drinking water for the public.[1] Pursuant to the act, the Environmental Protection Agency(EPA) is required to set standards for drinking water quality and oversee all states, localities, and water suppliers who implement these standards. SDWA applies to every public water system in the United States. There are currently more than 150,000 public water systems providing water to almost all Americans at some time in their lives. The Act does not cover private wells.

The SDWA does not apply to bottled water. Bottled water is regulated by the Food and Drug Administration (FDA) under the Federal Food, Drug, and Cosmetic Act. The SDWA requires EPA to establish National Primary Drinking Water Regulations (NPDWRs) for contaminants that may cause adverse public health effects.[2]

The regulations include both mandatory levels (Maximum Contaminant Levels, or MCLs) and non-enforceable health goals (Maximum Contaminant Level Goals, or MCLGs) for each included contaminant. MCLs have additional significance because they can be used under the Superfund law as "Applicable or Relevant and Appropriate Requirements" in cleanups of contaminated sites on the National Priorities List.

Future NPDWR standards will apply to non-transient non-community water systems because of concern for the long-term exposure of a stable population. It is important to note that EPA's decision to apply future NPDWRs to non-transient non-community water systems may have a significant impact on Department of Energy facilities that operate their own drinking water systems.

Prior to the SDWA there were few national enforceable requirements for drinking water. Improvements in testing were allowing the detection of smaller concentrations of contaminant and allowing more tests to be run. Many states had drinking water regulations prior to adoption of the federal SDWA.

The Safe Drinking Water Act, enacted by Congress in 1974, was one of several pieces of environmental legislation in the 1970s. Discovery of organic contamination in public drinking water and the lack of enforceable, national standards persuaded Congress to take action.

The 1986 SDWA amendments required EPA to apply future NPDWRs to both community and non-transient non-community water systems when it evaluated and revised current regulations. [3] The first case in which this was applied was the "Phase I" final rule, published on July 8, 1987. At that time NPDWRs were promulgated for certain synthetic volatile organic compounds and applied to non-transient non-community water systems as well as community water systems. This rulemaking also clarified that non-transient non-community water systems were not subject to MCLs that were promulgated before July 8, 1987. The 1986 amendments were signed into law by President Ronald Reagan on June 19, 1986.

In addition to requiring more contaminants to be regulated, the 1986 amendments included:
- Well head protection
- New monitoring for certain substances
- Filtration for certain surface water systems
- Disinfection for certain groundwater systems
- Restriction on lead in solder and plumbing
- More enforcement powers

In 1996, Congress amended the Safe Drinking Water Act to emphasize sound science and risk-based standard setting, small water supply system flexibility and technical assistance, community-empowered source water assessment and protection, public right-to-know, and water system infrastructure assistance through a multi-billion-dollar state revolving loan fund. [4] The amendments were signed into law by President Bill Clinton on August 6, 1996.

Main points of the 1996 amendments:

(1) Consumer Confidence Reports: All community water systems must prepare and distribute annual reports about the water they provide, including information on detected contaminants, possible health effects, and the water's source.

(2) Cost-Benefit Analysis: EPA must conduct a thorough cost-benefit analysis for every new standard to determine whether the benefits of a drinking water standard justify the costs.

(3) Drinking Water State Revolving Fund. States can use this fund to help water systems make infrastructure or management improvements or to help systems assess and protect their source water.

(4) Microbial Contaminants and Disinfection Byproducts: EPA is required to strengthen protection for microbial contaminants, including cryptosporidium, while strengthening control over the byproducts of chemical disinfection. EPA promulgated the Stage 1 Disinfectants and Disinfection Byproducts Rule and the Interim Enhanced Surface Water Treatment Rule to address these risks.

(5) Operator Certification: Water system operators must be certified to ensure that systems are operated safely. EPA issued guidelines in 1999 specifying minimum standards for the certification and recertification of the operators of community and non-transient, non-community water systems. These guidelines apply to state operator certification programs. All states are currently implementing EPA-approved operator certification programs.

(6) Public Information and Consultation: SDWA emphasizes that consumers have a right to

know what is in their drinking water, where it comes from, how it is treated, and how to help protect it. EPA distributes public information materials (through its Drinking Water Hotline, Safewater web site, and Resource Center) and holds public meetings, working with states, tribes, water systems, and environmental and civic groups, to encourage public involvement.

(7) Small Water Systems: Small water systems are given special consideration and resources under SDWA, to make sure they have the managerial, financial, and technical ability to comply with drinking water standards.

Notes

[1] 饮用水安全法案是美国主要的联邦法律，目的是确保公众的安全饮用水。

[2] 饮用水安全法案要求环保署为可能对公众健康产生不利影响的污染物质建立国家一级饮用水条例。

[3] 1986 年安全饮用水修正案要求环保局在评价和修订现行法律时致力于社区的和瞬时的非社区的水系统。

[4] 1996 年国会修订了安全饮用水法案，重点是健全的科学和以风险为基础的标准设定，小型水供应系统的灵活性和技术援助，水源水的评价和保护，公众的知情权，由数十亿美元的国家周转贷款资金援助的水系统基础设施。

Reading Material B

International Water Law and Diplomacy

A basic understanding of the fundamental concepts and principles of public international law is necessary in order to appreciate fully the issues that arise in the context of the law that governs international freshwater.[1] For example, it is important to know that the rules of international law apply to sovereign States, and it is primarily for States themselves to ensure compliance with international commitments. There is no "supra" authority to enforce such rules, except in very specific circumstances, such as a threat to international peace and security, where the United Nations can take action. Enforcement of international law is a central issue of concern. However, the first step to that exercise must be identification of the applicable rules.

These rules are found in treaties, international custom, general principles of law, and the writings of "learned publicists".Treaties usually provide the most readily accessible source of law, but the other sources cannot be ignored. In the law governing the non-navigational uses of international watercourses, rules of customary law are particularly important and are often invoked by States in the absence of "written" or "codified" law.[2] It is worth noting that not all treaties apply to all States. First, it must be ascertained whether the State concerned is a party to the treaty in question, and second, whether the latter has come into force and thus has become legally binding on the State.Finally, the normative content (requirements) of the treaty rules must be established in order to determine whether, or not, a State's actions are in accordance with its treaty obligations.

The cornerstone principle of international water law is a universally recognized rule of customary law, reflected in many international agreements, that governs States' behaviour with respect to international watercourses (McCaffrey, 1998; Caflisch, 1998). An important element of this principle is the requirement that watercourse States take all reasonable measures not to cause significant harm to other watercourse States. These substantive rules are supported by a set of procedural rules requiring, *inter alia*, prior notification, exchange of information and consultations concerning planned measures likely to adversely affect other watercourse States (Bourne, 1997).

The fundamental principles and procedural rules of water law are codified in the 1997 UN Watercourses Convention, a framework instrument that sets forth basic rights and obligations of watercourse States.[3] Adopted by UN General Assembly Resolution on 21 May 1997, the Con-vention was supported by 104 States, with only three States (Burundi, China, and Turkey) voting against (Wouters, 2000a). The 1997 Convention requires 35 ratifications and has yet to come into force. At present, Finland, Syria, Hungary, Jordan, Lebanon, Norway, South Africa, and Sweden are parties to the Convention; Luxembourg, Paraguay, Portugal, Venezuela, Germany, Namibia, Netherlands, Norway, Tunisia, and Yemen are signatories, who have yet to ratify it. The Convention has been recognized by the International Court of Justice (ICJ, 1997) and by a significant number of States as an authoritative statement of the fundamental principles of interna-tional water law. Regardless of when, and whether the Convention comes into force, it will continue to play an important role in the management of international watercourses.

International rules are often employed to meet regional requirements. A unique model for the protection and management of transboundary waters has evolved under the auspices of the UN Economic Commission for Europe (UN/ECE). The long history of European transboundary cooperation has resulted in a sophisticated legal system of water resources management, focusing primarily on limiting adverse transboundary impacts.Branko Bosnjakovic reviews the legal regime established under the 1992 Helsinki Convention on the Protection and Use of Transboundary Watercourses and International Lakes. The principal goal of the 1992 Helsinki Convention, which currently has 29 State parties, is to ensure the equitable and reasonable use of transboundary waters and limit transboundary pollution. The treaty objectives are to be achieved through a combination of national measures (legal, administrative, economic, financial, and technical) and multilateral arrangements, including joint activities, monitoring, exchange of information, etc. The 1992 Helsinki Convention, an "umbrella" treaty establishing a general framework for cooperation, has been supplemented by a number of basin-specific agreements and a recent Protocol on Water and Health (1999 London Protocol). The Parties to the Helsinki Convention are now developing a compliance verification strategy, including the development of monitoring systems (Wouters, 1999).The UN/ECE model provides one example of a legal framework that has evolved to respond to specific water resources problems in a regional context.

Most watercourse agreements do not provide for adequate compliance verification procedures. Patricia Jones considers this issue in the context of the US-Mexico boundary waters regime, comparing it with the system of environmental rules and practices adopted under the North American Free Trade Agreement (NAFTA) and the North American Agreement on Environmental Cooperation (NAAEC). She asks whether compliance mechanisms are necessary in international watercourse agreements, and considers what role an individual can play in ensuring that a State meets its treaty obligations. The latter issue is particularly challenging and demonstrates the interface of international and national legal systems in matters involving compliance. Whether or not a State has complied with its international obligations is determined, in the first instance, with an assessment of its national practice, generally accomplished through self-reporting (Wouters, 1999). [4] Jones' examination of the compliance practice regarding the environmental rules under NAFTA and NAAEC lead her to conclude that the US/Mexico transboundary watercourse regime could benefit from comparison.

Isabel Dendauw addresses the relatively new and intriguing problem of international trade in water in the context of the US-Canada transboundary relations. She considers whether the water and trade treaties that both Canada and the US are party to, permit or preclude the bulk export of water. In March 2000, the bilateral International Joint Commission issued a report recommending against the bulk transfer of water from the Great Lakes, setting forth strict criteria for the removal of water. The matter provoked a serious controversy in both Canada and the US, with the Council of Canadians fiercely opposing any bulk transfer of Canada's waters. Dendauw examines the provisions of the 1909 Boundary Waters Treaty, the NAFTA and the 1994 General Agreement on Tariffs and Trade (GATT), highlighting the contentious legal issues arising in this situation. It is obvious that trade in bulk water creates the potential for conflict between national conservation measures, on the one hand, and the multilateral regime of free trade, on the other. Dendauw concludes that it is difficult to forecast how a GATT or NAFTA dispute panel would rule on the matter of bulk water export, and suggests that such an activity might require, as a pre-requisite, joint co-operation between Canada and the U.S.A., including a shared coherent and principled approach to preserving the potentially affected ecosystem.

Notes

[1] 为了透彻地了解由国际淡水法律引起的争执，必须对公共国际法中的基本概念和原则有一个基本的了解。

[2] 在管理非航道用途国际河道的法律中，习惯法规则是特别重要的，而且经常被没有成文法令的国家所引用。

[3] 1997年的联合国水道公约将水法的基本原则和程序规则制定为法律，这是一个确定河道国家的基本权利和义务的框架法律。

[4] 一个国家是否遵守了它的国际义务，首先是靠本国的实践评价来确定的，通常以自我报告的形式来完成（乌特斯，1999）。

Unit 3   Analytical Technique and Methodology

When considering analytical methods it is important to appreciate the difference between accuracy and precision-accuracy measures the closeness of results to the true value whereas precision measures the reproducibility of results when the same sample is analyzed repeatedly. It is quite possible to have precise methods which are inaccurate or methods with poor precision but which provide a reasonably accurate result with repeated analyses of the same sample. Analytical methods and instrument manufacturers normally indicate accuracy and precision values although these are often obtained under ideal conditions and may not always be achieved under routine operation. [1]

Gravimetric Analysis

This form of analysis depends upon weighing solids obtained from the sample by evaporation, filtration or precipitation. Because of the small weights involved, a balance accurate to 0.0001 g is required together with a drying oven to remove all moisture from the sample. [2] Gravimetric analysis is thus not suited for field testing. Its main uses are for the measurement of:

(1) Suspended Solids (SS): a known volume of sample is filtered under vacuum through a preweighed glass-fibre paper with a pore size of 0.45 or 1.2 μm. Total SS are given by the increases in weight after drying at 103°C and volatile SS (VSS) are those lost on firing at 500°C;

(2) An indicator to show when the end point of the reaction has been reached. Various types of indicator are available, e.g. electrometric, acid-base, precipitation, adsorption and oxidation-reduction.

Colorimetric Analysis

When dealing with low concentrations, colorimetric analyses are often particularly appropriate and there are many determinations in water quality control which can be quickly and easily carried out by this form of analysis. [3]

To be of quantitative use a colorimetric method must be based on the formation of a completely soluble product with a stable Color. The Colored solution must conform with the following relationships.

(1) Beer's law: Light absorption increases exponentially with the concentration of the absorbing solution.

(2) Lambert's law: Light absorption increases exponentially with the length of the light path.

The Color produced may be measured by a variety of methods.

Visual Methods

Comparison tubes A standard range of concentrations of the substance under analysis is prepared and the appropriate reagent added. The unknown sample is treated in the same manner and matched to the standards by looking down through the solutions on to a white base.

Color discs In this case the standards are in the form of a series of suitably Colored glass filters through which a standard depth of distilled water or sample without Color-forming reagents is viewed. The sample in a similar tube is compared with the Color disc and the best visual match selected.

Both of these methods are dependent upon somewhat subjective judgements so that reproducibility between different analysts may not be good. The Color disc method is very convenient for field use and a wide range of discs and prepacked reagents is available.

Instrumental Methods

Absorptiometer or colorimeter This type of instrument comprises a glass sample cell through which a beam of light from a low-voltage lamp is passed. Light emerging from the sample is detected by a photoelectric cell whose output is displayed on a meter. The sensitivity is enhanced by inserting in the light path a Color filter complementary to the solution Color and the range of measurement can be extended by using sample cells of different length. [4]

Spectrophotometer This is a more accurate type of instrument using the same basic principle as an absorptiometer but with a prism being employed to give monochromatic light of the desired wavelength. The sensitivity is thus increased and on the more expensive instruments measurements can be undertaken in the infrared and ultraviolet regions as well as in the visible light wavebands.

With both types of instrument a blank of the sample without the last Color- forming reagent is used to set the zero optical density position. The treated sample is then placed in the light path and the optical density noted. A calibration curve must be obtained by determining the optical density of a series of known standards at the optimum wavelength, obtained from analytical reference books or by experiments. In any form of colorimetric analysis it is important to ensure that full Color development has taken place before measurements are made and that any suspended matter in the sample has been removed. [5] Suspended matter will of course prevent the transmission of light through a sample so that its presence will reduce the sensitivity of the determination and lead to erroneous results unless the blank has the identical concentration of suspended solids.

Electrode Techniques

The measurement of such parameters as pH and oxidation-reduction potential (ORP) by electrodes has been widespread for many years and the technology of such electrodes is thus well established. pH is measured by the potential produced by a glass electrode—an electrode with a special sensitive glass area and an acid electrolyte, used in conjunction with a standard calomel reference electrode. The output from the pH electrode is fed to an amplifier and then to a meter or digital display. A wide range of pH electrodes is available, including combined glass and reference units and special rugged units for field use. ORP is measured using a redox probe with a platinum electrode in conjunction with a calomel reference electrode.

More recent developments in electrode technology have resulted in the availability of a widening range of other electrodes, some of which are extremely useful in water quality control. Probably the most useful of these new electrodes is the oxygen electrode. An increasing number of specific ion electrodes for determinations such as NH_4^+, NO_3^-, Ca^{2+}, Na^+, Cl^-, Br^-, F^-, etc. are now available. These electrodes permit rapid measurements down to very low concentrations but they are relatively costly.

Important Words and Expressions

gravimetric [ˌɡrævɪˈmetrɪk]　adj.（测定）重量的

evaporation [ɪˌvæpəˈreɪʃən]　n. 蒸发，发散；消失

filtration [fɪlˈtreɪʃən]　n. 过滤；滤清

precipitation [prɪˌsɪpɪˈteɪʃən]　n. [化]沉淀；沉淀物；（雨、雪等的）降下；雨；雪

moisture [ˈmɔɪstʃə]　n. 湿气，潮气；水分

colorimetric [ˌkʌlərɪˈmetrɪk]　adj. 比色的；色度的

absorption [əbˈsɔːpʃən]　n. 吸收；吸收过程；吸收作用；全神贯注，专心致志，凝神专注(的事实和状态)(in)；合并；同化

absorptiometer [əbˌsɔːpʃɪˈɔmɪtə]　n. 吸收比色计；吸收计

spectrophotometer [ˌspektrəfəuˈtɔmɪtə]　n. [光] 分光光度计

emerging [ɪˈmɜːdʒɪŋ]　adj. 新兴的；出现的；形成的　v. 形成；浮现；显露（emerge 的ing 形式）；由…中脱出

monochromatic [ˌmɔnəukrəuˈmætɪk]　adj. 单色的

ultraviolet [ˌʌltrəˈvaɪəlɪt]　adj. 紫外的；紫外线的　n. 紫外线辐射，紫外光

distill [di'stil]   vt. 提取；蒸馏；使滴下   vi. 蒸馏；精炼；作为精华产生
complementary [ˌkɔmplə'mentəri:]   adj. 补足的，补充的
calomel ['kæləmel]   n. [无化] 甘汞；氯化亚汞

Notes

[1] 分析方法和仪器厂商经常给出其准确度和精密度，但这些通常只能在理想条件下取得，而在常规操作下不一定实现。

[2] 由于涉及重量微小，需要可精确到 0.0001g 的天平，并且需要烘箱以去除样品中的所有水分。

[3] 对于较低浓度的水，色度分析尤为合适，而且水质控制中有很多含量测定可采用这种分析方法快速简易的实现。

[4] 通过在光路上插入滤色镜补偿溶液的颜色，可提高灵敏度，且可通过采用不同长度的样品室扩大测定范围。

[5] 在任一形式的色度分析中，重要是要在测量前确保已实现完全显色，并且样品中所有悬浮物质已被去除。

Exercises

1. Answering the following questions in English according to the text:

(1) How can we get the calibration curve?

(2) What's the theory of measuring pH?

2. Using the following each word to make up the sentences, respectively:

(1) routine operation

(2) suspended matter

(3) sample

(4) water quality

3. Put the following English into Chinese:

(1) The principle of operation of the simplest (and historically the first) probe is that of a galvanic cell. If lead and silver electrodes are put in an electrolyte solution with a micrometer between, the reaction at the lead electrode would be:

$$Pb + 2OH^- \longrightarrow PbO + H_2O + 2e^-$$

At the lead electrode, electrons are liberated which travel through the micrometer to the silver electrode where the following reaction takes place:

$$2e^- + 1/2O_2 + H_2O \longrightarrow 2OH^-$$

(2) Turbidity gives an idea of the content matter in suspension. The turbidity may be expressed in terms of silica by comparing its transparency with an artificial suspension of silica. The measurement of turbidity by drops of mastic is particularly useful in ascertaining the content of the colloidal particles which will not settle and which cannot be filtered. That is why it is essential to carry out this test after filtering the liquid through paper in order to eliminate the influence of large particles, and thus to know exactly the extent of the turbidity due to the colloidal substances which are the most frequent causes of Color.

4. Put the following Chinese into English:

(1) 分光光度计

(2) 水样

(3) 悬浮固体

(4) 重现性

(5) DO 的浓度可以在实验室或在野外用标准湿式化学分析方法或者膜电极仪测量。也可以使用野外专用测量仪器，它的探头可以直接深入到溪流或是污水处理池里。电极的探头能感受到微小的电流，而电流与水中的溶解氧浓度成正比。

(6) 如果将水样的滤后部分放在蒸发皿中干燥，水中的固体物质作为残留物留在蒸发皿中。这些残留物通常称为总溶解固体，或 TDS。TDS 的浓度单位是 mg/L。可通过下式计算：

$$TDS=1000(A-B)/C$$

A=皿加上残留物的重量，mg；

B=空皿的重量，mg；

C=滤后水样的体积，mL。

5. Put the following abbr. into full phrases:

ORP；SS；VSS；TDS

Reading Material A

Physical and Chemical Parameter of Water

Pure water is tasteless, colorless, and odorless. Because water is a nearly universal solvent, organic and inorganic materials, including pollutants and gases, can become components of water as it moves through the hydrologic cycle. The quality of a source is measured by the kinds and quantities of these components found in the water. The components are generally categorized as physical, chemical, or biological.

Total Dissolved Solids

TDS refers to the total inorganic and organic particulate material in water. TDS is often used as a measure of mineral content and can be estimated with electrical conductivity tests. Although it is not a regulated measure of water quality, USEPA (United States Environmental Protection Agency) has established a nonenforceable secondary standard of 500 mg/L.

Turbidity

Turbidity in water results from suspended matter that causes the water to be opaque or cloudy. The suspended matter is often soil runoff in water sources. By itself, turbidity has no health effects, but it can interfere with disinfection and provide a medium for microbial growth. [1] Turbidity usually indicates the presence of microbes. The Surface Water Treatment Rule (SWTR) requires systems using surface water, or groundwater under the direct influence of surface water, to filter their water when certain water quality parameters are exceeded. [2] If turbidity goes above 5 nephelometric turbidity units (ntu), the system must filter the water. Systems that filter must ensure that the turbidity goes no higher than 1 ntu (0.5 ntu for conventional or direct filtration) in at least 95 percent of the daily samples of any two consecutive months.

Color

Color in water is caused by natural metallic ions, certain types of dissolved and colloidal organic matter leached from soil or decaying vegetation, and industrial wastes. [3] USEPA has established a nonenforceable secondary standard of 15 color units. Because substances that cause color are usually in solution, the color generally cannot be removed by mechanical filtration.

Tastes and odors

Tastes and odors are caused by salts or TDS, decomposed or synthetic organic material, or volatile chemicals. Tastes and odors are usually more closely related with biological properties of water than chemical properties. Generally, dead organic matter can be broken down into taste- and odor-free compounds in water with adequate dissolved oxygen. Odor-producing chemicals include solvents, pesticides, and benzene compounds. A taste or odor threshold of a substance in water is the lowest concentration that can be tasted or smelled. For odor, USEPA has established a nonenforceable secondary standard of 3 threshold odor number.

Temperature

The temperature of water affects biological activity rates, oxygen saturation, and mass transfer coefficients (which describe how molecules of a substance move across an interface from one phase to another). In the case of groundwater, a significant or relatively rapid shift in temperature, which closely correlates with climatological or surface water conditions, likely indicates that the source is influenced by surface water. [4] Water temperature is also an important environmental consideration; for example, fish species generally thrive in a relatively narrow temperature range.

pH

pH is a scale measure of the acidic or basic (alkaline) nature of the water, which ranges from 0 to 14, with 7 being neutral. pH measures intensity, not capacity, in the same way temperature measures how hot or cold water is. (Technically, pH is the negative log of the concentration of hydrogen ions, and pH refers to the potential of hydrogen.) The pH of natural rainfall is about 5.6. Naturally occurring substances, such as carbon dioxide or minerals, and artificially occurring pollution such as sulfur dioxide from industrial emissions, can react with water to reduce the pH of rainfall to as low as 3. Closely related to pH are the characteristics of water called alkalinity and acidity. Alkalinity measures water's ability to neutralize acids, that is, its ability to react with H^+ ions. Acidity measures water's ability to neutralize bases, or its ability to react with OH^- ions. For finished water, USEPA has established a nonenforceable secondary standard for pH of 6.5 to 8.5.

Cations

Cations are positively charged ions in solution, and anions are negatively charged. Common cations found in water include calcium (Ca^{2+}), magnesium (Mg^{2+}), and iron (Fe^{2+}). Common anions include chloride (Cl^-, bicarbonate (HCO_3^-), and carbonate (CO_3^{2-}) Cations and anions indicate the level of, or potential for, certain kinds of pollution or harmful substances in water, and other characteristics such as hardness. A number of similar numerical scales for rating water hardness have been devised and published.

Conductivity

Conductivity is a measure of electrical resistance, the property of a substance to conduct (carry) heat or electricity. The unit of measure is the siemens (formerly called mho), which is the reciprocal of resistivity (1 divided by resistivity). Conductivity provides an estimate of the TDS, or can be used to verify the TDS results obtained in physical analyses of water. Carbon dioxide, a minor gas in the atmosphere, is an end product of biological decomposition. In solution, it decreases pH and is a measure of the corrosiveness of water.

Notes

[1] 浊度本身对人体健康没有影响，但是它能干扰消毒并且为细菌生长提供媒介。

[2] 地表水处理规范要求，当某个水质指标超标时，采用地表水或受地表水影响的地下水的系统中，需对原水进行过滤。

[3] 水中的颜色来自于天然金属离子，某些从土壤或腐烂植物溶出的溶解或者胶状形态的有机物，以及工业废物。

[4] 至于地下水，如果温度发生与气候或地表水状态密切相关的明显或相对较快的变化，很可能意味着这个水源受到了地表水的影响。

Reading Material B
Development of Water Analysis Technique

There has been a growing trend in the past decade to concentrate analytical facilities in central laboratories and this applies in the water industry as much as it does in the medical sciences where many of these techniques were originally developed. The growth of central laboratories capable of processing hundreds of thousands of samples a year has been encouraged by the availability of reliable automated analytical systems. These systems can carry out a suite of determinations on a series of samples without human intervention once the samples have been loaded into the system. Results are logged on computers and archived or reported as required.

Many of the automated analytical systems utilize colorimetric determinations with automatic samplers feeding discrete samples into the reagent addition and Color development stages before entering the spectrophotometer flow-through cell. Individual metals can be determined to concentrations of 1 μg or less using automated atomic absorption spectrophotometers in which atoms are excited in a flame or electric arc to produce a characteristic emission.[1] In some analyses X-ray fluorescence spectroscopy may be used to improve sensitivity or to determine individual metals separately in a mixture.

Chromatography is widely employed in the detection and identification of individual organic compounds. It utilizes the concept of differential absorption of organic compounds to separate individual components in mixtures. Gas-liquid chromatography, in which volatile substances are released by heating, is particularly useful for trace organics in water. For quantitative determinations of organic substances in the ng/L range, as required by drinking water standards, gas- liquid chromatography can be combined with mass spectrometry in which molecules are converted to ions and then separated by their mass: charge ratio. [2] This enables identification and quantification of atoms and isotopes to provide a complete chemical analysis of a sample. High-technology analytical equipment such as that described above normally requires a controlled environment for it to operate reliably and it also needs skilled operators and maintenance technicians.

In pollution control work there is a need for on-site determinations or important quality parameters, often in remote situations with inhospitable environments. Equipment to fulfil such needs is required to operate for extended periods without attention other than routine cleaning and calibration. The attraction of probes or electrode sensors for such duties is obvious and much development work has been carried out by both instrument manufacturers and users. The production of reliable instruments has not been easy but they are now becoming available. The UK National Rivers Authority developed an automatic monitoring device which provides continuous records of dissolved oxygen, ammonia, pH, temperature and flow using probes which are automatically cleaned. Data are logged and telemetered to a control centre and a discrete sampler can be actuated automatically if preset levels are exceeded, thus providing samples for further investigation and legal action if appropriate. [3]

It is unlikely that it will ever be possible to provide remote monitoring of water for all possible contaminants which might be present. In relation to raw water supplies it is, however, very desirable to have some form of automatic warning of the presence of potentially toxic substances. To protect potable water supplies a number of devices have been developed which depend upon the effect of toxic substances on the metabolism or behavior of living organisms kept in a test chamber through which the water flows. Nitrifying bacteria are sensitive to many toxic substances and thus if exposed to them are likely to stop converting ammonia in the water into nitrate. An ammonia electrode placed at the outlet of a small column containing nitrifying bacteria will give rapid indication of a reduction in their activity. In a similar way, the respiration rate of fish, or in certain species changes in their electrical charge, can give early indication of stress due to undesirable substances in the water. It must be appreciated that such warnings simply indicate that the water has been contaminated and they cannot identify the particular contaminants. The warnings allow precautionary measures to be taken and must be followed up by the appropriate range of analyses to identify the substance causing the problem.

A major problem with conventional electrodes and probes is that they are inserted into the water or wastewater and thus as well as being prone to fouling and damage they may also alter the actual distribution of contaminants in the vicinity of the measurement.[4] The concept of non-invasive sensors has thus begun to receive attention. It is already possible to obtain a turbidity monitor which utilizes light scattering from a falling stream of water as the measuring technique. The use of images from satellite sensors appears to have potential for some water quality monitoring purposes, particularly as the ground resolution of such sensors improves. Satellite images have been used to provide land-use data for catchment modelling purposes and to detect pollution discharges. Images can be subjected to a range of spectral analyses which can highlight particular characteristics and such images have already been used to detect algal blooms in large reservoirs. Flow measurements in rivers and open channels can now be made using non-intrusive ultrasonic beams and it may well be that in the not too distant future the reflection and scattering of laser beams could provide information about the quality of waters and wastewaters.

Notes

[1] 采用自动原子吸收分光光度计，可使原子在火焰或电弧中被激发以产生特征发射，可以测定1μg或更低的特定金属浓度。

[2] 根据饮用水标准，定量测定在纳克每升范围的有机物质，可采用气体-液相色谱与质谱联用，将分子转化为离子，然后根据它们的质荷比分离。

[3] 数据被记录并传送到控制中心，如果超出预设值，离散采样器将自动启动，为进一步的调查研究和可能的法律诉讼提供样品。

[4] 使用传统电极和探针的一个主要问题是它们要插入水或废水中，这样不仅容易被污染和破坏，而且可能改变测量点附近污染物的实际分布。

Part Two
Water Supply and Sewerage System

Unit 4   Water Supply System

In general, water distribution systems can be divided into four main components: (1) water sources and intake works, (2) treatment works and storage, (3) transmission mains, and (4) distribution network. The common sources for the untreated or raw water are surface water sources such as rivers, lakes, springs, and man-made reservoirs and groundwater sources such as bores and wells. The intake structures and pumping stations are constructed to extract water from these sources. The raw water is transported to the treatment plants for processing through transmission mains and is stored in clear water reservoirs after treatment. The degree of treatment depends upon the raw water quality and finished water quality requirements. Sometimes, groundwater quality is so good that only disinfection is required before supplying to consumers. The clear water reservoir provides a buffer for water demand variation as treatment plants are generally designed for average daily demand.

Water is carried over long distances through transmission mains. If the flow of water in a transmission main is maintained by creating a pressure head by pumping, it is called a pumping main. On the other hand, if the flow in a transmission main is maintained by gravitational potential available on account of elevation difference, it is called a gravity main. There are no intermediate withdrawals in a water transmission main. Similar to transmission mains, the flow in water distribution networks is maintained either by pumping or by gravitational potential. Generally, in a flat terrain, the water pressure in a large water distribution network is maintained by pumping; however, in steep terrain, gravitational potential maintains a pressure head in the water distribution system.

A distribution network delivers water to consumers through service connections. Such a distribution network may have different configurations depending upon the layout of the area. Generally, water distribution networks have a looped and branched configuration of pipelines, but sometimes either looped or branched configurations are also provided depending upon the general layout plan of the city roads and streets. Urban water networks have mostly looped configurations, whereas rural water networks have branched configurations. On account of the high-reliability requirement of water services, looped configurations are preferred over branched configurations.[1]

The cost of a water distribution network depends upon proper selection of the geometry of the network. The selection of street layout adopted in the planning of a city is important to provide a minimum-cost water supply system. The two most common water supply configurations of looped water supply systems are the gridiron pattern and the ring and radial pattern; however, it is not possible to find an optimal geometric pattern that minimizes the cost. [2]

Generally, town water supply systems are single-input source, looped pipe networks. As stated, the looped systems have pipes that are interconnected throughout the system such that the flow to a demand node can be supplied through several connected pipes. The flow directions in a looped system can change based on spatial or temporal variation in water demand, thus unlike branched systems, the flow directions in looped network pipes are not unique. [3]

The looped network systems provide redundancy to the systems, which increases the capacity of the system to overcome local variation in water demands and also ensures the distribution of water to users in case of pipe failures. [4] The looped geometry is also favored from the water quality aspect, as it would reduce the water age. The pipe sizes and distribution system layouts are important factors for minimizing the water age. Due to the multidirectional flow patterns and also variations in flow patterns in the system over time, the water would not stagnate at one location resulting in reduced water age. The advantages and disadvantages of looped water distribution systems are given in Table 4.1.

Table 4.1 Advantages and Disadvantages of Looped Water Distribution Systems

Advantages	Disadvantages
Minimize loss of services, as main breaks can be isolated due to multidirectional flow to demand points	Higher capital cost
Reliability for fire protection is higher due to redundancy in the system	Higher operational and maintenance cost
Likely to meet increase in water demand-higher capacity and lower velocities	Skilled operation
Better residual chlorine due to inline mixing and fewer dead ends	
Reduced water age	

It has been described in the literature that the looped water distribution systems, designed with least-cost consideration only, are converted into a tree-like structure resulting in the disappearance of the original geometry in the final design. Loops are provided for system reliability. Thus, a design based on least-cost considerations only defeats the basic purpose of loops provision in the network. A method for the design of a looped water distribution system is described. This method maintains the loop configuration of the network by bringing all the pipes of the network in the optimization problem formulation, although it is also based on least-cost consideration only.

Important Words and Expressions

bore [bɔ:]　vt. 钻孔；使烦扰　n.（钻成的）孔，洞
pump [pʌmp]　vt. 打气；用抽水机抽…　n. 泵，抽水机；打气筒　vi. 抽水
disinfection [ˌdisinˈfekʃən]　n. 消毒，杀菌
buffer [ˈbʌfə]　n. [计] 缓冲区；缓冲器，[车辆] 减震器　vt. 缓冲
intermediate [ˌintəˈmi:djət, -dieit]　vi. 起媒介作用　adj. 中间的，中级的　n. [化学] 中

间物；媒介
  steep [sti:p] adj. 陡峭的 vt. 泡；浸；使…充满
  configuration [kən,figju'reiʃən] n. 配置；结构；外形
  loop [lu:p] vi. 打环 n. 环；圈
  gridiron ['grid,aiən] n. 烤架；格状物；橄榄球场；棋盘式街道布局；网状网
  temporal ['tempərəl] adj. 暂时的；当时的；现世的
  redundancy [ri'dʌndənsi:] n. [计][数] 冗余（等于 redundance）；裁员；人浮于事
  multidirectional [,mʌltidi'rekʃənəl] adj. 多方向的
  stagnate ['stægneit, stæg'neit] vi. 停滞；淤塞；变萧条 vt. 使淤塞；使沉滞；使萧条
  velocity [vi'lɔsəti] n. [力] 速率；迅速；周转率
  residual chlorine 余氯，残留氯

Notes

  [1] 由于供水服务可靠性要求高，环状（管网）优于枝状（管网）。

  [2] 环状供水系统中最常用的两种供水形式为方格状，环状和放射状。然而，（我们）不可能找到一个最佳的几何形状而使得成本最低。

  [3] 与枝状系统不同，在环状系统中，由于需水量在空间和时间上的变化，管道中的水流方向并非不变。

  [4] 环状管网可为系统提供余量，提高系统应对局部需水量变化的能力，并且保证管道故障时为用户供水。

Exercises

1. Answering the following questions in English according to the text：

  (1) What are the main parts of the water distribution system?

  (2) What are the two types of most common configurations of water supply network?

2. Using the following each word to make up the sentences, respectively：

  (1) Water service

  (2) Main

  (3) Pumping

  (4) Distribution

  (5) High- reliability

3. Put the following English into Chinese：

(1) A water supply for a town usually includes a storage reservoir at the source of the supply, a pipeline from the storage reservoir to the distribution reservoir near the town, and finally the distribution pipes buried in the streets, taking the water to the houses, shops, factories and offices. The main equipment is thus the two reservoirs and the pipeline between them. The function of the storage reservoir is keep enough water over one or several years to provide for all high demands in dry periods, and the distribution reservoir has the same function for the day or the week. The storage reservoir by its existence allows the supply sources to be smaller and less expensive. And the distribution reservoir similarly allows the pipeline and pumps to be smaller and cheaper than they would be if it did not exist.

(2) Pumps and pumping machinery serve the following purposes in water systems: 1) lifting water from its source (surface or ground), either immediately to the community through high-lift installations, or by low lift to purification works; 2) boosting water from low-service to high-service areas, to separate fire supplies, and to the upper floors of many-storied buildings; and 3) transporting water through treatment works, backwashing filters, draining component settling tanks, and other treatment units, withdrawing deposited solids and supplying water (especially pressure water) to operating equipment.

4. Put the following Chinese into English:

(1) 给水系统

(2) 环状管网

(3) 重力流

(4) 管网设计一般需要综合考虑地面标高、管径、水位等因素。此外，需水量按人均用水量估算，或者最好通过对管网节点水压和流量进行现场实测。管网系统分析通常采用计算机模拟完成，系统的数学模型在使用之前都要用实测数据进行校正。

(5) 在地形呈现急剧变化的地区（丘陵或山区）通常会把给水管网配水系统分成两个以上服务区域。这样可以避免地势低洼地区形成超高水压，而且能维持地势较高地区的正常水压。一般情况下，可将各个系统连接起来，但是在正常供水时用阀门将它们分开。

Reading Material A
Distribution System

Raw water (untreated) is collected from a surface water source (such as an intake on a lake or a river) or from a groundwater source (such as a water well drawing from an underground aquifer) within the watershed that provides the water resource.

Shallow dams and reservoirs are susceptible to outbreaks of toxic algae, especially if the water is warmed by a hot sun. The bacteria grow from storm water runoff carrying fertilizer into the river where it acts as a nutrient for the algae.[1] Such outbreaks render the water unfit for human consumption.

The raw water is transferred to the water purification facilities using uncovered aqueducts, covered tunnels or underground water pipes.

Virtually all large systems must treat the water; a fact that is tightly regulated by global, state and federal agencies, such as the World Health Organization (WHO) or the United States Environmental Protection Agency (EPA). Water treatment must occur before the product reaches the consumer and afterwards (when it is discharged again). Water purification usually occurs close to the final delivery points to reduce pumping costs and the chances of the water becoming contaminated after treatment.[2]

Traditional surface water treatment plant generally consists of three steps: clarification, filtration and disinfection. Clarification refers to the separation of particles (dirt, organic matter, etc.) from the water stream. Chemical addition (i.e. alum, ferric chloride) destabilizes the particle charges and prepares them for clarification either by settling or floating out of the water stream.[3] Sand, anthracite or activated carbon filters refine the water stream, removing smaller particulate matter. While other methods of disinfection exist, the preferred method is via chlorine addition. Chlorine effectively kills bacteria and most viruses and maintains a residual to protect the water supply through the supply network.

The product, delivered to the point of consumption, is called fresh water if it receives little or no treatment or drinking water if the treatment achieves the water quality standards required for human consumption. Once treated, chlorine is added to the water and it is distributed by the local supply network. Today, water supply systems are typically constructed of plastic, ferrous, or concrete circular pipe. However, other "pipe" shapes and material may be used, such as square or rectangular concrete boxes, arched brick pipe, or wood. Near the end point, the network of pipes through which the water is delivered is often referred to as the water mains.

The energy that the system needs to deliver the water is called pressure. That energy is transferred to the water, therefore becoming water pressure, in a number of ways: by a pump, by gravity feed from a water source (such as a water tower) at a higher elevation, or by compressed air.[4] The water is often transferred from a water reserve such as a large communal reservoir before being transported to a more pressurized reserve such as a watertower. In small domestic systems, the water may be pressurized by a pressure vessel or even by an underground cistern (the latter however does need additional pressurizing). This eliminates the need of a water-tower or any other heightened water reserve to supply the water pressure.

These systems are usually owned and maintained by local governments, such as cities, or other public entities, but are occasionally operated by a commercial enterprise (see water privatization). Water supply networks are part of the master planning of communities, counties, and municipalities. Their planning and design requires the expertise of city planners and civil engineers, who must consider many factors, such as location, current demand, future growth, leakage, pressure, pipe size, pressure loss, fire fighting flows, etc.-using pipe network analysis and other tools. Construction comparable sewage systems, was one of the great engineering advances that made urbanization possible. Improvement in the quality of the water has been one of the great advances in public health.

As water passes through the distribution system, the water quality can degrade by chemical reactions and biological processes. Corrosion of metal pipe materials in the distribution system can cause the release of metals into the water with undesirable aesthetic and health effects. Release of iron from unlined iron pipes can result in customer reports of "red water" at the tap. Release of copper from copper pipes can result in customer reports of "blue water" and/or a metallic taste. Release of lead can occur from the solder used to join copper pipe together or from brass fixtures. Copper and lead levels at the consumer's tap are regulated to protect consumer health.

Utilities will often adjust the chemistry of the water before distribution to minimize its corrosiveness. The simplest adjustment involves control of pH and alkalinity to produce water that tends to passivate corrosion by depositing a layer of calcium carbonate.[5] Corrosion inhibitors are often added to reduce release of metals into the water. Common corrosion inhibitors added to the water are phosphates and silicates.

Maintenance of a biologically safe drinking water is another goal in water distribution. Typically, a chlorine based disinfectant, such as sodium hypochlorite or monochloramine is added to the water as it leaves the treatment plant. Booster stations can be placed within the distribution system to ensure that all areas of the distribution system have adequate sustained levels of disinfection.

Like electric power lines, roads, and microwave radio networks, water systems may have a loop or branch network topology, or a combination of both. The piping networks are circular or rectangular. If any one section of water distribution main fails or needs repair, that section can be isolated without disrupting all users on the network.

Most systems are divided into zones. Factors determining the extent or size of a zone can include hydraulics, telemetry systems, history, and population density. Sometimes systems are designed for a specific area then are modified to accommodate development. Terrain affects hydraulics and some forms of telemetry. While each zone may operate as a stand-alone system, there is usually some arrangement to interconnect zones in order to manage equipment failures or system failures.

Water supply networks usually represent the majority of assets of a water utility. Systematic documentation of maintenance works using a Computerized Maintenance Management System is a key to a successful operation of a water utility.

Notes

[1] 雨水径流携带养分，滋生细菌，进入河流后为藻类提供养分。

[2] 水到达用户之前和之后（重新排放时）必须进行处理。水的净化一般接近最后使用点，以节省泵加压费用并减少水被二次污染的可能。

[3] 化学添加剂（如明矾、氯化铁）可使颗粒电荷失稳，使其沉降到水底或漂浮在水面而从水中去除。

[4] 将能量传递到水中，从而形成水压，可通过以下方式，如用水泵、水源重力给水（利用高位水塔）或者压缩空气。

[5] 最简单的调节方法包括控制 pH 值和碱度，使水易于产生碳酸钙沉淀层而钝化腐蚀。

Reading Material B

Groundwater Supply

The development of groundwater is more complicated than that of surface water. Groundwater is a resource that (1) is hidden from view; (2) is not amenable to delineation of basin boundaries from a topographic map; (3) is usually in a state of dynamic equilibrium; (4) does not necessarily follow surface watershed divides; (5) may comprise several aquifers in different geologic layers that have different areal extents, different flow directions, and different recharge or discharge areas; (6) may have significantly different water quality in different vertical aquifers in the same topographic location; (7) may have different hydraulic potential in different aquifers (such as confined and unconfined) in the same location; and (8) is affected by the quality of sediment and rock materials through which it passes. As a result, groundwater source identification, development, and continued management require consideration of numerous environmental factors. The primary options for groundwater sources of supply include Groundwater wells for direct withdrawal. Groundwater extraction wells are holes drilled into the ground to a formation that will permit water to be extracted from it. These water-bearing formations are called aquifers. In most aquifers, extraction of water can only be accomplished through the use of pumps because the groundwater surface is below the ground level. Artesian aquifers are aquifers that are under pressure. Artesian aquifers will flow to the surface, which may limit the amount of pumping needed. A collector well or subsurface drain (or horizontal well) that intercepts interflow in permeable materials or infiltrating surface water and discharges into a sump whose bottom is below the invert of the gallery screen and casing. [1] In filtration galleries, which are often exposed to the surface, but intercept groundwater. Groundwater development often begins when an individual digs a hole in the ground, pumps the water out of the ground, and uses it for domestic purposes or for irrigating the crop fields. As the population grows and additional holes are dug, the need for organized groundwater development arises in the face of reduced yield at the wells and poorer water quality. [2] A discussion of the water well development is provided here, followed by a methodology for planned development of groundwater.

A groundwater well is a hydraulic structure that allows water to be cost-effectively withdrawn from water bearing formations (aquifers). The utility of a well is not limited to water supply, wells are also used to monitor water levels and water quality, drain agricultural lands, prevent saltwater intrusions, recharge aquifers, discharge wastes, and relieve pressures under dams and levees.[3] Primary considerations for developing a groundwater well are:

(1) Location of potential groundwater aquifer that will yield a sufficient amount of water.

(2) Purpose of the proposed well and desired yield.

(3) Distance between the location of the well and where water is needed.

(4) Installing the casing to the production zone pump chamber casing.

(5) Placement of the well screen and gravel or filter pack (as needed).

(6) Installing a drive shoe to reinforce the bottom of the casing (if needed).

(7) Placement of grout for sealing to prevent surface water or poor-quality groundwater from entering the well.

(8) Installation of pump and column pipe-submersible pumps are commonly used as they reduce surface equipment and limit air intake in the raw water lines.

(9) Construction of elevated well seal or foundations (these can be used for vertical turbine pumps that are surface-mounted).

(10) Development of the well to minimize sand, silt and colloidal production during operation to limit the wear on the pump.

Detailed procedures for well design and construction can be found in text or reference books on groundwater, such as the AWWA M21 Groundwater, or the Groundwater Manual published by the US Department of Interior. The following design principles, if used, will likely result in a good well design, reduced construction and Operations and Maintenance (O&M) costs, and enhanced well performance:

Target highest yield, consistent with the current demand and demand growth, with minimum drawdown. Provide sand-free operation at maximum specific capacity. Provide good-quality water with proper protection from contamination. Use materials that will provide a long service life (approximately 25 years). Use drilling methods and construction techniques that befit the hydrogeologic conditions of the aquifer. Strike a balance between short- and long-term costs (that is, do not oversize a well for probable growth and do not use poor material to cut initial costs). Minimize head losses and drawdown by choosing proper screen opening, screen length, and distribution of screen openings. Mitigate the damage to natural hydraulic environment caused by drilling operation. Alter the hydraulic characteristics of the aquifer near the well to increase the rate of free flow of water to the well. Infiltration Galleries Infiltration galleries are constructed when subsurface conditions do not permit groundwater development using vertical production wells. Such conditions occur in thin aquifers or where a thin freshwater layer is underlain by saline water. A typical example is a river valley where thin alluvial deposits lie above bedrock where the water is plentiful, and the hydraulic conductivities are high, but the aquifer transmissivities are inadequate for well development because of the thinness of the aquifer.[4] In such cases, a subsurface drain or horizontal well is placed in permeable alluvial material and water is collected in a sump connected to a pump. Significant amounts of water can often be extracted through infiltration galleries because of high hydraulic conductivity of alluvial material and their proximity to a recharge source, such as a stream. Infiltration galleries can either be constructed under the streambed or adjacent to the stream or surface water body. The yield from infiltration galleries beneath a water body is normally twice the yield from galleries adjacent to the water body. However, constructing infiltration galleries is usually more difficult under a water body, Infiltration galleries below a water body tend to have higher turbidity and higher bacteria count because of less extensive filtration. Where such withdrawals are considered to directly affect the quantity or quality of surface flows, many of the considerations presented for direct surface water withdrawals will need to be followed, including meeting Surface Water Treatment Rule requirements.[5] This water would likely require filtration, which increases the cost of infiltration galleries.

Notes

[1] 集水井或者地下排水沟（或者水平井）拦截透水材料中的合流和渗入的地表水，并排到集水坑中，其底部在渠道筛管和套管之下。

[2] 随着人口的增长和更多的钻井，面对井的产水量减少和水质变差等问题，我们需要有组织地进行地下水的开发。

[3] 井的功能并不局限于供水；井也用于监测水位和水质，农田排水，防止海水入侵，补给含水层，排放废水，以及减轻大坝和防洪堤的压力。

[4] 一个典型的例子是位于基岩之上的冲积层形成的河谷，水量充足且渗透系数很高，但由于含水层太薄，其透过率不足以修建井。

[5] 这种取水方式会直接影响地表水的水质水量，需要依据许多直接取用地表水的注意事项，包括满足地表水处理规范的要求。

Unit 5 Wastewater Collection and Sewerage System Design

Wastewater may be classified into the following components：
• Domestic or sanitary wastewater. Wastewater discharged from residences, commercial (e.g., banks, restaurants, retail stores), and institutional facilities (e.g., schools and hospitals).
• Industrial wastewater. Wastewater discharged from industries (e.g., manufacturing and chemical processes).
• Infiltration and inflow. Water that enters the sewer system from groundwater infiltration, storm water that enters from roof drains, foundation drains, and submerged manholes.
• Storm water. Runoff from rainfall and snow melt.

Water consumption and wastewater production change with the seasons, the days of the week, and the hours of the day. Fluctuations are greater in small communities than in large communities, and during short rather than long periods of time.[1]

Industrial wastewaters can pose serious hazards to municipal systems because the collection and treatment systems have not been designed to carry or treat them. The wastes can damage sewers and interfere with the operation of treatment plants. They may pass through the wastewater treatment plant (WWTP) untreated or they may concentrate in the sludge, rendering it a hazardous waste.[2]

The depletion and degradation of urban water resources recently has led to the advocacy of a sustainable urban water system, characterized by lower water consumption, preservation of natural drainage, reduced generation of wastewater through water conservation and reuse, advanced water pollution control, and preservation and/or enhancement of the receiving water ecosystem.

Basic elements of the urban water system are shown in Figures 5.1(a) and 5.1(b) Three major water pollution control components are identified; urban drainage (conveying both surface runoff and municipal wastewaters), sewage treatment plants, and the receiving waters. The interdependency and

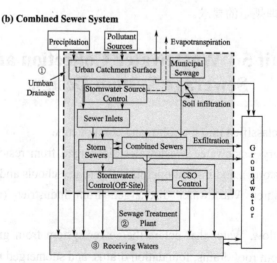

Figure 5.1 Separate and Combined Sewer Systems

connectivity among these components are shown by arrows indicating hydraulic transport by either gravity or pumping. For simplicity, only the major pathways of flow and pollutants are shown. Other transport modes, such as the mechanical removal of solids or sludge from various elements of the system, have been omitted. Urban drainage is provided for prevention of flooding, reduced inconvenience due to surface water ponding, alleviation of health hazards, and improved aesthetics.[3]

During the past century, two types of urban drainage systems have evolved - combined [Figure 5.l(a)] and separate [Figure 5.1(b)]. The combined system conveys both surface runoff and municipal wastewaters in a single pipe. In dry weather, the flow is transported to the sewage treatment plant and treated. In wet weather, as the runoff inflow into the combined sewers increases, the capacity of the collection system and of the treatment plant is exceeded and the excess flows are allowed to escape from the collection system into the receiving waters in the form of the so-called combined sewer overflows (CSOs).

In the separate sewer system, surface runoff is transported by storm sewers and discharged into the receiving waters, and municipal wastewaters are transported by sanitary sewers to the sewage treatment plant and treated prior to discharge into the receiving waters.

Both drainage systems exist in many variations. Interactions among catchments drainage, sewers, sewage treatment plants, and the receiving waters are shown in Figures 5.l(a) and 5.l(b). The interactions between storm sewer discharge and the receiving waters are particularly strong and related to the impact of urbanization on the hydrologic cycle. During urban development, urban surfaces are covered by impervious elements such as rooftops, streets, sidewalks and parking lots, and soils become consolidated by land use activities. Consequently, natural rainfall abstractions caused by vegetative canopy, depressions and infiltration into the ground are reduced and a higher proportion of rainwater is converted into direct runoff. Fast concentration of runoff on impervious surfaces, together with typical hydraulic improvements such as gutters, storm sewers and drains, result in the increased incidence and magnitude of floods. This impact is further aggravated by the straightening, deepening and lining of streams in urban areas.

Although the storm water and sewage are conveyed separately in separate systems [Figure 5.1(b)], some cross-connections are hardly avoidable. Influx of municipal sewage into separate storm sewers contributes to the pollution of storm water and the influx of storm water into sanitary sewers increases the flow rates, which may exceed the Sewage Treatment Plant (STP) capacity and lead to sewage bypasses. Sources of such influxes include cross-connections between the sanitary and storm sewers. There are also connections between sanitary and storm sewers and the groundwater - in the form of infiltration of groundwater (undesirably increasing flow rates), and sewer exfiltration leading to the pollution of groundwater. In a well designed and maintained separate sewer system, the cross-connections between storm and sanitary sewers are avoided, sewers are watertight to prevent infiltration and the interactions between storm water and sewage treatment plants are thereby minimized.

The main remaining interactions are those between storm water or STP effluent discharge and the receiving waters. Wet weather flows produce hydraulic and pollution shocks on the treatment plants which, while they do not affect the mechanical part of properly designed facilities, do affect especially the nitrification and denitrification processes of biological treatment by shortening the reaction time, reducing the return sludge flow and diminishing the biomass as sludge is flushed into the final clarifier. Furthermore, the biomass reactions are rather sensitive to fluctuations of concentration, temperature and pH value. All these factors can lead to reduced treatment efficiencies and increased discharge of pollutants into the receiving waters.

In combined sewer systems [Figure 5.l(a)], the interactions among the three major components are even stronger than in separate systems. In dry weather, the combined system functions like the separate system-the only flow generated is municipal sewage which is transported to the sewage treatment plant for treatment. In wet weather, surface runoff enters directly combined sewers. When the capacity of the system is exceeded, flows are either discharged directly into the receiving waters (as CSOs) with very adverse impacts, or enter CSO control facilities, which also interact with the STP.[4]

The pollution characteristics of CSOs, while somewhat similar to those of storm water, are strongly affected by domestic sewage and sewer sludge washout from combined sewers. Consequently, CSOs are particularly significant sources of solids, biodegradable organic matter, nutrients and faecal bacteria. Their impacts on the receiving waters are similar to those described in the preceding section, but much stronger in terms of oxygen depletion, eutrophication and increased productivity, and faecal pollution. It is desirable, therefore, to control CSOs prior to their discharge into the receiving waters. Such control facilities are typically operated in conjunction with the sewage treatment plant.

Important Words and Expressions

prerequisite [priˈrekwizit]　n. 先决条件，前提　adj.作为前提的，必备的
infiltration [ˌinfilˈtreiʃən]　n. 渗透；浸润物；渗透物；渗透活动
institutional [ˌinstiˈtjuːʃənəl]　adj. 公共团体的，机构的，学会的
GLUMRB 全称为 GREAT LAKES-UPPER MISSISSIPPI RIVER BOARD
密西西比河上游保护委员会
manufacturing [ˌmænjuˈfæktʃəriŋ]　n. 制造；产品；制造业　v. 制造，加工；粗制滥造；捏造；制造
per capita　每人
demographic [ˈdiːməˈgræfik]　adj. 人口统计学的
wastewater treatment plant (WWTP)　污水处理厂
depletion [diˈpliːʃən]　n. 消耗；用尽
advocacy [ˈædvəkəsi]　n. 拥护；提倡；鼓吹
interdependency [ˌintədiˈpendənsi]　n. 互相依赖
aesthetics [iːsˈθetiks]　n. 美学，审美学
impervious [imˈpəːviəs]　adj. 不能渗透的，不为所动的
exfiltration [ˌeksfilˈtreiʃən]　n. 漏出，渗漏，<俚>逃出敌军阵地
watertight [ˈwɔːtətait]　adj. 不漏水的，无懈可击的
nitrification [ˌnaitrəfiˈkeiʃən]　n. 氮化合，氮饱和，硝化作用
denitrification [diːˌnaitrifiˈkeiʃən]　n. 脱氮作用，反硝化作用
adverse [ˈædvəːs]　adj. 不利的，逆向的，有害的

faecal ['fiːkəl] adj. 排泄物的，渣滓的

conjunction [kən'dʒʌŋkʃən] n. 结合，关联，连词，（事件等的）同时发生

Notes

[1] 在小的社区中，（水的耗用和污水产生量的）波动变化要大于大的社区，且短时间内大于长时间。

[2] 它们（工业污水）可能会通过污水处理厂但未被处理而直接被排放，或者被浓缩在污泥里，成为危险的废物。

[3] 城市的排水系统用来防止内涝，减少由于地面汇集成水塘带来的不便，减少了对人类健康的危害，改善了美感。

[4] 当合流管道系统的容量已经无法满足排水量，过量的合流水或者带着负面影响，直接排放入收纳水体（即合流制溢流污水），或者进入污水处理厂联动的溢流设施。

Exercises

1. Answering the following questions in English according to the text：

When you have completed studying this chapter, you should be able to do the following without the aid of your textbook or notes：

(1) Name the types of sewers (lateral, main, etc.) on a map with a sewer plan layout.

(2) Name the parts (bell, spigot, etc.) of a sewer pipe.

2. Using the following each word to make up the sentences, respectively：

(1) Domestic wastewater

(2) Sanitary wastewater

(3) Industrial wastewater

(4) Manhole

(5) Pipe

3. Put the following English into Chinese：

(1) In the construction for new residential areas, the sewer is commonly placed on one side of the roadway in the right-of-way (ROW). Connections to the sewer from buildings on the opposite side of the street may be made by boring under the street. In established communities (or where local codes require), it may be found in alley ways behind the residence or in the street.

(2) Sewers should be at such a depth that they can receive the contributed flow by gravity. Where houses have basements, the invert of the sewer is placed a minimum of 3.0 to 3.5 m below grade. Where there is no basement, it is placed to provide sufficient cover to protect the pipe from live load and dead load damage. In the absence of other guidance, a rule of thumb is to use a sewer invert depth of 1.8 to 2.4 m below grade when basements are not present.

4. Put the following Chinese into English：

(1) 连接管

(2) 进水泵

(3) 地表径流

(4) 室内排水系统的作用是为了安全快速地排出生活污水、工业废水和雨水。通常这几种不同的废水由各自的排水系统排出。因此，室内排水系统可以分为生活排水系统，工业排水系

统和雨水排水系统。

(5) 设计一个排水系统的首要步骤是建立一个全局系统布置图，图中应包括排水区域、道路、街道、建筑物、其他公共设施、地形、土壤类型以及所有排水建筑物的地下室或最底层标高。对于未开发的或尚未列入发展计划中的排水区域应该采取在管网末端预留足够的检查井以便今后污水管道的接入。

5. Put the following abbr. into full phrases：
ROW；STP；CSOs；WWTP

Reading Material A

Sanitary Sewer Design

The design of a sewer system generally includes the following steps: preliminary investigations, a detailed survey, the actual design, and preparation of final drawings.

The various types of sewers in a typical wastewater collection system are described in Table 5.1 and are illustrated in Figure 5.2 and Figure 5.3.

Table 5.1 Nomenclature of sewers in a typical collection system

Name	Description
Lateral	Lateral sewers form the first element of a wastewater collection system. They collect the wastewater from buildings and convey it to a main sewer
Main	The main sewer conveys wastewater to trunk sewers of intercepting sewers
Force main	This term is used to describe a pressurized pipe that is used to convey wastewater
Trunk	Trunk sewers are large diameter sewers that are used to convey wastewater from main sewers to treatment facilities or to intercepting sewers
Interceptor	The interceptors are very large diameter sewers that are used to intercept a number of main or trunk sewers and convey wastewater to treatment facilities

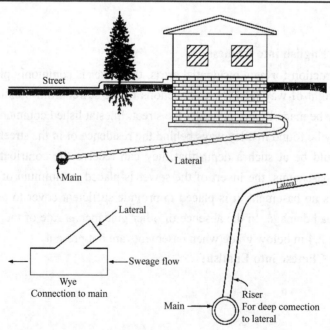

Figure 5.2 Lateral with exploded view of wye connection to main and an alternative connection for a deep main

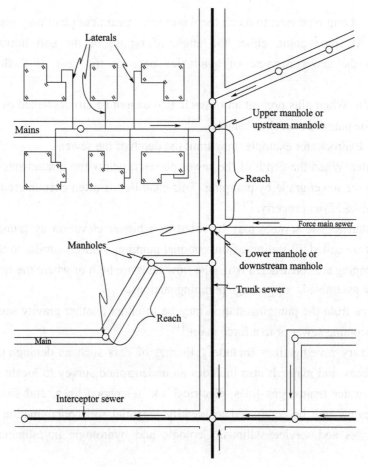

Figure 5.3 Nomenclature of sewers

Appurtenances:

• Manholes. Manholes are the most familiar appurtenance of a wastewater collection system. Although they have been built of brick and cast in place, current practice is to use precast concrete.[1] The standard manhole and the drop manhole are the typical configurations. The drop manhole is used when the inflow and outflow sewers differ in elevation by more than 0.6 m. This protects the workers who must enter from inadvertently taking a shower while they work. It also reduces volatilization of odoriferous compounds. The entire outside of the drop connection is encased in concrete to minimize differential settlement pressures between the drop pipe and the manhole that may fracture the connection.

The manhole cover is always round to prevent it from falling into the manhole. Current practice is to use a solid cast iron or ductile iron cover. The cover should not be perforated because of the potential for inflow from storm water. This also minimizes escape of odors. When there is potential for the manhole to be submerged, the cover is provided with a gasket and is bolted down. Alternatively, if the manhole is not in a roadway, the manhole may be constructed so that the top is above flood level.

Lift Stations and Pumping Stations. Several conditions result in the necessity to pump sewage in a gravity collection system. These include but are not limited to the following cases:

• Flat terrain. Long pipe runs to reach the wastewater treatment plant may result in sewers that are very deep. At some point, either the angle of repose of the soil limits the excavation perpendicular to the sewer because of available space or the cost of further excavation is prohibitive.[2]

• Hilly terrain. When hills present an obstacle that cannot be circumvented by gravity flow, the wastewater may be pumped over the obstacle.

• Obstacles. Bedrock, for example, may limit the depth of the sewer.

• Groundwater. When the depth of the sewer places it below the groundwater table, it may be desirable to raise the sewer grade by pumping. This condition is often encountered when sewers are to be provided for lakefront property. [3]

In these instances, the sewage may be lifted to a higher elevation by pumping. Thus, these pumping stations are called lift stations. Conventional pumping stations similar to those used for low service water pumping are constructed when the flow rates are high or where the wastewater must be screened. Factory-assembled, or package pumping stations.

The discharge from the pumping station may be to either another gravity sewer with a higher invert than the incoming sewer or to a force main. [4]

The preliminary investigations include gathering of data such as demographics, wastewater production estimates, and maps. It also includes an underground survey to locate obstacles such as existing sewers, water mains, gas lines, electrical and telephone lines, and similar features. An environmental review will be conducted to identify potential soil contamination from abandoned waste disposal sites and service stations. Geologic and hydrologic investigations may also be appropriate.

In order to prepare construction drawings, the following survey work must be conducted: location of streets, right-of-ways (ROW), basements and their elevations (usually estimated for residences), location of natural features such as streams and ditches, and construction of elevation profiles. In addition, benchmarks must be established for use during construction.

For sewer system layout, the map scale used is on the order of 1:1,000 to 1:3,000. For construction drawings, the map scale is on the order of 1:480 to 1:600. When there is significant relief, contours are shown at intervals ranging from 250 mm to 3 m. Elevations of street intersections, abrupt changes in grade, building foundations, and existing structures (sewers, lift stations, etc.) that new construction must connect with are included on the map. For projects encompassing more than one or two streets, aerial photogrammetry is often used.

The design of the sewer network in a collection system is an iterative process based on the required capacity of the system for the anticipated flow rates. Trial pipe diameters are selected for the network of pipes, and a hydraulic analysis is performed for the anticipated range of conditions.

Of the numerous issues that must be addressed in the network design, the following will be presented:

• Estimation of wastewater flow rates.

• Pipe material selection.

• Design criteria.

• Design equations.

- Collection system layout.
- Design of a lateral or branch.

Notes

[1] 尽管检查井以往由砖块建造，在工地上现场筑建，目前的实践趋势是使用预制混凝土取而代之。

[2] 平坦地形。敷设至污水处理厂之前的长距离污水主管可能会埋设很深，在某些地方，可能会由于几乎垂直的开挖角度限制或者是过高的大开挖成本，需要泵吸。

[3] 地下水。当污水管的埋设深度低于地下水位时，这时就可以用泵吸来抬高污水管。当污水管要埋设于湖泊边地块的时候经常遇到这种情况。

[4] 提升泵站的出水管要么排入另外的一套污水重力流系统，高程比进入的新管道高程还要高，要么就以压力管的形式敷设。

Reading Material B

Sewer Pipes and Jointing

The nomenclature of a typical sewer pipe with a bell and spigot joint is shown in Figure 5.4.

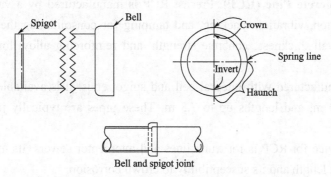

Figure 5.4   Nomenclature of a sewer pipe

Sewer Pipe Material Selection

The principal sewer material for pipes with small or medium diameters is polyvinyl chloride (PVC).[1] For larger pipe diameters, ductile iron pipe (DIP), high density polyethylene (HDPE) pipe, or reinforced concrete pipe (RCP) may be specified. Truss pipes are becoming m ore common for larger pipe diameters.

Vitrified clay pipe (VCP). This classic pipe material has demonstrated its durability in use in the United States for over a century. It has a high resistance to corrosion and abrasion. Its major disadvantage is its high mass per unit length that makes it more difficult to handle and increases installation costs. It is rarely installed today.

This pipe is made of clay or shale that has been ground, wet, molded, dried, and fired in a kiln. Near the end of the burning process, sodium chloride is added to the kiln. It vaporizes to form a hard waterproof glaze by reacting with the pipe surface. The firing of the clay produces a vitrification of the clay that makes it very hard and dense.

The pipe is manufactured with integral bell and spigot ends fitted with polymeric rings. It is available in diameters from 75 mm through 1,050 mm and lengths up to 3 m. Pipes are typically joined with push-on gasket joints.

Polyvinyl chloride pipe (PVC). This pipe is made by extrusion of polyvinyl chloride. It is available in diameters from 10 mm through 1.2 m and lengths up to 6 m. Rubber gasket bell and spigot type joints are used to connect the pipes.

This pipe has been in use for over half a century. It is almost exclusively the material of choice for pressure and vacuum sewers. Its advantages are corrosion resistance and low mass per unit length. It is subject to attack by certain organic chemicals and excessive deflection if improperly bedded.[2] The low mass per unit length gives it some cost advantage in installation.

Ductile iron pipe (DIP). This pipe material was discussed in Chapter 17. Its primary application for sewers is for force mains.[3] Because wastewater is often corrosive, current practice is to use a cement mortar lining and an asphaltic outer coating. Epoxy coating may be used in trunk sewers. DIP manufacturers recommend that the pipe be encased in a loose-fitting flexible polyethylene tube (0.2 mm thick) when the pipe is to be placed in corrosive soils.

High-density polyethylene (HDPE). This pipe material was discussed in Chapter 17. Its primary use is as an alternative pressure pipe for force mains.

Reinforced Concrete Pipe (RCP). Precast RCP is manufactured by a variety of techniques including centrifugation, vibration, packing, and tamping for consolidating the concrete in forms. Adjustment of the wall thickness, concrete strength, and reinforcing allow for a wide variety of strengths.

The pipe is manufactured with integral bell and spigot ends. It is available in diameters from 300 mm through 5.0 m, and lengths up to 7.5 m. These pipes are typically joined with push-on gasket joints.

The normal service for RCP is for trunk lines and interceptor sewers. Its major limitations are its high mass per unit length and its susceptibility to crown corrosion.

Truss Pipe. This pipe is made of PVC or acrylonitrile butadiene styrene (ABS). It consists of dual walls with a truss system between the walls. Sometimes the space between the walls is filled with cement. It is more rigid than PVC pipe but shares the same ease of construction.

Pipe Size

No public gravity sewer conveying raw wastewater shall be less than 200 mm in diameter. This size has been selected to minimize clogging when extraneous material enters the sewer.

Some engineers design sewer pipes to flow half full at the design capacity to provide a factor of safety. This practice is favored when designing laterals or branches that have the potential to be extended to accommodate growth. It is not justified for mains, trunk lines, or interceptors. [4]

Changes in Pipe Size

When a smaller pipe joins a larger one, the invert of the larger sewer should be lowered sufficiently to maintain the same energy gradient. An approximate method for securing this result is to place the 0.8 depth point of both sewers at the same location.

In no instance should a larger pipe discharge into a smaller pipe. Even though a smaller pipe at a steeper slope may be able to carry the larger flow, there is the potential for objects that will travel freely in the larger pipe to obstruct the smaller pipe.

Notes

[1] 对于中小管径的管道，首先考虑采用的是 PVC 管。

[2] 它可以承受一定程度的有机化学腐蚀，以及在不适当安装下的较大的偏斜。

[3] 它主要作为压力主干管的首要备选管材。

[4] 一些工程师在设计污水管时考虑到安全的因素采用非满管流。这种尝试对于设计支管和旁通管的时候比较适用，因为还可以容纳未来流量的增长。但不适用于主管、干管和截流管。

Unit 6 Stormwater Collection and Sewer Design

Historically, many communities elected to collect storm water and wastewater in combined sewers and convey the peak dry weather flow to the wastewater treatment plant while large surges of storm water were diverted directly to surface water bodies.[1] The resulting mixture of sewage and storm water has major adverse impacts on the receiving bodies of water. Current regulations prohibit this combination in new facilities.

Design Procedures for Storm Sewers

The design of storm sewers includes a number of steps, including the establishment of design objectives, preparation of input data, computation of runoff flows, and the sizing and layout of drainage elements.

Design objectives. Design objectives are generally established during the planning process. Traditionally, such objectives dealt only with runoff quantity and specified the desired levels of protection against flooding by specifying return periods of design rainfall events. Significant changes in this process were caused by adopting the major/minor drainage concept and water quality/environmental protection objectives.[2] The minor drainage, which includes underground sewers and small open channels and provides local convenience and prevention of water ponding, is typically designed for short return periods, from 1 to 10 years. The major drainage system conveys flood flows through urban areas and includes large sewers, the natural drainage system, swales, streets and other overland routes. This system is generally designed for return periods from 50 to 100 years.

Water quality objectives are much more difficult to define. Attempts to impose end-of-pipe water quality standards are rarely acceptable, because they neglect the linkage between drainage effluent quality and the environmental state, uses and self-purification capacity of the receiving waters.[3] Thus, there is more interest in defining drainage water quality objectives in terms of the receiving waters, quite often outside of the mixing zone. Additionally, in the ecosystem approach, traditional water quality objectives for the receiving stream, typically derived from the water uses, are expanded for ecological protection and enhancement of the stream, further increasing the expectations on runoff quality. Thus, the water quality objectives for urban runoff will probably continue to be driven by the water quality conditions in the receiving waters, established locally for specific watercourses.

Design Flows and Pollutant Loads

Using the established design objectives, runoff flows and their associated pollutant loads must be determined at various points in the drainage network. In current practice, various levels of sophistication are employed, depending on the design objectives and the size of the drainage area. Calculations of flows start with the preparation of rainfall data inputs used to calculate runoff hydrographs at inlets to the drainage network. These inlet hydrographs are then routed through the transport network.

Rainfall data are used in urban runoff calculations in various forms, depending on the design approach and computational procedure used. The most common forms include intensity-duration-frequency (IDF) curves, synthetic design storms, historical design storms, and actual or synthetic long-term rainfall records. Although the literature on rainfall data for storm sewer design is rather extensive the issues of uncertainties in rainfall inputs and their impact on calculated runoff flows have not been fully resolved. Uncertainties include errors in point measurements, and impacts of temporal and spatial distributions on estimates of catchment rainfall. Other uncertainties are introduced in the analysis of observed data by using various assumptions which may or may not be valid. It should be noted, however, that the impact of rainfall data uncertainties on calculated runoff flows is somewhat reduced by the fact that the catchment functions as a filter which dampens out some perturbations (real or spurious) in rainfall inputs.

IDF curves were among the earliest rainfall inputs used in runoff calculations, particularly as inputs to the rational method. The IDF curves are derived from rainfall records using frequency analysis, usually applied to annual rainfall maxima of durations ranging from 5 minutes to 24 hours. The main shortcoming of the IDF curves is the assumed constancy of rainfall intensities, which makes them unsuitable for computations of runoff hydrographs.

The development of synthetic design storms was necessitated by the need to use time-varying rainfall inputs to calculate runoff hydrographs. Design storms are generally defined as rainfall events developed for the design of specific facilities, such as sewer pipes or retention basins. Design storms are associated with certain return periods, and the calculated flow values are commonly (and erroneously) presumed to have the same return period as the storm. In spite of theoretical shortcomings of the design storm concept and evident uncertainties in return periods of various parameters of the calculated hydrographs, design storms are widely accepted in practice.

The criticism of synthetic storms as "events that never occurred" led to the adoption of historical design storms, which have the advantage that their severity and the resulting magnitudes of runoff flows and flood damages are well documented. Some shortcomings of the synthetic design storms, such as uncertainty regarding the storm return period and antecedent moisture, apply here as well. Furthermore, long-term climate change and its impacts on precipitation undermine the inherent assumption that the statistics of rainfall records containing these historical storms will not change.

The limitations of design storms and related single or multiple event simulations can be avoided by establishing design flows from frequency analysis of simulated runoff records. In this case, precipitation is converted into flows using one of the continuous simulation models described in the section on models. Rainfall inputs in these simulations are actual rainfall records or records simulated by rainfall models (the former are more readily accepted by practitioners). Simulated runoff records, in terms of water quantity and quality, are well suited for analysis of water quality in the receiving waters. Difficulties with long-term variations in precipitation and establishment of joint probabilities of runoff discharges and conditions in the receiving waters are unavoidable.

Design of Sewer System Structures

Sewer pipes - after computation of runoff flows and their characteristics, the layout of the sewer system is selected and its elements are designed. In general, each pipe is designed individually as an open-channel in which the design flow depth should be less than 0.85 of the pipe diameter.[4] Following the sizing of individual sewers, the system functioning is checked to assess its overall performance and whether any damages would occur when the pipe surcharging would cause damage at those points where the hydraulic grade line rises above the elevations of basements, or underpasses.

Sewer inlets are key elements in drainage design which divide runoff flow into two components - surface flow and subsurface flow conveyed by sewers. Temporary storage on the catchment surface is utilized to reduce flow peaks in sewers, and sewer surcharging is avoided by placing a limit on the maximum flow conveyed through inlets. Other considerations in inlet design include bicycle safety and pedestrian convenience - gutter flow over pedestrian crossings is to be avoided and multiple inlets are placed in sags to prevent the ponding of water. As a result the density of inlets in urban areas is fairly high, certainly higher than required for road drainage. This further emphasizes the need to restrict inlet capacities.

The ultimate goal of storm water management is to provide adequate drainage services in urban areas, while maintaining storm water flows and volumes at levels comparable to predevelopment conditions and controlling pollutant fluxes. Such a goal should be achieved under a number of constraints, including the given physical constraints (local physiography), cost-effectiveness, acceptable future maintenance burden, and a neutral impact on the environment.

Important Words and Expressions

purification [ˌpjuərəfiˈkeiʃən]   n. 洗净，净化；涤罪，洗罪；提纯，精炼；斋戒
self-purification [ˈselfpjuərəfiˈkeiʃən]   n. 自然净化
sophistication [səˌfistiˈkeiʃən]   n. 老练，精明，复杂，精密，有教养，诡辩，强词夺理
antecedent [ˌæntiˈsiːdnt]   n. 前情，先行词，祖先   adj. 在…之前的，居先的
moisture [ˈmɔistʃə]   n. 水分，潮气，湿度
precipitation [priˌsipiˈteiʃən]   n. 仓促，急躁，沉淀，降雨量，坠落，凝结，冰雹
inherent [inˈhiərənt]   adj. 固有的，内在的
open-channel   明渠
underpass [ˈʌndəˌpæs]   n. 地下通道，高架桥下通道或路段
inlet [ˈinlet]   n. 进口，水湾，入口
hydrograph [ˈhaidrəgræf]   n. 自记水位计，水位图，水位曲线
intensity-duration-frequency (IDF)   n. 强度-持续时间-频率
gutter [ˈgʌtə]   n. 排水沟，槽，贫民区
pedestrian [piˈdestriən]   adj. 徒步的，缺乏想象的   n. 行人

Notes

[1] 历史上，很多社区都选择了合流制排水管道来收集雨水和污水，它尽可能把最大的旱

季污水量输送至污水处理厂，同时大量汹涌的雨水被转移排入地面水体。

[2] 传统上来说，这样的目标只是明确径流流量和通过确定洪水重现期内明确想实现的抵御水灾的水平。在这个过程中重大的改进是引入主要/次要排水概念以及水环境质量/环境保护的目标。

[3] 水质量目标更加难以定义。推广实施末端管网水质标准的尝试几乎不被接受，因为它被认为忽略了管网出水水质，环境自身状况，用途，以及收纳水体的自净能力。

[4] 通常的，每个管道要单独作为非满流设计，管道中的水流深度不能超过其直径的0.85倍。

Exercises

1. Answering the following questions in English according to the text:
   (1) Illustrate the Sewer System Structures.
   (2) How to estimate the storm runoff?

2. Using the following each word to make up the sentences, respectively:
   (1) storm water
   (2) runoff
   (3) rainfall
   (4) inlet
   (5) drainage

3. Put the following English into Chinese:

(1) Runoff volume, peak flow or total hydrograph are most commonly predicted by computer methods. Runoff volumes (or depth of runoff over the catchment) can be predicted by simple regression techniques as well as by more complex simulation involving analysis of losses to infiltration and evaporation.

(2) The ageing of successive layers of sediment deposited by a time series of storms may substantially change the physical, chemical and biological properties of the sediment bed, which may create an enhanced pollution potential when moved. In addition to the time history of the storms, the deposition, erosion and transport of cohesive sediments in tanks is very much a function of the flow pattern and the distribution of bed velocity as the storm hydro graph is discharged through the tank.

4. Put the following Chinese into English:
   (1) 洪峰流量
   (2) 暴雨强度
   (3) 分流制排水系统
   (4) 污水支管将从各个建筑物收集的污水输送至污水截流管或污水干管中的管道。各地制定的地方标准规定了这些管道的铺设位置，这些管道一般铺设在位于街道中心下方的雨水管旁。污水支管应能输送其服务面积上目前人口数及预期人口数的污水量。
   (5) 通常，污水管道主要遵循重力流排水，并敷设于指定管道位置或街道下方。两边的土地坡度应朝向截流管。旁侧或支管接入到截流污水管后继续爬坡到分水岭。支管应敷设在所服务区域的指定位置或街道下为整个区域服务。

5. Put the following abbr. into full phrases:
   COD；SS；DS；TN；TKN；TP

Reading Material A

Estimating Storm Runoff

During the last 25 years a fairly good qualitative understanding of basic processes affecting runoff quality has evolved, and estimates of ranges or mean values of characteristic concentrations of various pollutants in storm water have been developed.[1] Urban runoff quality data bases have been established with such objectives as the characterization of urban runoff, evaluation of its potential to cause water quality deterioration, and assessment of selected runoff control measures.

Rainwater falling over the urban area scavenges various chemicals from the atmosphere, which reach the catchment surface and come in contact with other pollutants already accumulated on the surface.[2] Storm water runoff mobilizes such pollutants and transports them to sewer inlets as dissolved loads, suspended loads, or bed loads. After passing through sewer inlets, often equipped with catch basins functioning as sediment traps, runoff and dissolved or suspended pollutants enter the sewer system and eventually reach the receiving waters. Runoff composition changes during transport. First, transport of solids and chemicals by runoff can be either supply- or carrying-capacity limited. In the former case, runoff composition is affected by the availability of solids and chemicals on the catchment surface, in catch basins, and in sewers.

For drainage design and the assessment of its interaction with the receiving water quality, one must first compute runoff flows and then their physical/chemical characteristics. Such computations are usually done by simulation models.[3]

In calculations of runoff, certain distinct computational stages are recognized - calculation of rainfall excess, surface runoff hydrographs at inlets to the drainage system, and transport in drainage networks. Rainfall excess represents that part of rainfall that is directly converted into runoff. It is calculated by subtracting rainfall abstractions from precipitation. Rainfall abstractions differ for various surfaces and generally include interception, evaporation, evapotranspiration, depression storage, and infiltration.

Rainfall excess is routed along the catchment surface to obtain the so-called inlet hydrographs at the points of entry to the drainage network. These inlet hydro graphs are then routed through the drainage network using various levels of complexity, depending on the design objectives. In simple planning models, flow routing in transport elements is either neglected or approximated by the time-lagging of inflow hydro graphs using the calculated times of travel. The next level of complexity involves so-called storage routing, allowing for time offset of flow and changes in hydrograph shape. Finally, the most comprehensive flow routing is hydraulic flow routing, or the dynamic wave flow routing allowing considerations of pressurized flow in sewers.

The flow routing method used should be appropriate for the drainage system studied, and should account for interactions between the drainage, STP and the receiving waters. In separate systems, the interactions between drainage and STPs are limited. In this case, transport processes may be important for sewer sizing, determination of flood damages or surface water ponding, and calculations of temporal variations in runoff quality. In combined systems, transport calculations will be much more important, because the occurrence of overflows depends on discharges at overflow points. Also the sewer appurtenances may be rather complex and include such facilities as overflow structures, pumping stations and storage facilities. Intricacies of combined sewage transport will affect computations of inflows to the STP and such information is crucial for the assessment of plant operation.

Conventional design of urban drainage has focused on conveyance of runoff flows and neglected water quality considerations. Such considerations, however, form an integral part of storm water control which strives to reduce drainage costs and mitigate runoff impacts on receiving waters.

Urban storm runoff is a substantial source of surface-water pollution in the United States. Because collection and analysis of urban-storm-runoff data are expensive and time consuming, city planners and engineers need techniques to estimate storm-runoff loads and volumes where minimal or no data exist. As a result of the Clean Water Act amendments of 1977, the U.S. Geological Survey and the U.S. Environmental Protection Agency in cooperation with State and local governments collected and analyzed storm rainfall, runoff, and water-quality data in a number of cities throughout the United States to provide needed data for planning and design of water-related projects. The database generated from these studies and used here is comprised of measurements of 2813 storms at 173 urban stations in 30 metropolitan areas throughout the United States. Then, using this large database of urban runoff water-quality and quantity data to develop a set of regression models to estimate storm-runoff loads and volumes (dependent variables) from physical, land-use, and climatic characteristics (explanatory variables). This data base was also used to estimate long-term annual or seasonal loads.

Regional regression models were developed that related storm-runoff loads and volumes to easily measured physical, land-use, and climatic characteristics. In a simplified assessment, storm-runoff loads and volumes could be estimated from their mean values for each region. However, more accurate estimates of storm-runoff loads and volumes can be obtained by using regional multiple-regression analysis to relate these dependent variables to physical, land-use, and climatic characteristics. Regional analyses account for spatial variations in storm-runoff loads and volumes that are caused by regional differences in characteristics directly or indirectly affecting storm-runoff loads and volumes. Accuracy of the estimates of storm-runoff loads and volumes (as measured by the standard error of estimate) is a function of the difference between measured and estimated storm-runoff loads and volumes.

The dependent variables include storm-runoff loads for 11 chemical constituents, expressed in pounds: chemical oxygen demand (COD), suspended solids (SS), dissolved solids (DS), total nitrogen (TN), total ammonia plus organic nitrogen (total Kjeldahl nitrogen) (TKN), total phosphorus (TP), dissolved phosphorus (DP), total recoverable cadmium (CD), total recoverable copper (CU), total recoverable lead (PB), and total recoverable zinc (ZN); and storm-runoff volumes (RUN), expressed in cubic feet, have been analyzed. The dependent variables were selected according to their frequency of availability in the database and according to the general importance of the variable in urban planning. [4]

Initially, all data were analyzed together, and the most accurate regression models were selected for each constituent. Then the data were stratified on a regional basis to determine whether the regression models could be improved. Regionalization on the basis of statistically aggregated patterns and physical settings has been beneficial in-many hydrologic studies. The best regional divisions were selected after testing the following possible bases for regionalization: physiographic divisions, geographic divisions, total contributing drainage areas, impervious areas, 2-year 24-h rainfall, mean annual rainfall, and mean minimum January temperatures. The resultant regionalized models were compared with the regression models incorporating all the data.

Analysis of covariance was carried out on data in certain regions to determine whether the models for these regions were significantly different from one another.

As a result, linear regression models were developed for the estimation of storm-runoff loads and volumes from physical, land-use, and climatic characteristics of urban watersheds throughout the United States. One use of these models is to estimate storm-runoff loads and volumes at gaged and ungaged urban watersheds. The most significant explanatory variables in all linear regression models were total storm rainfall and total contributing drainage area. Impervious area, land-use, and mean annual climatic characteristics were also significant explanatory variables in some linear regression models. Models for dissolved solids, total nitrogen, and total ammonia plus organic nitrogen as nitrogen were the most accurate models for most areas, whereas models for suspended solids were the least accurate. The most accurate models were those for the more arid western United States, and the least accurate models were those for areas that had large quantities of mean annual rainfall.

Notes

[1] 在过去的 25 年中，一种非常好的定性的关于影响降雨量的形成的理论一直在发展，而且关于暴雨中各种污染物的特征值浓度的范围或平均值的预测理论也在发展。

[2] 降临在城市区域的雨水从大气中搜集了各种各样的化学物质，雨水达到流域的表面后便开始与原来表面上已经聚集的其他污染物开始互相作用。

[3] 为了实现排水设计以及它与收纳水体混合作用后的效果评估，人们必须通过计算雨量以及他们的物理和化学特征值。这样的计算往往要通过建立模型来实现。

[4] 雨水径流负荷中的因变量参数包括 11 种，这些参数以每立方米雨水中的质量来计量分析：生化需氧量，悬浮固体浓度，溶解性固体，总氮，总凯氏氮，总磷，溶解性磷，总可恢复性镉，总可恢复性铜，总可恢复性铅，总可恢复性锌，雨水径流体积。这些参数是根据它们在数据库里出现的频率以及在城区系统设计中的重要性来选择的。

Reading Material B

Combined Sewer System

When combined sewer systems were introduced in 1855, they were hailed as a vast improvement over urban cesspool ditches that ran along city streets and spilled over when it rained.[1] These networks of underground pipes were designed to dry out streets by collecting rainwater runoff, domestic sewage from newly invented flush toilets, and industrial wastewater all in the same pipe. Waste- and stormwater was then discharged directly into waterways; in the early twentieth century, sewage treatment plants were added to clean the wastewater before it hit streams. Combined sewer systems were-and still are-a great idea, with one catch: when too much stormwater is added to the flow of raw sewage, the result is frequently an overflow. These combined sewer overflows (CSOs) have become the focus of a debate regarding the best techniques to manage growing volumes of sewage and stormwater runoff in many older U.S. communities.[2]

In dry weather, a combined sewer system sends a town's entire volume of wastewater to a sewage plant, which treats and discharges it into a waterway. Rain and snowmelt, however, can fill up a combined sewer. The sewers have been specifically designed with escape overflow pipes so that the mixture of sewage and stormwater doesn't back up into buildings, including homes. The resulting CSO dumps raw sewage into lakes, rivers, and coastal waters, potentially harming public health and the environment.

In April 1994, the U.S. Environmental Protection Agency (EPA) issued the CSO Control Policy, the national framework for control of CSOs, through the National Pollutant Discharge Elimination System permitting program. This policy mandated that communities dramatically reduce or eliminate their CSOs, and the agency began working with municipalities to improve antiquated sewage systems so they could reach Clean Water Act goals. Under this policy, communities with combined sewer systems must establish a short-term plan to control these discharges as well as a long-term control plan.[3]

The EPA's mandate on CSOs leaves communities with two basic options, communities with CSOs can build separate underground pipes for sewage and storm water; or they can keep their combined pipes and somehow build more capacity. "Blending," or "bypassing," is one engineering technique that many sewerage operators have used to handle peak flows. During wet weather, utilities route a portion of peak wastewater flows around the biological treatment units, then combine the rerouted flows with the portion of wastewater that went through biological treatment. After blending, the effluent is usually disinfected and discharged into water bodies.

In November 2003, the EPA proposed a new federal policy that would have authorized municipal sewage plants around the country to blend wastewater in certain circumstances and under certain conditions-for example, only during periods of heavy rain or snowmelt, and only if plants were already meeting effluent standards required for permitting. The EPA said that its proposed policy was already common practice in many communities.

On 19 May 2005, the EPA announced that it would not finalize the sewage blending policy as proposed in November 2003. Blending is not a long-term solution, it will continue to review policy and regulatory alternatives to create feasible approaches to treat wastewater.

In 1970, the UK Technical Committee on Storm Overflows and the Disposal of Storm Sewage concluded "it would be unrealistic to contemplate eliminating, over the next few decades, all storm overflows, either by enlarging the sewer capacity or by providing separate sewers for surface water. The cost of any such project would be prohibitive." Subsequently, combined sewer systems have continued to be developed and large European populations are connected to combined sewer systems.

Current policy is to maintain and upgrade the existing combined systems and to consider CSOs in the context of catchment-wide integrated pollution control (IPC). The approach to IPC has been given a central focus by the publication of the latest European Community (EC) Directives, and in the UK the present approach to IPC is very much one of achieving Environmental Quality Standards (EQS) to meet agreed Environmental Quality Objectives (EQO). To achieve the latter it is necessary to control the discharge from CSOs and to provide effective treatment of wastewater effluent to minimize the pollution impact on receiving waters. In each of the EC member states, however, major differences in the legal, organizational, operational and financial management practices, together with a wide range of cultural and geographical differences, have significantly influenced the development and implementation of such pollution control strategies.

In combined sewers, when dry weather flows are low (at night, for instance) solids deposition may take place, causing operational problems such as a reduction in hydraulic capacity, the increased possibility of surcharge and surface flooding, and the premature operation of, and the subsequent increase in, pollutants discharged from, CSOs. It is desirable, therefore, to maintain a self cleansing velocity on at least one occasion per day - usually during peak dry weather flow. In the U.K., the design of combined sewers has been based on the concept of a self-cleansing velocity, or on the use of a minimum shear stress criterion to initiate sediment movement.

Referring to Figure 6.1, for a given time-varying inflow, the hydraulic performance of a CSO structure may be computed from the continuity equation stating that inflow minus outflow (equals the continuation flow plus the spilled flow) equals the rate of change of storage volume.

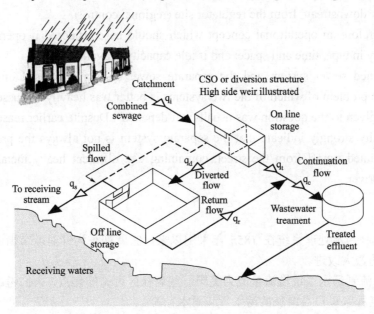

Figure 6.1 Typical configuration of combined sewer inputs to receiving waters

Storage tanks have become a common design feature in many European sewerage systems, and are increasingly being used in North America. The concept is one of including an additional "storage" volume for flow and pollutant load retention in the form of an oversized sewer pipe or storage chamber, which is incorporated into the sewerage system, often at CSO sites.[4] Tanks are normally either on-line (continually in operation) or off-line (to which flow is diverted during high-flow periods via a diversion structure).

Operation of conventional sewer systems focuses on simple local controls (e.g. flow pumping in low lying areas) and systems maintenance. While this simplicity has obvious advantages, in other cases, the concomitant disadvantages, in the form of poorly utilized system capacities or system failures, may be even more important. Consequently, operation of sewer systems in real time has been introduced during the last 25 years.

An urban drainage system (UDS) is controlled in real time if currently monitored process data is used to operate regulators during the flow process. Typically, the task is to activate a number of pumps, sluice gates, weirs, etc. to allow adverse effects (e.g. flooding, CSOs) only if the system is at capacity and at locations where the least damage is caused.

In static systems this can rarely be achieved, and as a result moveable (self-operating) regulators have been introduced to maintain a pre-set flow or water level. Common to many of those regulators is their use of measurement data taken directly at the regulator site (e.g. a float gauge). Such a system is termed local control. Under local control, regulators are not (and sometimes cannot be) remotely manipulated from a control centre. Local control is a good solution if the system has only one regulator (e.g. inflow equalization tank at a treatment plant). However, if several regulators operate independently from each other it might happen that, for example, an upstream pond is emptying into a downstream pond which is already overflowing. In that case, better operation is possible if the ponds are operated conjunctively. This must be done based on process measurements further up and/or downstream from the regulator site (regional control).

RTC is therefore an operational concept which should be considered if operational problems exist; if they vary in type, time and space; and if idle capacity is available.

The combined sewer system and the separate sewer system are based on the analysis of simulations. The problem of which of the two systems is better was heavily discussed over the years and the answer given to the question was usually: "it depends". Despite earlier reasoning, studies on river water quality strongly indicate that the separate system is not always the preferable solution because the polluted runoff from the street, containing e.g. different heavy metals, is discharged directly into the river.

Notes

[1] 当合流制污水处理系统在 1855 年采用以来,它就被誉为针对城市街道的雨天经常溢流的污水沟渠的最大改进。

[2] 这些合流制污水系统溢流量成为美国一些老社区讨论的焦点,人们考虑如何采用最好的方法管理好老社区里日益增长的污水量和雨水径流。

[3] 在这个法案(清洁水资源法案)的要求下,敷设有合流制排水系统的社区必须制定一个短期的计划,来减少合流制污水系统溢流量,同时也要制定长远计划达到方案中的目标。

[4] 储水池是为水流创造新的存储体积以及截留污染物负荷,其形式是一个特大的污水管或者存储室,经常在合流系统的溢流设施处与之合建。

Unit 7   Pumps and Pumping Stations

Pumping machinery and pumping station are very important components in water supply system and drainage system.

Pumps

Pumps are devices that increase the static pressure of fluids. In other words, pumps add energy to a body of fluid in order to move it from one point to another.

Today most water and wastewater pumping is done by either centrifugal pumps or propeller pumps. How the water is directed through the impeller determines the type of pump. The three typical impeller types for pumps are axial, radial and mixed. A description of each of these flow-types follows.

(1) Axial-Flow Pumps

Pumps of the axial- flow type have impellers that lift the water up a vertical riser pipe and direct the flow axially through the impeller parallel to the pump axis and drive shaft. Horizontally mounted, axial-flow pumps are high-capacity pumps that are typically used for low head, high discharge applications such as flood control.

(2) Radial-Flow Pumps

Radial (centrifugal) flow pumps have impellers that force the liquid to discharge radially, from the hub to the periphery, by using centrifugal force to move water up a riser pipe. Impellers of this type are called radial flow or radial vane impellers. The pumps handle any range of head and discharge, but are most suited to high head applications.

(3) Mixed-Flow Pumps

The mixed- flow type has impellers with vanes which are shaped such that the pumping head is developed partly by centrifugal force and partly by a lifting action of the vanes. They are either open type or closed type. The pumps are used primarily for immediate head and discharge applications.

(4) Propeller versus Impeller

Propeller pumps are used for low-head pumping, as is typical for highway stormwater pumping stations. The propellers are generally of the vertical single-stage, axial- and mixed-flow type. Two-stage, axial- flow pumps may also be used. Propellers are usually referred to as mixed- flow impellers with a very small radial- flow component. A true propeller, in which the flow strictly parallels the axis of rotation, is called an axial-flow impeller. Impellers are called radial vane or radial. As the impeller turns, the centrifugal action creates a vacuum at the impeller "eye" and causes the fluid to be discharged radially to the periphery with increasing velocity.[1] The high velocity at the blade tips is converted to pressure in the casing. A higher impeller speed results in a higher blade velocity, which means higher pressures. The impellers of centrifugal pumps may be of the radial- or mixed-flow type.

Duty Point

If the head/discharge (H/Q) characteristic is available, and a study of the system has led to the preparation of a system resistance curve the duty point may be found by plotting the two curves on the same H/Q axes:

It is not always possible to match the system with an available pump such that the operating point is coincident with that of maximum efficiency.[2] Pump manufacturers supply selection diagrams which indicate the suitable range of duties for each pump.

Pump Selection

Select pump based on total head (not discharge pressure) and flow rate. The flow rate will depend on your maximum requirement. Total head is the amount of energy that the pump needs to deliver to account for the elevation difference and friction loss in your system.

Pump Stations

Pumping stations are buildings or places that house pumps or other equipment designed to move water and other fluids from one location to another. Pump stations are sometimes called lift stations. The particular type of equipment residing in a specific pumping station will depend on its exact function, and on the type of fluid that requires pumping. [3] Different pumps may be needed, for example, at a sewage pumping station that deals with sludge and slurry, when compared with a water pumping station.

Pumping stations typically have a dedicated function. Many pumping stations form important structural parts of the public water supply system, typically serving to pump water out of a reservoir, and into a system of pipes. Some pumping stations transport domestic sludge, liquid industrial waste, or agricultural slurry. Other uses of pumping stations include managing the water supply of canals, pumping water uphill in certain types of hydroelectric systems, providing irrigation to farming land, and draining water from low-lying land. The components in pumping station can be grouped as follows.

(1) Pumping machinery
- Pumps and other mechanical equipment, i.e. valves, pipe work, vacuum pumps
- Motors, switchgears, cable, transformer and other electrical accessories

(2) Ancillary Equipment
- Lifting equipment
- Water hammer control device
- Flowmeter
- Diesel generating set

(3) Pumping station
- Sump/intake/well/tube well/bore well
- Pump house
- Screen
- Penstock/gate

Water supply pumping station

Water pumping is a term used to describe the process of moving water from one area – usually a body of water, a well, or a container – to another area. From obtaining water for drinking, cooking, and bathing to draining water from a swimming pool, lake, or a flooded basement, water pumping can be used for a wide range of tasks. [4] Energy is required in order to move water for these purposes, and water pumping typically works by using pressurized pumping systems that are designed to shift water.

Pumping stations can be grouped as follows:
- pumping water from a water source such as a river;
- for lifting water (high quantity, low pressure) from a well;
- for pumping water into a supply system, elevated water tank or water tower;
- to increase pressure.

Pumping stations for the first two functions are generally of 2-20 m lifting capacity. Pumping stations for obtaining water from a water source have two types depending on the source:
- pumping from surface water (river, canal, lake, reservoir, etc.);
- pumping from subsurface water (soil water, deep seated spring, cavern water, spring water,

marginal water, etc.).

Sewage pumping station

Sewage lift/pump stations are used for pumping wastewater or sewage from a lower to higher elevation, particularly where the elevation of the source is not sufficient for gravity flow and/or when the use of gravity conveyance will result in excessive excavation and higher construction costs. [5]

Stormwater pumping stations

Stormwater pumping stations are necessary for the removal of stormwater from sections of highway where gravity drainage is impossible or impractical. However, stormwater pumping stations are expensive to operate and maintain and have a number of potential problems that must be addressed. Therefore, the use of stormwater pumping stations is recommended only where no other practicable alternative is available. Alternatives to pumping stations include siphons, recharge basins, deep and long storm drain systems and tunnels.

Important Words and Expressions

pump [pʌmp]   n. 泵   vt.& vi. 用抽水机汲水；用泵输送
pumping station   泵站
centrifugal [sen'trifjəgəl, -'trifə-]   adj. 离心的
propeller [prə'pelə]   n. 螺旋桨，推进器；
impeller [im'pelə]   n. 叶轮
axial ['æksiəl]   adj. 轴向的，轴周围的
radial ['reidiəl]   adj. 径向的
drive shaft   n. 传动轴，主动轴
hub [hʌb]   n. 轮轴；中心
periphery [pə'rifəri:]   n. 边缘；圆周；外围；边缘地带
vane [vein]   n. 叶片，叶轮
head [hed]   n. 水头；扬程
discharge [dis'tʃɑ:dʒ]   vt.& vi. 放出；流出   n.（气体、液体如水从管子里）流出；流量
resistance [ri'zistəns]   n. 抵抗；阻力
friction ['frikʃən]   n. 摩擦；摩擦力
duty ['dju:ti]   n. 功率；效率
slurry ['slə:ri]   n. 泥浆，浆
structural part   结构零件
hydroelectric [,haidrəui'lektrik]   adj. 水力发电的
vacuum ['vækjuəm]   n. 真空
switchgear ['switʃgiə]   n. 接电装置，开关设备
cable ['keibl]   n. 电缆
transformer [træns'fɔ:mə]   n. 变压器
ancillary ['ænsə,leri]   adj. 辅助的；补充的；附属的
hammer ['hæmə]   n. 铁锤，榔头
flowmeter ['fləumi:tə]   n. 流量计

diesel generating set   柴油发电机组
penstock ['penstɔk]   n. 阀门
container [kən'teinə]   n. 容器
wet well   湿井；排水井
siphon ['saifən]   n. 虹吸管
recharge [ri:'tʃɑ:dʒ]   n. 补给，补充；回灌

Notes

[1] 当叶轮进行转动，在叶轮的"眼睛"处由于离心作用产生真空，使得水流以加速度的方式径向流向四周。

[2] 可用的水泵的工况点不总是和系统的最大效率相一致。

[3] 在具体的泵站中，安装设备的特定类型取决于泵站的确切作用和需要提升的液体的类型。

[4] 从获取饮用水、烹饪用水以及洗澡用水到将水从游泳池、湖泊或者淹没的地下室中排出，水泵的用途很广泛。

[5] 污水提升泵站用于从低处向高处抽取废水或污水，特别是在取水点不能够形成重力流或者是依靠重力流将产生过度的开挖和较大的建设成本时。

Exercises

1. Answering the following questions in English according to the text:

(1) In water and wastewater treatment, what pumps are the most commonly used?

(2) What is the definition of pumping station?

2. Using the following each word to make up the sentences, respectively:

(1) single-suction

(2) discharge

(3) velocity

(4) submerge

(5) self-priming

3. Put the following English into Chinese:

(1) Flow recorders may supplement the flow meter device to record pump performance, condition of pump, and energy usages rates. For complex installations, flow recorders may be part of a remotely located controller or part of remote stations which monitor other data such as speed indication, vibration monitoring, and bearing or casing temperature indicators. Flow recorders will be used to indicate flow fluctuations over the course of a day. Technological advances have made transducer output measurement possible with self-balancing recorders and computer-compatible data-gathering systems.

(2) Common uses of vane pumps include high pressure hydraulic pumps and automotive uses including, supercharging, power steering and automatic transmission pumps. Pumps for mid-range pressures include applications such as carbonators for fountain soft drink dispensers and espresso coffee machines. They are also often used as vacuum pumps for providing braking assistance in large trucks and diesel powered passenger cars (whose engines do not generate intake vacuum) through a braking booster, and in most light aircraft to drive gyroscopic flight instruments, the

attitude indicator and heading indicator.

4. Put the following Chinese into English:
   (1) 水泵吸水管
   (2) 卧式水泵
   (3) 地下式泵房
   (4) 水泵种类繁多，在各行各业中被广泛使用。
   (5) 大中型水厂中，常需设置多台水泵联合工作。

Reading Material A

Centrifugal Pump

General

According to Reti, the Brazilian soldier and historian of science, the first machine that could be characterized as a centrifugal pump was a mud lifting machine which appeared as early as 1475 in a treatise by the Italian Renaissance engineer Francesco di Giorgio Martini. True centrifugal pumps were not developed until the late 17th century, when Denis Papin made one with straight vanes. The curved vane was introduced by British inventor John Appold in 1851.

This type of pump is so named because the pressure head is generated by centrifugal action. The impeller is made up of a number of curved vanes which are supported on both sides by plates known as shrouds. It rotates inside a casing or volute: low enters the pump through the centre or eye of the impeller. Energy is given to the liquid as the blades of the impeller transport it outwards in a radial direction.

Centrifugal pumps move fluids by stirring them faster and faster in a circular motion and then changing the increased speed of the fluid into pressure.[1] Depending on the design of the particular pump, centrifugal pumps are capable of either very high or very low discharge pressures and very high or very low volume discharges.

As the water gains speed (kinetic energy), it pushes outward against the walls of the pump casing. This is due to centrifugal force - the same force that causes a stone on the end of a string to pull outward on its string when swung in a fast, circular orbit. As the water moves outward, it makes room for more water and at the same time creates a suction, which draws more water in at the suction eye of the impeller. When the water is discharged at the tip of the impeller into the volute, it is moving very fast, that is, it contains a large amount of kinetic energy.[2] In the volute, which widens at the discharge end, the water must spread out to fill the chamber. In the course of spreading out, the water slows down. When the water is forced to slow down, the kinetic energy (speed or motion) does not just disappear; it is transformed into pressure. This pressure carries the water out of the pump through the discharge piping.

Centrifugal pump classifications

Centrifugal pumps are classified according to certain design features. For example, pumps can be referred to as vertical or horizontal, single-suction or double-suction, single stage, double-stage, or multi-stage, volute or diffuser, and radial-flow, axial-flow, or mixed flow.[3] The name of the pump might also include formation about the impeller: whether it is closed, open, or semi-open. The mechanical design of the casing provides the added classifications of axially split, radially split, or occasionally solid. It is not unusual, then, to hear a pump referred to as a vertical, double suction, single stage diffuser pump with closed impellers.

Vertical and horizontal refer to the position of the shaft during normal operation. The shaft is vertical and the motor is positioned above the pump itself. This arrangement allows the pump to be submerged in the fluid without causing water damage to the motor. Vertical pumps may be used where floor space is limited.

Horizontal pumps have their motors beside them on the same horizontal level and their shafts run parallel to the ground. Horizontal centrifugal pumps are further classified as (1) end suction, (2) side suction, (3) bottom suction, and (4) top suction. Vertically mounted centrifugal pumps are almost always bottom suction pumps.

When the suction nozzle is placed on the side of the pump with its centerline horizontal, the pump is called a side suction pump. When the suction points vertically downward, the pump is classified a bottom suction pump. The most common type of pump, with its suction horizontal and its centerline coincidental with the shaft is an end suction pump. [4]

Pressure and Head

If the discharge of a centrifugal pump is pointed straight up into the air the fluid will pumped to a certain height - or head - called the shut off head. This maximum head is mainly determined by the outside diameter of the pump's impeller and the speed of the rotating shaft. The head will change as the capacity of the pump is altered.

The kinetic energy of a liquid coming out of an impeller is obstructed by creating a resistance in the flow. The first resistance is created by the pump casing which catches the liquid and slows it down. When the liquid slows down the kinetic energy is converted to pressure energy. It is the resistance to the pump's flow that is read on a pressure gauge attached to the discharge line. A pump does not create pressure, it only creates flow. Pressure is a measurement of the resistance to flow.

In Newtonian fluids (non-viscous liquids like water or gasoline) the term head is used to measure the kinetic energy which a pump creates. Head is a measurement of the height of the liquid column the pump creates from the kinetic energy the pump gives to the liquid. The main reason for using head instead of pressure to measure a centrifugal pump's energy is that the pressure from a pump will change if the specific gravity (weight) of the liquid changes, but the head will not. The pump's performance on any Newtonian fluid can always be described by using the term head.

Centrifugal Pump Safety

The following precautions should be observed prior to starting a centrifugal pump:

• Ensure the pump is filled and vented, to prevent gas binding and cavitation due to air and gas in the pump casing.

• Cooling water and lubricating systems should be verified operable before starting the pump. This check should include checking lubricating oil levels and flow, and cooling water temperatures to the bearings. Introduce cooling water to pump bearings and lubricating oil systems slowly.

• Bearings should be near normal operating temperature when the pump is started.

The suction valve of a centrifugal pump must be verified open prior to pump start, to ensure an adequate flow path to the pump impeller. The suction valve must remain open while the pump is running. The discharge valve should be closed when a centrifugal pump is started, to prevent excessive starting torque and load on the motor.[5] During pump start, observe pump motor current to ensure it drops to the normal operating range after the starting surge.

The discharge valve should not be closed for an extended period unless minimum (recirculating) flow is verified adequate. Some recirculating flow is necessary to prevent overheating the pump.

Notes

[1] 通过离心泵（叶片）搅动使液体成快速的圆周运动，然后转化液体增加的速度成为压力。

[2] 当水从叶轮的顶端进入蜗壳时，它运动得非常快，也就是说，水获得了大量的动能。

[3] 例如，水泵可以被称作立式泵或卧式泵，单吸式泵或双吸式泵、单级泵、双级泵或多极泵，蜗壳泵或扩散泵、径向流泵、轴流泵或混流泵。

[4] 最常见类型的泵是单吸泵，它的水平吸水口的中心线和泵轴是一致的。

[5] 为了防止发动机上过大的启动转矩和负荷，当离心泵开启时排出阀应该被关闭。

Reading Material B
Pump Station Design
Types of pumping station

(1) Wet well/Dry well: This consists of two separate underground chambers, the sump (or wet well) containing the liquid to be pumped and the dry well where the pump, motor and associated pipe work are located. This type usually has an associated superstructure where the control gear is located.

(2) Submersible: This consists of two underground chambers one much larger than the other. In these installations the pump and motor are located in the larger chamber, submerged within the liquid to be pumped. The smaller chamber contains valves and over pumping facilities. This type usually has its control gear located in a small kiosk above the station.

In each of the above it is usual to have two or more pumps connected in parallel, operating independently or together depending on the required outflow.

Under normal operating conditions the pumps operate automatically, being brought into operation by water level detecting devices. These range from electrodes and mercury tilting switches to ultra sonics. The operating levels are determined from consideration of inflow, outflow and sump capacity.

All the electrical switchgear is connected to a control panel which can be used to control the station manually if required. The panel will normally keep a record of operational information such as hours run etc.

One variation on the above stations would be found in a borehole type installation. In this type the pump is immersed in the liquid to be pumped and consists of several impellers mounted vertically above one another. In this way the pump acts as several pumps connected in series, thereby considerably increasing the lift (head) potential.

Pumping station design stages

(1) Determine peak and dry weather flows to station

(2) Select station type

(3) Select rising main diameter and determine friction and static head lift

(4) Select No. and configuration of pumps

(5) Determine sump plan area for chosen configuration

(6) Determine maximum water level in station based on incoming pipe invert level– 0.5m

(7) Determine volume required in sump for various operational scenarios based on 15 starts per hour

(8) Work out stop and start levels for control purposes

(9) Determine exact chamber configuration

(10) Check station & rising main for night flows

Design criteria

The design of the pumping station must conform to the current city of standard, and all other related standards, codes and regulations, unless authorized and approved by the City Engineer and other approval authorities.[1] Provide a plastic laminate fact sheet with information such as lowest basement elevation, hydraulic grade line, and overflow invert elevation. Overflow pipe information shall include pipe size, location, and flow rates at 25, 50, 75 and 100 percent capacities, at 1 metre above overflow pipe obvert. Include other pumping station information as required by the City Engineer. A plastic laminate with a process flow diagram indicating valves and key interlocks shall also be included.

Site layout and servicing Pumping stations are to be located outside the 100-year flood limits unless approved by the City Engineer and other regulatory agencies. The site shall have good vehicular access and maneuvering area, and minimize potential adverse environmental impacts. The facilities layout shall allow for future expansion, and comply with front, rear and side yard set backs according to the applicable zoning and site plan standard and requirements, and convenient location of portable generator.[2] Building construction shall be architecturally pleasing, in relation to surrounding community, and low maintenance. Permanent structures shall be masonry or concrete construction. Temporary structures shall not be of wood frame construction. Cladding for temporary structures shall be of pre-formed FRP or pre-finished metal. Include provisions to protect the building from vehicles. Building insulation requirements, interior finish, and minimum interior building temperature shall be as directed by the City Engineer. Building design, layout and construction materials shall be to the satisfaction of the City Engineer. Facility design and layout shall have regards to making confined space entry user friendly, optimizing sight and retrieval lines and comply with OHSA regulation. Landscaping of the site shall be low maintenance and architecturally pleasing, well-graded, minimal grass areas and landscaped to the satisfaction of the City Engineer. Site drainage shall not drain onto adjacent private property. Fencing shall be 1.8m high chain link fence with lockable gates that are sized appropriately. Include warning and municipal address signage as per current City standards. Barbed wire fence shall be used as per current City fence by-law PS-1, and as directed by the City Engineer. Provide adequate exterior lighting of the pumping station facilities such as access, parking, provide security hardware and alarms for all exterior doors, windows and exterior equipment to the satisfaction of the City Engineer. Exterior lighting may be controlled by motion sensor or photo-eye as directed by the City Engineer. All control equipment and panels shall be indoors unless approved by the City Engineer. All utility meters such as gas, hydro, water meter reader, shall be mounted on the exterior of the building.

Access to the site shall include provision for parking of maintenance vehicles and standby/emergency equipment. Roads shall be asphalt surfaced in parking and maneuvering areas and provide convenient removal and storage of snow, and turn around for trucks, tankers and heavy equipment. All utilities including phone and computer communications servicing the site shall be underground unless authorized by the City Engineer. Design, installation and planning of services shall be according to requirements of applicable codes, regulations and the local utility authority.

Flow Capacity

The pumping station flow capacity shall be based on the peak hourly flow rate and consider low flow conditions, as approved by the City Engineer. The flow capacity of the pumping station should be able to maintain a desirable cleansing velocity of 0.9 m/s with a minimum velocity of 0.60 m/s, and a maximum velocity of 3.0 m/s in all piping. The design of new pumping stations shall allow for future modification or expansion to meet the requirements of the tributary area of the pumping station. [3]

Cost Effective Design

Development in pumping technology and the submersible motor sewage pump has provided the designer of a sewerage system with an opportunity to evaluate various combinations of pumping stations, rising mains and sewers to give the most economical scheme based on construction, operating and maintenance costs.[4] For small schemes the most attractive combination can very often be assessed by a site inspection but for larger schemes reliable unit rates must be established for all the main variable items and alternatives examined and cost such that the final design is cost effective. Cost must, however, be subject to the engineering requirements of the scheme being satisfied.

Emergency Storage

Pump station failure may occur for a number of reasons including failure of power supply, switchboards, a number of pumps or failure of the pump station pipe work or rising main. Emergency storage shall be provided to allow Hunter Water sufficient time to respond to such failures and to mitigate the potential for overflow to occur. Emergency storage is considered to include both wet well storage and storage in upstream gravity sewers.

Notes

[1] 除了被城市工程师审定和核准，和其他正式的授权，泵站的设计必须符合现行的城市标准和所有其他相关标准、规范和条例。

[2] 根据区域和位置设计标准和要求，以及便于便携式发电机布置条件，设施的布置可允许将来的发展和满足前后左右距离要求。

[3] 新泵站设计应该允许将来的改建或扩建来满足泵站支流区域的需求。

[4] 抽水技术和潜水排污泵的发展给污水系统设计者提供了一个机会依据建设，运行和维护成本去评估各种泵站，压力干管和污水管，从而制定最经济的计划。

Part Three
Physical-Chemical Treatment Process

Unit 8   Coagulation and Flocculation

There are three types of substances which can be found in water. These substances are chemicals in solution, colloidal solids, and suspended solids. Coagulation/flocculation will remove colloidal and suspended solids.

In the water treatment industry, the terms coagulation and flocculation imply different mechanisms. Although the words "coagulation" and "flocculation" are often used interchangeably they refer to two distinct processes. Coagulation indicates the process through which colloidal particles and very fine solid suspensions are destabilized so that they can begin to agglomerate if the conditions are appropriate. Flocculation refers to the process by which destabilized particles actually conglomerate into larger aggregates so that they can be separated from the wastewater.

Coagulation

Coagulation is the destabilization of colloidal particles brought about by the addition of a chemical reagent (coagulant). The purpose of destabilization is to lessen the repelling character of the particles and allow them to be attached to other particles so that they may be removed in subsequent sedimentation processes.[1]

The particulates in raw water, which contribute to color and turbidity, are mainly clays, silts, viruses, bacteria, humic acids, minerals (including asbestos, silicates, silica, and radioactive particles), and organic particulates. At pH levels above 4.0, such particles or molecules are generally negatively charged. Coagulation is employed for the removal of waste materials in suspended or colloidal form. Colloids are presented by particles over a range of 0.1-1.0 nm. These particles do not settle out on standing and cannot be removed by conventional physical treatment processes. Colloids present in wastewater can be either hydrophobic or hydrophilic. The hydrophobic colloids possess no affinity for the liquid medium and lack stability in the presence of electrolytes. They are readily susceptible to coagulation. Hydrophilic colloids, such as proteins, exhibit a marked affinity for water. The absorbed water retards flocculation and frequently requires special treatment to achieve effective coagulation.

Electrical properties of the colloids create a repelling force and prevent agglomeration and settling. Stabilizing ions are strongly adsorbed to an inner fixed layer which provides a particle charge that varies with the valence and number of adsorbed ions. Ions of an opposite charge form a diffuse outer layer which is held near the surface by electrostatic forces. The stability of a colloid is due to the repulsive electrostatic forces and in the case of hydrophilic colloids to solvation in which an envelope of water retards coagulation.[2]

The advantages of coagulation are that it reduces the time required to settle out suspended solids and is very effective in removing fine particles that are otherwise very difficult to remove. Coagulation can also be effective in removing many protozoa, bacteria and viruses.

Flocculation

Flocculation is stimulation by mechanical means to agglomerate destabilized particles into compact, fast settleable particles (or flocs). Flocculation or gentle agitation results from velocity differences or gradients in the coagulated water, which causes the fine moving, destabilized particles to come into contact and become large, readily settleable flocs.[3] It is a common practice to provide an initial rapid (or) flash mix for the dispersal of the coagulant or other chemicals into the water. Slow mixing is then done, during which the growth of the floc takes place. Design contact times for flocculation range from 15 or 20 minutes to an hour or more.

Coagulation and flocculation occur in successive steps intended to overcome the forces stabilizing the suspended particles, allowing particle collision and growth of floc. If step one is incomplete, the following step will be unsuccessful.

Coagulation Mechanisms

Coagulation can be accomplished through any of four different mechanisms. The following section details these various mechanisms.

(1) Double-layer compression

The mechanism of double-layer compression relies on compressing the diffuse layer surrounding a colloid. This is accomplished by increasing the ionic strength of the solution through the addition of an indifferent electrolyte. The added electrolyte increases the charge density in the diffuse layer. The diffuse layer is 'compressed' toward the particle surface, reducing the thickness of the layer. Therefore, the zeta potential, ZP, is significantly decreased.

(2) Adsorption and charge neutralization

Adding coagulants with a charge opposite to that on the colloidal particles can cause adsorption of the ions on to the colloidal particles and neutralize surface charge. This leads to easier aggregation. However, the coagulant dosage should be proportional to the quantity of colloids present. If overdose is applied, charge reversal on the colloids occurs and the colloids are not destabilized.

(3) Enmeshment by a precipitate (Sweep-floc coagulation)

Chemical compounds such as aluminum sulfate [$Al_2(SO_4)_3$], ferric chloride ($FeCl_3$), and lime (CaO or Ca($OH)_2$) are frequently used as coagulants to form the precipitates of $Al(OH)_3$, $Fe(OH)_3$ and $CaCO_3$. These precipitates physically entrap the suspended colloidal particles as they settle, especially during subsequent flocculation. When the colloidal particles themselves serve as nuclei for the formation of the precipitate, the flocs are formed around colloidal particles and the sweep-floc coagulation process can be enhanced.[4] Thus, the rate of precipitation increases with increasing concentration of colloidal particles (turbidity) in the solution.

(4) Interparticle bridging

Since synthetic polymeric compounds have large molecular sizes and multiple electrical charges along a molecular chain of carbon atoms, they are effective for the destabilization of colloids in water.

Perikinetic and Orthokinetic Flocculation

The flocculation process can be broadly classified into two types, perikinetic (also known as microflocculation) and orthokinetic (also known as macroflocculation).

Perikinetic flocculation refers to flocculation (contact or collisions of colloidal particles) due to Brownian motion of colloidal particles. The random motion of colloidal particles results from their rapid and random bombardment by the molecules of the fluid. The random thermal motion of fluid molecules is also known as Brownian motion or movement. Perikinetic flocculation is significant for particles that are in the size range from 0.001 to about 1μm. It is normally not a major factor in the transport associated with flocculation in water treatment.

Orthokinetic flocculation refers to contacts or collisions of colloidal particles resulting from bulk fluid motion, such as stirring. In systems of stirring, the velocity of the fluid varies both spatially (from point to point) and temporally (from time to time). Orthokinetic flocculation can be brought about by (1) induced velocity gradients and (2) differential settling. Particles can be brought together (i.e., flocculated) by inducing velocity gradients in a fluid containing the particles to by flocculated. Faster-moving particles will overtake slower-moving particles in a velocity field. If the particles that collide stick together, a larger particle will be formed that will be easier to be removed by gravity separation.

Factors Affecting Coagulation

For all raw water types, there are several water quality parameters that affect coagulation performance, including the amount of particulate material, the amount and nature of the NOM present, and the bulk chemical and physical properties of the water.

Important Words and Expressions

solution [sə'lu:ʃən] n. 溶解，溶液
coagulation [kəuˌægju'leiʃən] n. 凝结，凝结物，混凝
flocculation [flɔkju'leiʃən] n. 絮凝，絮结产物
destabilize [di:'steibilaiz] vt. 使打破平衡，使不稳定；使动摇
agglomerate [ə'glɔməˌret] adj. 成团的；结块的 n. <化>凝聚物；聚集体 vt.&vi.（使）聚集；（使）聚结；（使）凝聚；（使）结块
conglomerate [kən'glɔməˌreit] vt. 使聚结；使成团
aggregate ['ægrigit] vt. 使聚集，使积聚
reagent [ri:'eidʒənt] n. 反应物，试剂
coagulant [kəu'ægjulənt] n. 凝结剂
sedimentation [ˌsedimen'teiʃən] n. 沉淀，沉降
turbidity [tə:'biditi] n. 混浊，混乱；浑浊度；浊度
humic acids 腐殖酸
asbestos [æs'bestəs, æz'bestəs] n. 石棉
silicate ['silikit] n. 硅酸盐

silica ['silikə]   n. 硅石，二氧化硅；硅氧
hydrophobic [,haidrəu'fəubik]   adj. 憎水的，疏水的
hydrophilic [,haidrəu'filik]   adj. 亲水的
affinity [ə'finiti:]   n. 亲和力；亲合力
electrolyte [i'lektrə,lait]   n. <化>电解液，电解质
susceptible [sə'septəbl]   adj. 易受影响的；易受感染的
retard [ri'ta:d]   vt. 使减速，妨碍，阻止，推迟   vi. 减慢，受到阻滞
valence ['veiləns]   n.（化合）价，原子价
electrostatic forces   静电力
repulsive [ri'pʌlsiv]   adj. 推斥的，排斥的
solvation [sɔl'veiʃən, sɔl-]   n. 溶合；溶化；溶剂化作用；溶剂离解作用
stimulation [,stimju'leiʃən]   n. 刺激（作用）；促进
floc [flɔk]   n. 絮状物
enmeshment [in'meʃmənt]   n. 网住；绊住；包络（作用）
aluminum sulfate   硫酸铝
ferric chloride   氯化铁
lime [laim]   n. 石灰
nuclei ['nju:kliai]   n. 核，核心，原子核（nucleus 的复数形）；中心，核心
interparticle bridging   颗粒间架桥
synthetic [sin'θetik]   adj. 合成的；人造的
polymeric [,pɔli'merik]   adj. 聚合的
perikinetic [,perikai'netik]   adj. 与布朗运动有关的，异向的
orthokinetic [ɔ:θəkai'netik]   adj. 同向的
bombardment [bɔm'ba:dmənt]   n. 撞击；轰击；冲击
NOM 天然有机物

Notes

[1] 混凝是靠外加的化学试剂（混凝剂）来减少胶体粒子的稳定性。脱稳的目的是减少胶体粒子之间的排斥力而使其能够结合更多的胶体粒子，使它们在随后的沉淀过程中得以去除。

[2] 胶体的稳定性是由于静电斥力而对于溶液中的亲水性胶体，水膜阻止了混凝。

[3] 絮凝或者由于速度或水力梯度不同形成的缓慢搅拌导致了良好的水力运动，使得胶体粒子可以聚集变大从而容易形成絮凝物。

[4] 当胶体粒子本身作为核形成沉淀时，胶体粒子周围可形成絮凝体并且卷扫的混凝过程可以加快。

Exercises

1. Answering the following questions in English according to the text:

(1) What is difference between coagulation and flocculation?

(2) What are the two types of flocculation?

2. Using the following each word to make up the sentences, respectively:

(1) coagulation

(2) coagulant
(3) neutralization
(4) turbidity
(5) hydrolytic

3. Put the following English into Chinese:

(1) Heterocoagulation is a destabilization mechanism that is similar to the process of surface charge neutralization by the adsorption of oppositely charged soluble species. However, in this case, the process involves one particle depositing on another of opposite charge. For example, large particles with a high negative surface charge may contact smaller particles with a relatively low positive charge. Because the particles have opposite surface charge, electrostatic attraction enhances particle-particle interaction. As the stabilizing negative charge of the larger particles is reduced by the deposited positive particles, the suspension of larger particles is destabilized.

(2) Alum may react in different ways to achieve coagulation. When used at relatively low doses (<5mg/L), charge neutralization (destabilization) is believed to be the primary mechanism involved. At higher dosages, the primary coagulation mechanism tends to be entrapment. In this case, aluminum hydroxide ($Al(OH)_2$) precipitates forming a "sweepfloc" that tends to capture suspended solids as it settles out of suspension. The pH of the water plays an important role when alum is used for coagulation because the solubility of the aluminum species in water is pH dependent. If the pH of the water is between 4 and 5, alum is generally present in the form of positive ions (i.e., $Al(OH)^{2+}$, $Al_8(OH)^{4+}$, and Al^{3+}). However, optimum coagulation occurs when negatively charged forms of alum predominate, which occurs when the pH is between 6 and 8.

4. Put the following Chinese into English:

(1) 电性中和作用机理
(2) 水中胶体颗粒的稳定性
(3) 有机高分子混凝剂
(4) 为促使水中胶体颗粒脱稳以及悬浮颗粒的相互聚集，常需要投加一些化学药剂。
(5) 在水处理中，混凝是影响处理效果最为关键的因素。

5. Put the following abbr.into full phrases：

NOM；ZP

Reading Material A

Coagulant and Flocculant

Coagulant is process in which destabilization is achieved by the addition of salts which reduce, neutralize or invert the electrical repulsion between particles. Flocculants absorb on particles and cause destabilization either by bridging or charge neutralization.

The chemistry of coagulation and flocculation is primarily based on the electrical properties of the particles. Like charges repel each other while opposite charges attract. Most particles present in water have a negative charge, so they tend to repel each other.[1] As a result, they stay dispersed in the water. The purpose of most coagulant chemicals is to neutralize the negative charges on the colloidal particles to prevent those particles from repelling each other. The amount of coagulant which should be added to the water will depend on the zeta potential, a measurement of the magnitude of electrical charge surrounding the colloidal particles. You can think of the zeta potential as the amount of repulsive force which keeps the particles in the suspension. If the zeta potential is large, then more coagulants will be needed. The combination of positive and negative charge results in a neutral, or lack of charge. As a result, the particles no longer repel each other.

The next force which will affect the particles is known as van der Waal's forces. Van der Waal's forces refer to the tendency of particles in nature to attract each other if they come close enough. [2] Once the particles in water are not repelling each other and due to their motion in water, they will come close to each other (collide) so that van der Waal's forces of attraction can make the particles stick to each other. When enough particles have joined together, they become floc and will settle out of the water.

The most commonly used coagulants are aluminum sulfate and ferric sulfate, although other coagulants are available.

Types of Coagulants

There are two types of coagulant chemicals, the primary coagulants and the coagulant aids. Primary coagulants neutralize the electrical charges of particles in the water which causes the particles to clump together. Chemicals commonly used for primary coagulants include aluminum or iron salts and organic polymers. The most common aluminum salt used for coagulation is aluminum sulfate, or alum. Coagulant aids are "added after the primary coagulant to produce a stronger and more settleable floc. These chemicals can also help reduce the amount of primary coagulant needed and the amount of sludge produced during the treatment process". Organic polymers, such as polyaluminum hydroxychloride (PACl), are typically used to enhance coagulation in combination with a primary coagulant. The advantage of these organic polymers is that they have a high positive charge and are much more effective at small dosages. [3] Even though they may be more expensive, a smaller amount may be needed, thereby saving money. Organic polymers also typically produce less sludge. Even after these chemicals are used to treat water, the water will progress through other steps, including filtration and disinfecting (at which point more chemicals will be used). Chemically, coagulant chemicals are either metallic salts (such as alum) or polymers. Polymers are man-made organic compounds made up of a long chain of smaller molecules. Polymers can be either cationic (positively charged), anionic (negatively charged), or nonionic (neutrally charged.).

Different sources of water need different coagulants, but the most commonly used are alum and ferric chloride. Aluminum salts are cheaper but iron salts are more effective over wider pH range. The resulting inorganic polymers may have some advantages over alum or ferric chloride for turbidity removal in cold waters or in low-alkalinity waters. Organic polymers tend to be large molecules composed of chains of smaller "monomer" groups. Because of their large size and charge characteristics, polymers can promote destabilization through bridging, charge neutralization, or both. Polymers are often used in conjunction with other coagulants such as alum or ferric chloride to optimize solids removal.

The choice of the coagulant to be used for any particular water should preferably be based upon experiment on different coagulants. Cost may be a consideration when selecting chemicals. The system should perform an economic analysis when comparing chemicals and not just compare unit cost. For instance, a polymer may cost more per unit than alum, but less polymer may be needed than alum. Therefore, the total cost for polymer may not be much different than the total cost for alum.

Coagulant Aids

Flocculants (also known as flocculant aids or coagulant aids), which assist in the joining and enmeshing of the particles together. Primary coagulants are always used in the coagulation/flocculation process. Coagulant aids, in contrast, are not always required and are generally used to reduce flocculation time. Coagulant aid can be used for better coagulation and more decrease in turbidity. So that if low turbidity is required it's possible to make bigger flocks by adding coagulant aid to make more particles sediment in addition to increase the rate of sedimentation. A polymeric (anionic) coagulant, this type of coagulant aid, in addition to neutralize the positive charges in water, causes the formation of flocks more quickly and increases the rate of sedimentation by bridging and connecting the already formed flocks so that with the network formed during sedimentation they take other tiny particles which couldn't form flocks inside them and make them sediment among with themselves. Synthetic organic polymers have been used as an effective coagulant aid in drinking water purification systems .However, organic polymers have potential limitations. Polymer formulations contain contaminants from the manufacturing process such as residual monomers, other reactants, and reaction by-products that could potentially negatively impact human health. Polymers and product contaminants can react with other chemicals added to the water treatment process to form undesirable secondary products. Thus, in recent years, there has been considerable interest in the development of natural coagulants.

Coagulant aids may improve coagulation process and turbidity removal. But it should be considered that coagulant aids should not increase water treatment costs significantly. Their accessibility and preparation procedure should also be considered when selecting a coagulant aid. Nearly all coagulant aids are very expensive, so care must be taken to use the proper amount of these chemicals. It should be noted that the coagulant aid dosage in comparison to coagulant dosage is very low and we should determine the optimum dosage for different types of water using the jar test.

A couple of coagulant aids will be considered below.

Lime is a coagulant aid used to increase the alkalinity of the water. The increase in alkalinity results in an increase in ions (electrically charged particles) in the water, some of which are positively charged. [4] These positively charged particles attract the colloidal particles in the water, forming floc.

Bentonite is a type of clay used as a weighting agent in water high in color and low in turbidity and mineral content. This type of water usually would not form floc large enough to settle out of the water. The bentonite joins with the small floc, making the floc heavier and thus making it settle more quickly.

The proper type and concentration of coagulant are essential to the coagulation process. The coagulant choice will depend on the conditions at the plant. Coagulants are dosed in solution at a rate determined by raw water quality near the inlet of a mixing tank or flocculator. The coagulant is rapidly and thoroughly dispersed on dosing by adding it at a point of high turbulence. The water then passes into the sedimentation tank to allow aggregation of the flocs, which settle out to form sludge. Coagulants need accurate dosing equipment to function efficiently and the dose required depends on raw water quality that can vary rapidly.[5] The choice of coagulant and determination of optimum operating conditions for a specific raw water have to be determined by bench-scale coagulation tests ('jar tests').

Notes

[1] 水中的大部分颗粒带负电，因此它们趋向于排斥彼此。
[2] 如果自然界的颗粒距离足够近，范德华力有使颗粒之间相互吸引的趋势。
[3] 这些有机聚合体的优点是它们带有高价正电荷并且在小剂量时更有效。
[4] 水中碱性的升高会引起电荷离子的提高，一些电荷离子带正电。
[5] 混凝剂需要精确的计量设备使其作用充分发挥，并且所需混凝剂量随快速改变的原水水质而改变。

Reading Material B
Coagulation Facilities

Coagulation depends on the rapid reaction through which the coagulant destabilizes the colloids. Coagulation requires the rapid dispersion of the coagulant throughout the water. This is accomplished through very intense agitation and mixing. High shear rates are beneficial to coagulation. Flocculation depends on the frequency of collision of the destabilized colloids to form larger floc particles. The frequency of collision depends on the intensity of the agitation and the shear rate. However, too high a value of the agitation intensity and shear rate may break up the floc just formed. Therefore, moderate shear rates and agitation intensities are used in flocculators.

Flocculator is a piece of equipment that aids or performs flocculation, or the removal of contaminants in water by the use of flocculating agents to encapsulate and remove these solids or contaminants from solution.[1]

Classification of power sources

The power dissipated inside a tank must be supplied from the outside in some way. In principle, this external power can be supplied by means of three primary different sources, i.e.
- ➢ Mechanical agitation (e.g., impellers, paddles, turbines)
- ➢ Power delivered by a compressed gas (e.g., through gas dispersers, sparged gas diffusers)
- ➢ Power delivered by the liquid (e.g., venture mixers, hydraulic jumps, water jets)

Types of flocculators

The agitation required for flocculation is usually provided by either hydraulic or mechanical means.

(1) Mechanical mixing flocculators
- Vertical shaft with impeller (turbine or propeller type blades)
- Paddle type with either horizontal or vertical shafts
- Walking Beam Flocculator

Submerged impellers (mixers) mounted on vertical shafts. Many different types of impellers exist. Impellers are classified on the basis of shape, dimensions, type of flow pattern generated, flow intensity, power consumption under aerated, nonaerated conditions and their ability to disperse a gas effectively.[2] Mechanical paddle mixers in a flocculation basin with a detention time of 20 to 60 minutes are widely used in practice. Mechanical flocculators, consist of revolving paddles connected to horizontal or vertical shafts, driven by electric motor.

(2) Gravitational or hydraulic flocculator

Baffle type mixing basins are examples of gravitational flocculation. Water flows by gravity and baffles are provided in the basins which induce the required velocity gradients for achieving floc formation.[3]

The most common hydraulic flocculator is the baffled basin in which a sinuous channel is equipped with either around-the-end or over-the-under baffles. The flocculation energy is derived primarily from the 180°change in direction of flow at each baffle.

The baffle spacing should be increased gradually with channel length to achieve tapered flocculation. The floor of the channel should slope towards the outlet. The advantage of the baffle basin is its simplicity because there is no mechanical or moving equipment, and near plug flow conditions occur with low short-circuiting. The disadvantages are that most headloss occurs at the 180°bends and therefore the value may be too high at the bends and inadequate in the straight channels for good flocculation, G value will vary as the flow Q varies(but this could be partly overcome by providing removable baffles) and settlement of suspended solids in the channel.

There are two types of gravitational type baffled flocculator in practice as follows:
- Horizontal flow baffled flocculator
- Vertical flow baffled flocculator

Horizontal flow baffled flocculator

The horizontal flow flocculator consists of several around the end baffles with in between spacing of not less than 45 cm to permit cleaning. Clear distance between the end of each baffle and the wall is about 1.5 times the distance between the baffles, but never less than 60 cm. Water depth shall not be less than 1.0m and the water velocity is in the range of 10 to 30 cm/s. The detention time is between 15 to 20 minutes. This type of flocculator is well suited for very small treatment plants. It is easier to drain and clean. Paddles mounted on horizontal shafts are often encountered in flocculation tanks.

Vertical flow baffled flocculator

This type of flocculator is used for medium to large size treatment plants. In vertical flow baffled flocculator the distance between the baffles is not less than 45cm. Clear space between the upper edge of the baffles and the water surface or lower edge of the baffles and the basin bottom is almost 1.5 times the distance between the baffles.[4] Water depth varies between 1.5 to 3 times the distance between the baffles and the water velocity is in the range of 10 to 20 cm/s. The detention time is between 10 to 20 minutes.

Generalized approach to the design of coagulation and flocculation devices
- Carry out jar tests to determine dosage of coagulant.
- Assume values for G and the residence time.
- Size the tank for the residence time selected.
- Choose the type of equipment appropriate for the process (e.g., high speed impeller for rapid mix or paddle agitator for flocculation).
- Size the equipment on the basis of the power dissipation that will result in the desired G

value.

Type of flocculator basic design criteria

Vertical shaft gave value up to $100\ s^{-1}$, maximum tip speed of 2m/s, approximately 5m x 5m to 10m × 10m basin surface area per unit, downward flow pattern preferable for propeller unit, stator baffles should be provided for turbine units.

Horizontal-shaft paddle gave value up to $50s^{-1}$, maximum tip speed of 1 m/s, number of paddles adjusted for tapered mixing; paddle area should not exceed 20% of tank section area

Baffled channel

Tapered mixing by adjusting baffles, maximum flow velocity of approximately 0.75 m/s, end-around baffle used when total head loss across tank is limited. Diffused air and water jets Gave = $95\text{-}20s^{-1}$ or Gave · t = 105-106, may be used for auxiliary mixing when plant is overloaded.

Table 8.1 shows flocculator design guidelines.

Table 8.1 Flocculator design guidelines

Type of Flocculator	Advantages and Disadvantages
Vertical shaft	Easy maintenance and few breakdowns. Suitable for high-energy input. Suitable for direct filtration and conventional treatment. Many units required for a large plant. High capital cost for variable-speed reducers and support slabs
Horizontal-shaft Paddle	Generally produces a large-size floc. Simple mixing it. Suitable for conventional treatment. Need for precise installation and maintenance. Difficult to increase energy input. Problems with leakage and shaft alignment
Baffled channel	Performs well if the plant flow rate is reasonably constant. Little maintenance. A lack of flexibility for mixing intensity. High head loss for the over-and-under baffle
Diffused air and water jets	Simple installation and less capital cost. Limited amount of operational data available. High local velocities for water jet flocculators. High operational cost for air diffuser flocculators

Notes

[1] 絮凝池是通过用絮凝剂去压缩和去除水中固体或污染物，从而帮助或完成絮凝或污染物去除的一种装置。

[2] 叶轮种类很多，根据外形、尺寸、产生的流动类型、流动强度、曝气和非曝气情况下的能量消耗和它们有效的分散气体的能力进行分类。

[3] 水依靠重力流动，在池中安装挡板使速度梯度达到絮凝物形成条件。

[4] 隔板上边缘和水表面或隔板下边缘和池底的间隔距离大约是隔板间距离的 1.5 倍。

Unit 9 Sedimentation

The impurities in water may be either dissolved or suspended. The easiest way to remove the suspended material is to let the force of gravity do the work. Under quiescent conditions, when flow velocities and turbulence are minimal, particles that are denser than water will be able to settle to the bottom of a tank. This process is called sedimentation, and the layer of accumulated solids at the bottom of the tank is called sludge. The settling basins, the settling tanks or sedimentation tanks are ponds constructed for the purpose of removing entrained solids by sedimentation. Clarifiers are settling basins built with mechanical means for continuous removal of solids being deposited by sedimentation.

The speed at which suspended particles settle toward the bottom of a tank depends on their size as well as on their density.[1] The larger and heavier particles will naturally settle faster than smaller or lighter particles. The forces opposing the downward force of gravity include buoyancy and friction (drag). The temperature and viscosity of the water are additional factors that affect the particle-settling rate.

The nature of the sedimentation process also varies with the concentration of suspended particles and their tendency to interact with one another. In a dilute suspension, where the particles are free to settle without interference, the process is called free settling or *discrete settling*. As the concentration increases, the particles tend to interact and interfere with the free movement of one another; this is sometimes called *hindered settling*.[2] In a sedimentation tank there may be up to four different zones or types of settling that occur at different depths, and exact mathematical analysis of the process can be quite complicated. This section discusses some common factors related to discrete particle settling.

Particle Settling Theory

The settling of discrete, non-flocculating particles can be analyzed by means of the classic laws of sedimentation formed by Newton and Stokes.

- Size, shape and specific gravity of the particles do not change with time.
- Settling velocity remains constant.

If a particle is suspended in water, it initially has two forces acting upon it:

(1) force of gravity: $F_g = \rho_p g V_p$

(2) the buoyant force quantified by Archimedes as: $F_b = \rho g V_p$

If the density of the particle differs from that of the water, a net force is exerted and the particle is accelerated in the direction of the force: $F_{net} = (\rho_p - \rho) g V_p$

This net force becomes the driving force. Once the motion has been initiated, a third force is created due to viscous friction. This force, called the drag force, is quantified by:

$$F_d = C_D A_p \rho v^2 / 2 \tag{9-1}$$

Where F_g = gravitational force, MLT^{-2} (kg·m/s^2)

ρ_p = density of particle, MLT^{-3} (kg/m^3)

ρ = density of water, MLT^{-3} (kg/m^3)

V_p = volume of particle, L^3 (m^3)

g = acceleration due to gravity, LT^{-2} (9.81 m/s^2)

F_d = frictional drag force, MLT^{-2} (kg·m/s^2)

C_D = drag coefficient (unitless)

A_p = projected area of the particle, L^2 (m^2)

v = particle settling velocity, LT^{-1} (m/s)

Because the drag force acts in the opposite direction to the driving force and increases as the square of the velocity, acceleration occurs at a decreasing rate until a steady velocity is reached at a point where the drag force equals the driving force:[3]

$$(\rho_p - \rho) g V_p = C_D A_p \rho v^2 / 2 \tag{9-2}$$

For spherical particles,

$$V_p = \pi d^3 / 6 \quad \text{and} \quad A_p = \pi d^2 / 4 \tag{9-3}$$

Thus,
$$v^2 = \frac{4g(\rho_P - \rho)d}{3C_D\rho} \tag{9-4}$$

Expressions for C_D change with characteristics of different flow regimes. For laminar, transition, and turbulent flow, the values of C_D are:

$$C_D = \frac{24}{Re} \text{(laminar)} \tag{9-5}$$

$$C_D = \frac{24}{Re} + \frac{3}{Re^{1/2}} + 0.34 \text{(transition)} \tag{9-6}$$

$$C_D = 0.4 \text{(turbulent)} \tag{9-7}$$

Where Re is the Reynolds number:

$$Re = \frac{\rho v d}{\mu} \tag{9-8}$$

Reynolds number less than 1.0 indicate laminar flow, while values greater than 10 indicate turbulent flow. Intermediate values indicate transitional flow.

Stokes Flow

For laminar flow, terminal settling velocity equation becomes:

$$v = \frac{(\rho_P - \rho)gd^2}{18\mu} \tag{9-9}$$

which is known as the stokes equation.

Transition Flow

Need to solve non-linear equations:

$$v^2 = \frac{4g(\rho_p - \rho)d}{3C_D\rho} \tag{9-10}$$

$$C_D = \frac{24}{Re} + \frac{3}{Re^{1/2}} + 0.34 \tag{9-11}$$

$$Re = \frac{\rho v d}{\mu} \tag{9-12}$$

Calculate velocity using Stokes law or turbulent expression.
- Calculate and check Reynolds number.
- Calculate C_D.
- Use general formula.
- Repeat from step 2 until convergence.

Factors Affecting Sedimentation

Several factors affect the separation of settleable solids from water. Some of the more common types of factors to consider are:

Particle Size

The size and type of particles to be removed have a significant effect on the operation of the sedimentation tank. Because of their density, sand or silt can be removed very easily. The velocity of the water-flow channel can be slowed to less than one foot per second, and most of the gravel and grit will be removed by simple gravitational forces. In contrast, colloidal material, small particles that stay in suspension and make the water seem cloudy, will not settle until the material is coagulated and flocculated by the addition of a chemical, such as an iron salt or aluminum sulfate. [4]

The shape of the particle also affects its settling characteristics. A round particle, for example, will settle much more readily than a particle that has ragged or irregular edges.

All particles tend to have a slight electrical charge. Particles with the same charge tend to repel each other. This repelling action keeps the particles from congregating into flocs and settling.

Water Temperature

Another factor to be considered in the operation of a sedimentation basin is the temperature of the water being treated. When the temperature decreases, the rate of settling becomes slower. The result is that as the water cools, the detention time in the sedimentation tanks must increase. As the temperature decreases, the operator must make changes to the coagulant dosage to compensate for the decreased settling rate. In most cases temperature does not have a significant effect on treatment. A water treatment plant has the highest flow demand in the summer when the temperatures are the highest and the settling rates are the best. When the water is colder, the flow in the plant is at its lowest and, in most cases, the detention time in the plant is increased so the floc has time to settle out in the sedimentation basins.

Several types of water currents may occur in the sedimentation basin:

• Density currents caused by the weight of the solids in the tank, the concentration of solids and temperature of the water in the tank.

• Eddy currents produced by the flow of the water coming into the tank and leaving the tank.

The currents can be beneficial in that they promote flocculation of the particles. However, water currents also tend to distribute the floc unevenly throughout the tank; as a result, it does not settle out at an even rate. [5]

Some of the water current problems can be reduced by the proper design of the tank. Installation of baffles helps prevent currents from short circuiting the tank.

Important Words and Expressions

sedimentation [ˌsedimen'teiʃən]　n. 沉淀，沉降；沉积；淤积；沉降法

tendency ['tendənsi]　n. 倾向，趋势；（话或作品等的）旨趣，意向；性情；癖好

quiescent [kwiː'esənt]　adj. 不活动的，静态的，休眠的

discrete settling　自由沉淀

hindered settling　拥挤沉淀

reagent [riː'eidʒənt]　n. 反应物，试剂

coefficient [ˌkəui'fiʃənt]　n. 系数；（测定某种质量或变化过程的）率；程度；协同因素　adj. 共同作用的；合作的

boundary ['baundəri]　n. 分界线；范围；（球场）边线

buoyant ['bɔiənt,'bu:jənt]   adj. 轻快的； 活泼的；有浮力的，易浮的
unevenly [' ʌn'i:vənli]   adv. 不规则地；不稳定地；不平行地
laminar['læminə]   adj. 薄片装的，薄层的；层状的，板状的；流线的；层流的
turbulent ['tə:bjulənt]   adj. 湍流的，激流的；混乱的，骚乱的；吵闹的；强横的

Notes

[1] 池中悬浮颗粒沉淀到池底的速度取决于它们的大小和密度。

[2] 当浓度增加时，颗粒倾向于相互作用，干扰其他颗粒的自由运动，这有时被称为拥挤沉淀。

[3] 由于摩擦阻力与驱动力方向相反，且随速度的平方增大，加速度下降，直到达到一个稳定的速度使得摩擦阻力与驱动力相等。

[4] 与之相反，胶体物质、细小颗粒悬浮在水中，使水看上去呈云状浑浊，这时只有投加如铁盐或硫酸铝之类的化学药剂对之进行混凝和絮凝才能使之沉淀。

[5] 水流对促进颗粒的絮凝有好处。然而，水流也会使絮体在整个池内分布不均匀，结果絮体不能在平均速度下沉淀下来。

Exercises

1. Answering the following questions in English according to the text:

(1) Introduce particle settling theory briefly.

(2) What are the factors affecting sedimentation?

2. Using the following each word to make up the sentences, respectively:

(1) discrete settling

(2) suspension

(3) laminar

(4) viscous

(5) floc

3. Put the following English into Chinese:

(1) On the basis of the concentration and the tendency of particles to interact, four types of gravitational settling can occur: 1) discrete particle, 2) flocculent, 3) hindered (also called zone), and 4) compression. Because of the fundamental importance of the separation processes in the treatment of wastewater, the analysis of each type of separation process is discussed separately. In addition, tube settlers, used to enhance the performance of sedimentation facilities, are also described.

(2) Under the influent of gravity, any particle having a density greater than 1.0 will settle in water at an accelerating velocity until the resistance of the liquid equals the effective weight of the particle. Thereafter, the settling velocity will be essentially constant and will depend upon the size, shape, and density of the particle, as well as the density and viscosity of the water. For most theoretical and practical computations of settling velocities in sedimentation basins, the shape of the particles is assumed to be spherical. Settling velocities of particles of other shapes can be analyzed in relation to spheres.

4. Put the following Chinese into English:

(1) 颗粒沉淀

(2) 自由沉淀

(3) 拥挤沉淀

(4) 水中悬浮颗粒依靠重力作用，从水中分离出来的过程称为沉淀。

(5) 严格而言，自由沉淀时单个颗粒在无边际的水体中的沉淀。此时颗粒排挤开同体积的水，被排挤的水将以无限小的速度上升。

Reading Material A

Types of Settling and Hindered Settling

Types of Settling

The removal of suspended and colloidal materials from wastewater by gravity separation is one of the most widely used unit operations in wastewater treatment. A summary of gravitational phenomena is presented in Table 9.1. Sedimentation is the term applied to separation of suspended particles that are heavier than water, by gravitational settling. The terms sedimentation and settling are used interchangeably. A sedimentation basin may also be referred to as a sedimentation tank, clarifier, settling basin, or settling tank. Accelerated gravity settling involves the removal of particles in suspension by gravity settling in an accelerated flow field. The fundamentals of gravity separation are introduced in this section. Solid liquid separation process in which a suspension is separated into two phases: (1) clarified supernatant leaving the top of the sedimentation tank (overflow), (2) concentrated sludge leaving the bottom of the sedimentation tank (underflow). [1]

Table 9.1　Types of gravitational phenomena utilized in wastewater treatment

Type of separation phenomenon	Description	Application/occurrence
Discrete particle settling	Refers to the settling of particles in a suspension of low solids concentration by gravity in a constant acceleration field. Particles settle as individual entities, and there is no significant interaction with neighboring particles[2]	Removal of grit and sand particles from wastewater
Flocculent settling	Refers to a rather dilute suspension of particles that coalesce, or flocculate, during the settling operation. By coalescing, the particles increase in mass and settle at a faster rate	Removal of a portion of the TSS in untreated wastewater in primary settling facilities, and in upper portions of secondary settling facilities. Also removes chemical floc in settling tanks
Ballasted flocculent settling	Refers to the addition of an inert ballasting agent and a polymer to a partially flocculated suspension to promote rapid settling and improved solids reduction.[3] A portion of the recovered ballasting agent is recycled to the process	Removal of a portion of the TSS in untreated wastewater, wastewater from combined systems, and industrial wastewater. Also reduces BOD and phosphoru
Hindered settling(also called zone settling)	Refers to suspensions of intermediate concentration, in which inter-particle forces are sufficient to hinder the settling of neighboring particles. The particles tend to remain in fixed positions	Occur in secondary settling facilities used in conjunction with biological treatment facilities
Compression settling	Refers to settling in which the particles are of such concentration that a structure is formed, and further settling can occur only by compression of the structure. Compression takes place from the weight of the particles, which are constantly being added to the structure by sedimentation from the supernatant liquid	Usually occurs in the lower layers of a deep solids or biosolids mass, such as in the bottom of deep secondary settling facilities and in solids-thickening facilities
Accelerated gravity settling	Removal of particles in suspension by gravity settling in an acceleration field	Removal of grit and sand particles from wastewater
Flotation	Removal of particles in suspension that are lighter than water by air or gas flotation	Removal of greases and oils, light material that floats, thickening of solids suspensions

Sedimentation is used for the removal of grit, TSS in primary settling basins, biological floc removal in the activated-sludge settling basin, and chemical floc removal when the chemical coagulation process is used. Sedimentation is also used for solids concentration in sludge thickeners. In most cases, the primary purpose is to produce a clarified effluent, but it is also necessary to produce sludge with a solids concentration that can be handled and treated easily.

On the basis of the concentration and tendency of particles to interact, four types of gravitational settling can occur: (1) discrete particle, (2) flocculent, (3)hindered (also called zone), and (4) compression. Discrete particle settling - particles settle individually without interaction with neighboring particles. Flocculent particles – flocculation causes the particles to increase in mass and settle at a faster rate. Hindered or zone settling –the mass of particles tends to settle as a unit with individual particles remaining in fixed positions. Compression – the concentration of particles is so high that sedimentation can only occur through compaction of the structure.

Hindered (Zone) Settling

In systems that contain a high concentration of suspended solids, both hindered or zone settling and compression settling usually occur in addition to discrete(free) and flocculent settling. The settling phenomenon that occurs when a concentrated suspension initially of uniform concentration throughout, is placed in a graduated cylinder, is illustrated on Figure 9.1.

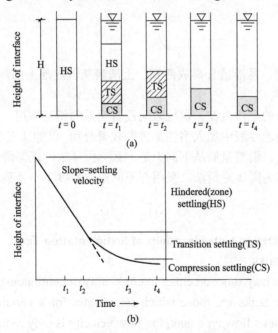

Figure 9.1 Definition sketch for hindered (zone) settling: (a) settling column in which the suspension is transitioning through various phases of settling and (b)the corresponding interface settling curve

Because of the high concentration of particles, the liquid tends to move up through the interstices of the contacting particles, As a result, the contacting particles tend to settle as a zone or "blanket", maintaining the same relative position with respect to each other. The phenomenon is known as hindered settling. As the particles settle, a relatively clear layer of water is produced above the particles in the settling region. The scattered, relatively light particles remaining usually settle as discrete or flocculent particles, as discussed previously. In most cases, an identifiable interface develops between the upper region and the hindered settling region on Figure 9.1. The rate of settling in the hindered settling region is a function of the concentration of solids and their characteristics.

As settling continues, a compressed layer of particles begins to form on the bottom of the cylinder in the compression settling region. The particles apparently form a structure in which there is close physical contact between the particles. As the compression layer forms, regions containing successively lower concentrations of solids than those in the compression region extend upward in the cylinder.[4] Thus, in actuality the hindered settling region contains a gradation in solids concentration from that found at the interface of the settling region to that found in the compression settling region.

Because of the variability encountered, settling tests are usually required to determine the settling characteristics of suspensions where hindered and compression settling are important considerations. On the basis of data derived from column settling tests, two different design approaches can be used to obtain the required area for the settling/thickening facilities. In the first approach, the data derived from one or more batch settling tests are used. In the second approach, known as the solids flux method, data from a series of settling tests conducted at different solids concentrations are used. [5] It should be noted that both methods have been used where existing plants are to be expanded or modified. These methods are, however, seldom used in the design of small treatment plants.

Notes

[1] 固液分离过程中，悬浮液分离成两相：上清液从沉淀池上部流出（溢流），浓缩污泥从沉淀池底部排出（底流）。

[2] 颗粒以一个单独的个体沉淀，颗粒之间没有明显的相互作用。

[3] 只在部分絮凝的悬浮液中加入惰性加重剂或聚合物，以加速沉淀,提高固体的去除量。

[4] 当压缩区形成时，沿着量筒从下向上是一系列固体浓度逐渐降低的区域。

[5] 第二种方法也称为固体通量法，采用在不同固体浓度下一系列沉淀试验的数据。

Reading Material B

Design Considerations of Sedimentation Tank

Types of Settling Tanks

• Sedimentation tanks may function either intermittently or continuously. The intermittent tanks also called quiescent type tanks are those which store water for a certain period and keep it in complete rest. In a continuous flow type tank, the flow velocity is only reduced and the water is not brought to complete rest as is done in an intermittent type.

• Settling basins may be either long rectangular or circular in plan. Long narrow rectangular tanks with horizontal flow are generally preferred to the circular tanks with radial or spiral flow.

Long Rectangular Settling Basin

• Long rectangular basins are hydraulically more stable, and flow control for large volumes is easier with this configuration.

• A typical long rectangular tank have length ranging from 2 to 4 times their width. The bottom is slightly sloped to facilitate sludge scraping. A slow moving mechanical sludge scraper continuously pulls the settled material into a sludge hopper from where it is pumped out periodically.[1]

A long rectangular settling tank can be divided into three different functional zones:

Inlet zone Region in which the flow is uniformly distributed over the cross section such that the flow through settling zone follows horizontal path.

Settling zone Settling occurs under quiescent conditions.

Outlet zone Clarified effluent is collected and discharge through outlet weir.

Inlet and Outlet Arrangement

Inlet devices Inlets shall be designed to distribute the water equally and at uniform velocities. A baffle should be constructed across the basin close to the inlet and should project several feet below the water surface to dissipate inlet velocities and provide uniform flow;

Outlet Devices Outlet weirs or submerged orifices shall be designed to maintain velocities suitable for settling in the basin and to minimize short-circuiting. Weirs shall be adjustable, and at least equivalent in length to the perimeter of the tank. However, peripheral weirs are not acceptable as they tend to cause excessive short-circuiting.

Weir Overflow Rates

Large weir overflow rates result in excessive velocities at the outlet. These velocities extend backward into the settling zone, causing particles and flocs to be drawn into the outlet. Weir loadings are generally used up to 300 m^3/d/m. It may be necessary to provide special inboard weir designs as shown in Figure 9.2 to lower the weir overflow rates.

Figure 9.2 Inboard weir arrangement to increase weir length

Circular Basins

• Circular settling basins have the same functional zones as the long rectangular basin, but the flow regime is different. When the flow enters at the center and is baffled to flow radially towards the perimeter, the horizontal velocity of the water is continuously decreasing as the distance from the center increases. [2] Thus, the particle path in a circular basin is a parabola as opposed to the straight line path in the long rectangular tank.

- Sludge removal mechanisms in circular tanks are simpler and require less maintenance.

Settling Operations

- Particles falling through the settling basin have two components of velocity:

(1) Vertical component: $v_t = \dfrac{(\rho_p - \rho)gd^2}{18\mu}$

(2) Horizontal component: $v_h = Q/A$

The path of the particle is given by the vector sum of horizontal velocity v_h and vertical settling velocity v_t.

- Assume that a settling column is suspended in the flow of the settling zone and that the column travels with the flow across the settling zone. Consider the particle in the batch analysis for type-1 settling which was initially at the surface and settled through the depth of the column Z_0, in the time t_0. [3] If t_0 also corresponds to the time required for the column to be carried horizontally across the settling zone, then the particle will fall into the sludge zone and be removed from the suspension at the point at which the column reaches the end of the settling zone.

All particles with $v_t > v_0$ will be removed from suspension at some point along the settling zone.

- Now consider the particle with settling velocity $< v_0$. If the initial depth of this particle was such that $Z_p/v_t = t_0$, this particle will also be removed. Therefore, the removal of suspended particles passing through the settling zone will be in proportion to the ratio of the individual settling velocities to the settling velocity v_0. The time t_0 corresponds to the retention time in the settling zone.

$$t = \dfrac{v}{Q} = \dfrac{LZ_0W}{Q} \tag{9-13}$$

Also,

$$t_0 = \dfrac{Z_0}{v_0} \tag{9-14}$$

Therefore,

$$\dfrac{Z_0}{v_0} = \dfrac{LZ_0W}{Q} \quad \text{and} \quad v_0 = \dfrac{Q}{LW} \tag{9-15}$$

or

$$v_0 = \dfrac{Q}{A_s} \tag{9-16}$$

Thus, the depth of the basin is not a factor in determining the size particle that can be removed completely in the settling zone. The determining factor is the quantity Q/A_s, which has the units of velocity and is referred to as the overflow rate q_0. This overflow rate is the design factor for settling basins and corresponds to the terminal setting velocity of the particle that is 100% removed.

Design Details

(1) Detention period: for plain sedimentation: 3 to 4 h, and for coagulated sedimentation: 2 to 2.5 h.

(2) Velocity of flow: Not greater than 30 cm/min (horizontal flow).

(3) Tank dimensions: L: B = 3 to 5:1. Generally L= 30 m (common) maximum 100 m. Breadth= 6 to 10 m. Circular: Diameter not greater than 60 m. generally 20 to 40 m.

(4) Depth 2.5 to 5.0 m (3 m).

(5) Surface Overflow Rate: For plain sedimentation 12000 to 18000 L/d/m² tank area; for thoroughly flocculated water 24000 to 30000 L/d/m² tank area.

(6) Slopes: Rectangular 1% towards inlet and circular 8%.

Notes

[1] 典型的矩形槽的长度是宽度的 2~4 倍。底部略微倾斜以便于刮泥。缓慢移动的机械刮泥机不断将污泥刮进周期性排泥的污泥斗。

[2] 圆形沉淀池像矩形池一样具有相同的功能区，但是流动机理是不同的。当水流进入中心不断向四周流动，水平流速不断下降同时中心距离增加。

[3] 假设沉淀筒悬浮在沉淀区的水流中，随水流通过沉淀区。对于沉淀类型Ⅰ中颗粒批量分析，颗粒起初在液面，经过 t_0 时间沉淀到沉淀筒 Z_0 的位置。

Unit 10　　Filtration

Filtration is used to separate nonsettleable solids from water and wastewater by passing it through a porous medium. The most common system is filtration through a layered bed of granular media, usually a coarse anthracite coal anthracite coal underlain by finer sand.

Gravity granular-media filtration

Gravity filtration through beds of granular media is the most common method of removing colloidal impurities in water processing and tertiary treatment of wastewater.[1] The mechanisms involved in removing suspended solids in a granular-media filter are complex, consisting of interception, straining, flocculation, and sedimentation. Initially, surface straining and interstitial removal result in accumulation of deposits in the upper portion of the filter media. Because of the reduction in ore are, the velocity of water through the remaining voids increases, shearing off pieces of captured floc and carrying impurities deeper into the filter bed. The effective zone of removal passes deeper and deeper into the filter. Turbulence and resulting increased particle contact within the pores promotes flocculation, resulting in trapping of the larger floc particles. Eventually, clean bed depth is no longer available and breakthrough occurs, carrying solids out in the underflow and causing termination of the filter run. [2]

Direct filtration

The process of direct filtration does not include sedimentation prior to filtration. The impurities removed from the water are collected and stored in the filter. Although rapid mixing of chemicals is necessary, the flocculation stage is either eliminated or reduced to a mixing time less than 30min. Contact flocculation of the chemically coagulated particles in the water takes places in the granular media. Successful advances in direct filtration are attributed to the development of coarse-to-fine multimedia filters with greater capacity for "in-depth" filtration, improved backwashing systems using mechanical or air agitation to aid cleaning of the media, and the availability of better polymer coagulants.

Surface waters with low turbidity and color are most suitable for processing by direct filtration. Based on experiences cited in the literature, waters with less than 40 units of color, turbidity consistently below 5 units, iron and manganese concentrations of less than 0.3 and 0.05 mg/L, respectively, and algal counts below 2,000/mL can be successfully processed. Operational problems in direct filtration are expected when color exceeds 40 units or turbidity is greater than 15 units on a continuous basis. Potential problems can be alleviated during a short period of time by application of additional polymer. Tertiary filtration of wastewaters containing 20-30mg/L suspended solids following biological treatment can be reduced to less than 5 mg/L by direct filtration.[3] For inactivation of viruses and a high degree of bacterial disinfection, filtration of chemically conditioned wastewater precedes disinfection by chlorine.

The feasibility of filtration without prior flocculation and sedimentation relies on a comprehensive review of water quality data. The incident of HCE origin turbidities caused by runoff from storms and blooms of algae must be evaluated. Often, pilot testing is valuable in determining efficiency of direct filtration compared to conventional treatment, design of filter media, and selection of chemical conditioning.

Filter Backwashing

During the service cycle of filter operation, particulate matter removed from the applied water accumulates on the surface of the grains of fine media and in the pore spaces between grains.[4] With continued operation of a filter, the materials removed from the water and stored within the bed reduce the porosity of the bed. This has two effects on filter operation: it increases the headloss through the filter, and it increases the shearing stresses on the accumulated floc. Eventually the total hydraulic headloss may approach or equal the head necessary to provide the desired flow rate through the filter, or there may be a leakage or breakthrough of floc particles into the filter effluent. Just before either if these outcomes can occur, the filter should be removed from service for cleaning. In the old slow-sand filters the arrangement of sand particles is fine to coarse in the direction of filtration (down); most of the impurities removed from the water collect on the top surface of the bed, which can be cleaned by mechanical scraping and removal of about 12.7 mm of sand and floc. In rapid sand filters, there is somewhat deeper penetration of particles into the bed because of the coarser media used and the higher flow rates employed. However, most of the materials are stored in the top few inches of a rapid sand filter bed. In dual-media and mixed-media beds, floc is stored throughout the bed depth to within a few inches of the bottom of the fine media.

Rapid sand, dual-media, and mixed-media filters are cleaned by hydraulic backwashing (up flow) with potable water. Thorough cleaning of the bed makes it advisable in the case of dual-or mixed-media filters to use auxiliary scour or so-called surface wash devices before or during the backwash cycle. Backwash flow rates of 36.6 to 48.8 m/h should be provided. A 20 to 50 percent expansion of the filter bed is usually adequate to suspend the bottom grains. The optimum rate of washwater application is a direct function of water temperature, as expansion of the bed varies inversely with viscosity of the washwater. For example, a backwash rate of 43.9 m/h at 20℃ equates to 38.3 m/h at 5℃ and 48.8 m/h at 35 ℃. The time required for complete washing varies from 3 to 15 minutes.

Following the washing process, water should be filtered to waste until the turbidity drops to an acceptable value.[5] Filter-to-waste outlets should be through an air-gap-to-waste drain, which may require from 2 to 20 minutes, depending on pretreatment and type of filter. This practice was discontinued for many years, but modern recording turbidimeters have shown that this operation is valuable in the production of a high-quality water. Operating the washed filter at a slow rate at the start of a filter run may accomplish the same purpose. A recording turbidimeter for continues monitoring of the effluent from each individual filter unit is of great value in controlling this operation at the start of a run, as well as in predicting or detecting filter breakthrough at the end of a run.

The time from start to full backwash flow should be at least 30 seconds and perhaps longer, and should be restricted by devices built into the plant. This is frequently done by means of an automatically regulated master wash valve, controlled hydraulically or electrically and designed so that it cannot open too fast. Alternatively, a speed controller could be installed on the operator of each washwater valve.

Important Words and Expressions

nonsettleable [nɔn'setləbl]   a. 非沉降性的，不沉淀的
porous ['pɔːrəs]   adj. 多孔渗水的；能渗透；有气孔的
impurities [im'pjuəritiːz]   n. 杂质（impureity 的复数）
tertiary ['təːʃ(ə)ri]   a. 第三（位，级，纪）的
interstitial [,intə(ː)'stiʃ(ə)l]   a. 空[孔]隙的，缝隙间
voids [vɔidz]   n. 空洞，孔洞；空隙率，结点间（void 的复数） v.使无效；排泄，清空
turbulence ['təːbjələns]   n. 骚乱，动荡；湍流；狂暴
agitation [ædʒi'teiʃ(ə)n]   n. 激动；搅动；煽动；烦乱
polymer ['pɔlimə]   n. [化]聚合物
feasibility [,fiːzə'biliti]   n. 可行性；可能性
pore [pɔː]   vi. 细想；凝视；熟读   n.气孔；小孔   vt. 使注视
penetration [peni'treiʃ(ə)n]   n. 渗透；突破；侵入；洞察力
viscosity [vi'skɔsitiː]   n. 黏性，黏度

Notes

[1] 通过粒状滤料床的重力过滤方法，是水处理和废水的三级处理中去除胶体杂质最常见的方法。

[2] 最终，清洁的滤层厚度不足，杂质发生穿透，底部出水携带固体颗粒，过滤周期结束。

[3] 对悬浮物浓度 20～30mg/L 的生化处理出水进行三级过滤处理，经过直接过滤后悬浮物能减少至 5 mg/L。

[4] 在滤池的工作周期内，被去除的进水中的悬浮物，聚集在细颗粒滤料的表面以及颗粒间的空隙中。

[5] 随着反冲洗的进行，冲洗水应当排入废水中，直到浊度下降到一个可接受的值为止。

Exercises

1. Answering the following questions in English according to the text：
　　(1) Difine the in-depth filtration.

(2) Discuss the mechanisms involved in removing suspended solids in a granular media filter.

2. Using the following each word to make up the sentences, respectively:

(1) rapid filter

(2) backwashing

(3) direct filtration

(4) agitation

(5) filter media

3. Put the following English into Chinese:

(1) A typical scheme for processing surface supplies to drinking-water quality consists of flocculation with a chemical coagulant and sedimentation prior to filtration. Under the force of gravity, often by a combination of positive head and suction from underneath, water passes downward through the media that collect the floc and particles. When the media become filled or solids break through, a filter bed is cleaned by backwashing where upward flow fluidizes the media and conveys away the impurities that have accumulated in the bed. Destruction of bacteria and viruses depends on satisfactory turbidity control to enhance the efficiency of chlorination.

(2) Fluidization is defined as upward flow through a granular bed at sufficient velocity to suspend the grains in the water. During the process of fluidization, the upward flow overcomes the gravitational force on the grains, and the energy loss is due to fluid motion. The viscous energy loss is proportional to the velocity of flow, and the kinetic energy loss is proportional to the square of the velocity.

The pressure loss through a fixed bed is a linear function of flowrate at low superficial velocities when flow is laminar. As the flowrate increases further, the resistance of the grains to wash-water flow increases until this resistance equals the gravitational force and the grains are suspended in the water. Any further increase in upward velocity results in additional expansion of the bed while maintaining a constant pressure drop equal to the buoyant weight of the media.

4. Put the following Chinese into English:

(1) 多层滤料滤池

(2) 水中杂质和混凝剂浓度

(3) 正压水头和下部吸水头

(4) 无烟煤和砂是常用的多孔介质滤料。

(5) 反冲洗形成的上向水流使滤料流化，并带走聚集滤床内的杂质。

5. Put the following abbr. into full phrases:

(1) gravity filtration

(2) flocculation

(3) backwashing

(4) sedimentation

(5) effluent

Reading Material A

Rapid Filters

The first filters built for water purification used very fine sand as the filter media. Because of the tiny size of the pore spaces in the fine sand, water takes a long time to flow through the filter bed, and when the surface becomes clogged with suspended particles, it becomes necessary to manually scrape the sand surface to clean the filter. [1] These units, called *slow sand filters*, take up a considerable amount of land area because of the slow filtration rates. Slow sand filters are still used in several existing treatment plants. They are effective and relatively inexpensive to operate.

In modern water treatment plants the *rapid filter* has largely replaced the slow sand filter. As its name implies, the water flow through the filter bed much faster (about 30 times as fast) than it flows through the slow sand filter. This naturally makes it necessary to clean the filter much more frequently. But instead of manual cleaning by scraping of the surface, rapid filter are cleaned by reversing the direction of flow through the bed. This is shown schematically in Figure 10.1.

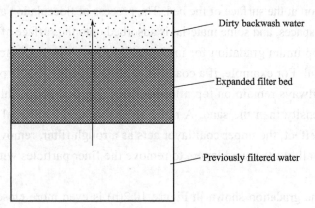

Figure 10.1 Schematic diagram of the backwash or cleaning cycle of a rapid filter

During filtration, the water flows download through the bed under the force of gravity. When the filter is washed, clean water is force upward, expanding the filter bed slightly and carrying away the accumulated impurities. This process is called *backwashing*. Cleaning by a backwash operation is a key characteristic of a rapid filter.

Many rapid filters currently in operation use sand as the filter medium and are called *rapid filters*. But the sand grains (are pore spaces) are larger than those in the older, slow sand filters. In a rapid sand filter, the effective size of the sand is about 0.5 mm and the uniformity coefficient is 1.5. A difficulty that arises when using only sand in the rapid filter is that, after backwashing, the larger sand grains settle to the bottom first, leaving the smaller sand grains at the filter surface. This pattern of filter medium gradation is shown in Figure 10.2(a).

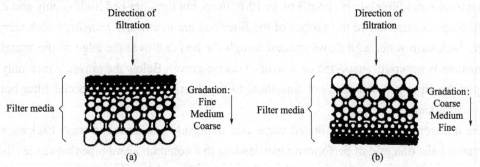

Figure 10.2 (a) Typical gradation of a rapid sand bed. Solids removal occurs primarily by straining action at the top of the sand bed;(b) Typical coarse-to-fine gradation in a mixed-media filter.
It is preferable to the sand bed because it provide in-depth filtration

Because of this small-to-large gradation of sand grains in the direction of flow, most of the filtering action takes place in the top layer of the bed. This results in inefficient use of the filter. The filter run time (period of time between backwashes) is reduced, and frequent backwashes are required. Also, if some of the suspended material happens to penetrate the upper layer of fine sand, it is then likely to pass through the entire filter bed.

A preferable size distribution of the filter material is shown in Figure 10.2(b). The large-to-small particle gradation allows the suspended particles to reach greater depths with the filter bed. This in-depth filtration, as it is called, provides more storage space for the solids, offers less resistance to flow, and follows longer filter runs. The process of filtration becomes more than just a physical straining action at the surface of the bed. The process of flocculation and sedimentation also occur within the pore spaces, and some material is adsorbed onto the surface of the filter medium.

To achieve the optimum gradation for in-depth filtration, it is necessary to use two or more different filter material. For example, if a coarse layer or anthracite coal is placed above the sand, the coal grains will always remain on top after backwashing occurs. [2] This is because the coal has a much lower density than the sand. A rapid filter that uses both coal and sand is called a dual-media filter. In effect, the upper coal layer acts as a rough filter, removing most of the large impurities first. This allows the sand layers to remove the finer particles without getting clogged too quickly.

The coarse-to-fine gradation shown in Figure 10.2(b) is even more closely obtained by using three filter materials: coal, sand, and garnet (a very dense material). After backwashing, the top layer of the filter bed is mostly coarse coal, the middle is mostly medium sand, and the bottom layer is mostly very fine grain of garnet. This is called a mixed-media filter. Filter material ranges in size from about 2mm at the top to about 0.2mm at the bottom. In recent years, dual-and mixed-media filters have been used to replace existing rapid sand filter in many treatment plants.

Filter Design

Rapid filer, whether of sand, dual media, or mixed media, are usually built it in boxlike concrete structures, as illustrated in Figure 10.3. Multiple filter boxes or units are arranged on both sides of a central *piping gallery*, and a *clear well* used for storing filter water is often located under the filters. Since only one unit is backwashed at a time, the filtration process can occur continuously as water flows through the treatment plant.

A typical rapid filter box is about 3 m, or 10 ft, deep, but the filter bed itself is only about 0.75m, or 2.5ft, deep. Located above the surface of the filter bed are *washwater troughs*, which carry away the dirty backwash water as it flows upward trough the bed and over the edge of the troughs. The filter medium is generally supported on a layer of coarse gravel. Below the gravel, which only serves to support the filter bed and does not contribute to the filtering action, is a special filter bottom or *underdrain system*.

The underdrains collect the filtered water and uniformly distribute the wash backwash cycle. They may consist of a grid of perforated pipes leading to a common heard pipe that carries the water into the clear well. In many filter, the underdrain consist of specially manufacture porous tile blocks or steel plates with nozzles to help to distribute the backwash water. A cross-section of a typical filter unit is shown in Figure 10.4.

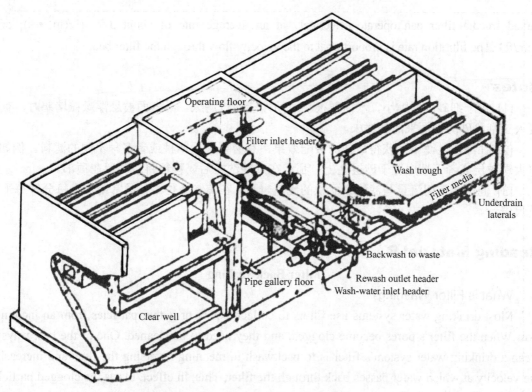

Figure 10.3 Perspective view of a typical rapid filter facility
The filtered water is temporarily stored in the clear well.
Multiple filter boxes provide operational flexibility; only one filter is backwashed at a time

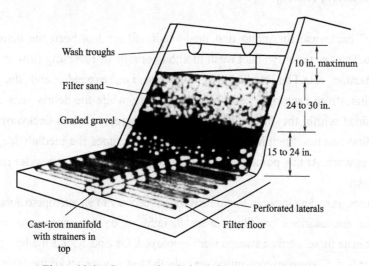

Figure 10.4 Cross-sectional view of a typical sand filter box

The effective of filtration and the length of a filter run depend on the filtration rate. Lower filtration rates generally allow longer filter runs and produce higher quality water, but they require larger filters. Filtration rate is often expressed as the flow rate of water divided by the surface area of the filter. In customary units, this is usually in terms of gallons per minute per square foot (gpm/ft^2 or gal/ft^2/min). [3] In SI metric units, it is liters per square meter per second [L/(m^2 · s)]. Rapid sand filter are usually designed to operate at an average rate of about 1.4 [L/(m^2 · s)] or 2 gpm/ft^2, whereas mixed-media filter can operate effectively at an average rate of about 3.5 [L/(m$^2 \cdot$ s)] or 5 gpm/ft^2. The filtration rate is proportional to the velocity flow through the filter bed.

Notes

[1] 由于细砂的空隙小，水需要很长时间才能通过滤床，当表面被悬浮颗粒堵塞时，有必要人工刮除砂的表面来清洁滤床。

[2] 在深层过滤中为获得最佳的级配效果，有必要采用两种或者多种不同的滤料。例如，将大颗粒层或者无烟煤置于砂层之上，那么在反冲洗之后煤颗粒将总是留在顶部。

[3] 滤速通常用流量与滤池表面积的比值表示。在美制单位中，通常用加仑每分钟每平方英尺表示。

Reading Material B

Filter Backwashing

What is Filter Washing?

Most drinking water systems use filters to collect, catch, or gather particles from an incoming flow. When the filter's pores become clogged, and they need to be cleaned. One of the best ways to clean a drinking water system's filter is to backwash it, meaning reversing the flow and increasing the velocity at which water passes back through the filter, This, In effect, blasts the clogged particles off of the filter.[1] Although every filter is unique, the principles of backwashing are similar for all of them.

Filter Backwashing History
Water Only

"Water only" backwash for mono and dual media filters has been the historical "minimal" backwash method. The "water only" backwash method consists of reversing flow in a filter bed to its theoretical fluidization rate. The media then fluidizes, i.e., expands, and the media particles theoretically separate from each other, and from the debris, while the debris goes out to waste, and the media is retained within the filter cell. As the flow increases when backwash is initiated, the energy required first reaches "incipient headloss". This overcomes the media's inertia, and gets the particles moving upward. At this point, headloss decreases somewhat as the water rate increases.[2]

Surface Wash

Surface washers were developed in the mid-twentieth century in an attempt to enhance "water only" backwash. Surface encrustations on filters were thought to be the source and cause of mudball formation. To eliminate these, surface sweeps were employed. Obviously, this method can only affect the surface of the filter bed. Surface sweeps influence only the top few inches of the filter. "Surface sweeps cannot reach the location where mudballs often accumulate, [that is] the interface of the two media."

Air Scour

In the 1970's, air scour was developed in an attempt to cleanse the entire filter media and break up surface encrustations. The introduction of air prior to water backwash was marginally effective at improving backwash efficiency over "water only" methods. The air scour method was a slight improvement over the surface sweeps in that it broke up surface incrustations in corners. When viewed from above, air scour appears to be violently agitating the entire filter bed, so it looks better too. Air scour has been found to be effective for preventing the type of mudballs that form on the surface of the bed and previously were found to be "rolled" into larger agglomerations and balls by the action of the surface sweeps.[3]

Collapse Pulsing Action

A mathematical model was developed by Amirtharajah, et al, to determine the optimum air/water rates, using fluid and soil mechanics theories. This theoretical model was later verified with experimental testing. The most surprising discovery was that under the action of simultaneous air and water, the filter beds undergo a "collapse pulsing action". The primary variables for attaining this collapse pulsing action were found to be media gradation and water temperature.

Simultaneous Air/Water Backwash

In the 1990's, filter backwash research was conducted by Amirtharajah, et al, at Georgia Tech under an AWWA Research Foundation(AWWARF) grant. This research was summarized in an AWWARE publication entitled Optimum Backwash of Dual Media Filters and GAC Filter-Adsorbers With Air Scour. His study proved that "backwashing filters with simultaneous air plus water at sub-fluidized rates provides the best cleaning of the filter media".

What was surprising was that using high simultaneous rates of air and water (i.e., water at or near fluidization combined with air) did not significantly increase the amount of debris released from the bed. What showed the best results was simultaneous air and water at sub-fluidized rates, typically water rates on the order of 3 to 5 gpm/sf of filter bed area, coupled with air rates at 2 to 3 cfm/sf. This finding revolutionized the art of filter backwashing.

Filter Geometry

The only limitation of the AWWARF research was that time of the backwash was assumed to be limited by filter geometry with little wash water conservation possible. Most existing rapid sand gravity filters are designed for "water only" backwash with maximum 50% allowable room for media expansion below the backwash troughs. This means that to practice simultaneous air and water backwash, water needs to be drained down to 6" above the surface of the media, air scour applied, and then water introduced simultaneously until the water surface rises to the bottom of the backwash trough. At this point the air must be turned off and "water only" backwash must commence. If the air is not turned off, then media loss will occur. Collapse pulsing action is so violent that it expands media all the way to the water surface.

Sustained Simultaneous Air/Water Backwash

In the late 1970's research was begun on baffled backwash trough technology suitable for sustained simultaneous air and water backwash. The development of a successful baffled trough allowed the length of the simultaneous air/water backwash step to be extended beyond the filter's geometric rise limitation.[4] This ability allows operators to control the length of collapse pulse backwashing for optimum adjustable filter cleaning. This also was found to minimize wash water production and prevent mudball formation. This sustained simultaneous air/water backwash system centers around a proven baffled trough and is the first engineered system available that promotes collapse pulse action, while eliminating media loss and minimizing wash water production.

When to Backwash

The cleanliness or cloudiness (turbidity) of the water coming out of the filter just before it goes into the clear well is the best way to determine when to backwash. A good rule of thumb is 0.1 nephelometric turbidity units (NTU) on each individual filter's effluent. This may sound a little exterme when the combined filter effluent (CFE) for conventional and direct filtration systems is 0.3 NUT. But 0.1 NUT gives the operator time to react to any problems within the treatment system.

Head loses on the filter also indicates the need to backwash. Head loss is usually measured with a negative pressure gauge. As the filter gets clogged, more negative pressure is created. The pressure usually starts near zero pounds per square inch (psi) or approximately one foot of head loss on the clean filter. Then the pressure will increase in a linear fashion in the negative direction to approximately -2.5 to -4 psi on rapid-rate, gravity filters and some pressure filters or about 6 to 10 feet of head loss. This calculation may be different depending on the filter type and make.

Some small plants will just have a clear tube with water indicating pressure differences. The water level in the tube rises as the pressure difference increases. For every one psi measure, there is 0.434 psi of pressure difference. The clear tube can be marked with the pressure difference in negative psi, or it could have a single mark, indicating it is time to backwash.

A couple of other indicators really only work when a water system has consistent raw water turbidity. These indicators are gallons filtered or run time. When the raw water is consistent, operators usually can tell when to backwash based on the pump's run time.

Notes

[1] 清洗饮用水系统滤池的最佳方式之一是进行反冲洗，这意味着水流反向提速流过滤池，从而使滤池中的阻塞的滤料膨胀。

[2] 这克服了滤料的惯性，使得颗粒向上运动。从这点上来讲，随着流量的增加，水头损失在一定程度上降低。

[3] 气洗已被证实能够有效地防止在滤床表面形成泥球，之前已发现这些泥球通过表面扫洗可以"滚"成更大的颗粒群或者更大的泥球。

[4] 研发一个成功的隔板槽，可使气/水反冲洗过程的长度，不受滤池几何高度的限制。

Unit 11   Chemical Oxidation

Chemical oxidation in wastewater treatment typically involves the use of oxidizing agents such as ozone (O_3), hydrogen peroxide (H_2O_2), permanganate (MnO_4), chloride dioxide (ClO_2), chlorine (Cl_2) or (HOCl), and oxygen (O_2), to bring about changes in the chemical composition of a compound or a group of compounds.[1] Included in the following discussion is an introduction of the fundamental concepts involved in chemical oxidation, an overview of the uses of chemical oxidation in wastewater treatment, and a discussion of the use of chemical oxidation for the reduction of BOD and COD, the oxidation of ammonia, and oxidation of nonbiodegradable organic compounds.

Fundamentals of Chemical Oxidation

The purpose of the following discussion is to introduce the basic concepts involved in chemical oxidation reactions. The topics to be discussed include (1) oxidation-reduction reactions, (2) half reaction potentials, (3) reaction potentials, (4) equilibrium constants for redox equations for redox equations, and (5) rate of oxidation-reduction reactions.

Oxidation-Reduction Reactions Oxidation-reduction reactions (known as redox equations) take place between an oxidizing agent and a reducing agent. In oxidation-reduction reactions both electrons are exchanged as are the oxidation states of the constituents involved in the reaction. While an oxidizing agent causes the oxidation to occur, it is reduced in the process. Similarly, a reducing agent that causes a reduction to occur is oxidized in the process. For example, consider the following reduction:

$$Cu^{2+} + Zn \rightleftharpoons Cu + Zn^{2+} \qquad (11\text{-}1)$$

In the above reaction copper (Cu) changes from a +2 to zero oxidation state and the zinc (Zn) changes from zero to a +2 state. Because of the electrons gain or loss, oxidation-reduction reactions can be separated into two half reactions. The oxidation half reaction involves the loss of electrons while the reduction half reaction involves the gain of electrons. The two half reactions that comprise Eq. (11-1) are as follows:

$$Zn - 2e^- \rightleftharpoons Zn^{2+} \text{ (oxidation)} \qquad (11\text{-}2)$$

$$Cu^{2+} + 2e^- \rightleftharpoons Cu \text{ (reduction)} \qquad (11\text{-}3)$$

Referring to the above equations, there is a two-electron change.

Half-Reaction Potentials Because of the almost infinite number of possible reactions, there are no summary tables of equilibrium constants for oxidation-reduction reactions. What is done instead is the chemical and thermodynamic characteristics of the half reactions, such as those given by Eq. (11-2) and Eq.(11-3), are determined and tabulated so that any combination of reactions can be studied.[2] Of the many properties that can be used to characterize oxidation-reduction reactions, the electrical potential (i.e., voltage) or emf of the half reaction is used most commonly. Thus, every half reaction involving an oxidation or reduction has a standard potential E^0 associated with it. The potentials for the half reactions given by Eq. (11-2) and Eq. (11-3) are as follows:

$$Cu^{2+} + 2e^- \rightleftharpoons Cu \quad E^0 = 0.34 \text{ volt} \qquad (11\text{-}4)$$

$$Zn - 2e^- \rightleftharpoons Zn^{2+} \quad E^0 = 0.763 \text{ volt} \qquad (11\text{-}5)$$

The half-reaction potential is a measure of the tendency of a reaction to proceed to the right. Half reactions with large positive potential, E^0, tend to proceed to the right as written. Conversely, half reactions with large negative potential, E^0, tend to proceed to the left.

Reaction potentials The half-reaction potentials, discussed above, can be used to predict whether a reaction comprised of two half reactions will proceed as written. The tendency of a reaction to proceed is obtained by determining the E^0 reaction for the entire reaction as given by the following expression.

$$E^0_{reaction} = E^0_{reduction} - E^0_{oxidation} \qquad (11\text{-}6)$$

Where $E^0_{reaction}$ = potential of the overall reaction

$E^0_{reduction}$ = potential of the reduction half reaction

$E^0_{oxidation}$ = potential of the oxidation half reaction

For example, for the reaction between copper and zinc [see Eq(11-1)] the $E^0_{reaction}$ of the reaction is determined as follows:

$$E^0_{reaction} = E^{02+}_{Cu,Cu} - E^{02+}_{Zn,Zn} \qquad (11\text{-}7)$$

$$E^0_{reaction} = 0.34 - (-0.763) = 1.103 \text{ volts} \qquad (11\text{-}8)$$

The positive value for the $E^0_{reaction}$ is taken as an indication that the reaction will proceed as written. The magnitude of the value, as will be illustrated subsequently, can be taken as a measure of the extent to which the reaction as written will proceed. For example, if Eq.(11-1) had been written as follows:

$$Cu + Zn^{2+} \rightleftharpoons Cu^{2+} + Zn \quad (11-9)$$

The corresponding $E^0_{reaction}$ for this reaction is

$$E^0_{reaction} = E^{02+}_{Zn,Zn} - E^{02+}_{Cu,Cu} \quad (11-10)$$

$$E^0_{reaction} = -0.763 - 0.34 = 1.103 \text{ volts} \quad (11-11)$$

Because the $E^0_{reaction}$ for the reaction is negative, the reaction will proceed in the opposite direction from what is written.

Equilibrium constants for redox equation The equilibrium constant for oxidation-reduction reactions is calculated using the Nernst equation as defined below.

$$\ln K = \frac{nFE^0_{reaction}}{RT} \quad (11\text{-}12a)$$

$$\log K = \frac{nFE^0_{reaction}}{2.303RT} \quad (11\text{-}12b)$$

Where K = equilibrium constant

n = number of electrons exchanged in the overall reaction

F = Faraday's constant

= 96485 a.s/g eq = 96485 C/g eq (Note: C=coulomb)

$E^0_{reaction}$ = reaction potential

R = universal gas constant

= 8.3144 J (abs)/(mole · K)

T = temperature, K (273.15+°C)

Rate of oxidation-reduction reactions As noted previously, the half-reaction potentials can be used to predict whether a reaction will proceed as written. Unfortunately, the reaction potential provides no information about the rate at which the reaction will proceed. Chemical oxidation reactions often require the presence of one or more catalysts for the reaction to proceed or to increase the rate of reaction. Transition metal cations, enzymes, pH adjustment, and a variety of proprietary substances have been used as catalysts.

Applications

In the past, chemical oxidation was used most commonly to (1) reduce the concentration of residual organics, (2) control odors, (3) remove ammonia, and (4) reduce the bacterial and viral content of wastewater. Chemical oxidation is especially effective for the elimination of odorous compounds (e.g., oxidation of sulfides and mercaptans). Now chemical oxidation is commonly used to (1) improve the treatability of nonbiodegradable (refractory) organic compounds, (2) eliminate the inhibitory effects of certain organic and inorganic compounds to microbial growth, and (3) reduce or eliminate the toxicity of certain organic and inorganic compounds to microbial growth and aquatic flora. The chemical oxidation of BOD and COD, ammonia, and refractory organic compounds is considered in this section.

Chemical oxidation of BOD and COD The overall reaction for the oxidation of organic molecules comprising BOD, for example, with chlorine, ozone, and hydrogen peroxide, can be represented as follows:

$$\text{Organic Molecule (e.g., BOD)} \xrightarrow[H_2O_2]{Cl,O_3} \text{Intermediate oxygenated molecules} \xrightarrow[H_2O_2]{Cl,O_3} \text{Simple end products (e.g., } CO_2, H_2O, \text{etc.)} \quad (11\text{-}13)$$

Multiple arrows in the direction of the reaction are used to signify that a number of steps are involved in the overall reaction sequence. The use of oxidizing agents such as oxygen, chlorine, ozone, and hydrogen peroxide is termed "simple oxidation". In general the overall reaction rates are usually too slow to be applicable generally for wastewater treatment. Advanced oxidation processes (AOPs), which typically involve the use of the hydroxyl radical for the oxidation of complex organic molecules, are considered in other literatures.

Chemical oxidation of nonbiodegradable organic compounds The dosages increase with the degree of treatment, which is reasonable when it is considered that the organic compounds that remain after biological treatment are typically composed of low-molecular-weight polar organic compounds and complex organic compounds built around the benzene ring structure. Because of the complexities associated with composition of wastewater, chemical dosages for the removal of refractory organic compounds cannot be derived from the chemical stoichiometry, assuming that it is known. [3] Pilot-plant studies must be conducted when either chlorine, chlorine dioxide, or ozone is to be used for the oxidation of refractory organics to assess both the efficacy and required dosages.

Chemical oxidation of ammonia The chemical process in which chlorine is used to oxidize the ammonia nitrogen in solution to nitrogen gas and other stable compounds is known as breakpoint chlorination. Perhaps the most important advantage of this process is that, with proper control, all the ammonia nitrogen in the wastewater can be oxidized. However, because the process has a number of disadvantages including the buildup of acid (HCl) which will react with the alkalinity, the buildup of total dissolved solids, and the formation of unwanted chloro-organic compounds, ammonia oxidation is seldom used today. [4]

The breakpoint chlorination process can be used for the removal of ammonia nitrogen from treatment-plant effluents, either alone or in combination with other processes. To avoid the large chlorine dosages required when used alone, break-point chlorination can be used following biological nitrification to achieve low levels of ammonia in the effluent. To optimize the performance of this process and to minimize equipment and facility costs, flow equalization is usually required. Also, because of the potential toxicity problems that may develop if chlorinated compounds are discharged to the environment, it is usually necessary to dechlorinate the effluent.

Important Words and Expressions

oxidation [ɔksi'deiʃən]   n. 氧化

hydrogen peroxide   过氧化氢

permanganate [pəˈmæŋgəneit]   n. 高锰酸

ammonia [əˈməunjə]   n. 氨

nonbiodegradable [ˈnɔnˌbaiəudiˈgreidəbl] adj. 不能生物降解的
oxidation-reduction reaction 氧化还原反应
half reaction potential 半反应电势
redox [ˈredɔks] n. 氧化还原作用
oxidizing agent 氧化剂
reducing agent 还原剂
thermodynamic [ˈθəːməudaiˈnæmik] adj. 热力学的
voltage [ˈvəultidʒ] n. 电压
emf abbr 电动势 (electromotive force)
standard potential 标准电势
cation [ˈkætaiən] n. 阳离子
enzyme [ˈenzaim] n. 酶
catalyst [ˈkætlist] n. 催化剂
sulfide [ˈsʌlˌfaid] n. 硫化物
mercaptan [məˈkæptæn] n. 硫醇
refractory [riˈfræktəriː] adj. 执拗的, 倔强的, 难驾驭的; 难治疗的; 耐熔的, 难熔炼的
inhibitory [inˈhibitəri] adj. 抑制的
aquatic flora 水生植物区系、水生植物志
advanced oxidation processes (AOPs) 高级氧化工艺
benzene [ˈbenˌziːn] n. 苯
stoichiometry [ˌstɔikiˈɔmitri] n. 化学计算(法); 化学计量学
nitrogen [ˈnaitrədʒən] n. 氮
alkalinity [ˌælkəˈliniti] n. 碱度
chloro-organic compound 氯化有机化合物
nitrification [ˌnaitrəfiˈkeiʃən] n. 硝化作用
dechlorinate [diːˈklɔːrineit] vt. 脱氯

Notes

[1] 废水处理中的化学氧化法是使用臭氧（O_3）、过氧化氢（H_2O_2）、高锰酸盐（MnO_4）、二氧化氯（ClO_2）、氯（Cl_2）或者（$HOCl$）和氧（O_2）等具有代表性的氧化剂，使一种化合物或一组化合物的化学组分发生变化。

[2] 取而代之的是半反应的化学特性和热力学特性，例如式（11-2）和式（11-3）给出的反应是确定的，并做成了表格，因而可以对任何一种反应组合进行分析。

[3] 因为废水组分的复杂性，对于去除难处理的有机化合物，即使化学计量为已知，也不可根据化学计量计算所需的化学药剂量。

[4] 然而，由于该过程也具有若干缺点，包括它将产生与碱度反应的酸（HCl）、形成总溶解固体、形成一些有害的氯化的有机化合物等，所以目前，氨的氧化法已很少采用。

Exercises

1. Answering the following questions in English according to the text：

(1) What are the fundamentals of chemical oxidation?

(2) What is the application of chemical oxidation in wastewater treatment?

2. Using the following each word to make up the sentences, respectively:

(1) oxidation

(2) reduction

(3) catalyst

(4) redox

(5) breakpoint

3. Put the following English into Chinese:

(1) The primary function of chemical oxidation is to destroy a pollutant e.g. mineralization of an organic matter or to modify its structure so as to be accommodated by conventional treatment methods or natural processes. That is why the role of chemical oxidation in the control of industrial wastewaters has become increasingly important. One of the advantages of chemical oxidation is its almost innumerable modes of operation as far as the oxidants, combination of methods and environmental conditions are concerned. As a result of these chemical oxidation applications to industrial wastewaters has long been a focus of research giving rise to a significant accumulation of knowledge and literature.

(2) Chemical oxidation processes play several important roles in the treatment of drinking water. The most common chemical oxidants used in water treatment are chlorine, ozone, chlorine dioxide, and permanganate. Ozone is sometimes used in conjunction with hydrogen peroxide or ultraviolet irradiation in what are called advanced oxidation processes (AOPs) to produce radicals that have powerful oxidative properties. Mixed oxidant technologies are also available. Free chlorine has traditionally been the oxidant (and disinfectant) of choice in the United States, but concerns about the formation of potentially harmful halogenated disinfection byproducts (DBPs) produced by reactions between free chlorine and NOM (exacerbated in some cases by the presence of bromide) have caused many water systems to adopt alternative chemical oxidants (and disinfectants) to lower halogenated DBP formation.

4. Put the following Chinese into English:

(1) 氧化还原反应

(2) 半反应电位

(3) 不可生物降解的有机化合物

(4) 用氯将溶液中的氨氮氧化为氮气和其他一些稳定化合物的化学过程称为折点加氯。

(5) 废水处理中的化学氧化法是使用臭氧、过氧化氢、高锰酸钾、二氧化氯、氯或次氯酸和氧等具有代表性的氧化剂，使一种化合物或一组化合物的组分发生变化。

5. Put the following abbr.into full phrases:

Emf; ORP; AOPs

Reading Material A

Disinfection of Drinking Water

Disinfection is used n water treatment to reduce pathogens (disease-producing microorganisms) to an acceptable level. Disinfection is not the same as sterilization. Sterilization implies the destruction of all living organisms. Drinking water need not be sterile. Three categories of human enteric pathogens are normally of consequence: bacteria, viruses, and amebic cysts. Purposeful disinfection must be capable of destroying all three.

Chlorination

The addition of chlorine or chlorine compounds to water is called chlorination. Chlorination is considered to be the single most important process for preventing the spread of waterborne disease.

Molecular chlorine, Cl_2, is a greenish-yellow gas at ordinary room temperature and pressure. In gaseous form it is very toxic, and even in low concentrations it is a severe irritant. But when the chlorine is dissolved in low concentrations in clean water, it is not harmful, and if it is properly applied, objectionable tastes and odors due to the chlorine and its by-products are not noticeable to the average person. [1]

Although chlorine is effective in destroying pathogens and preventing the spread of communicable disease, there may be an indirect noninfectious health problem caused by the chlorination process. [2] Natural waters often contain trace amounts of organic compounds, primarily from natural sources such as decaying vegetation. These substances can react with the chlorine to form compounds called trihalomethanes (THMs), which may cause cancer in humans. Chloroform is an example of a THM compound.

The EPA has set standards that limit the maximum amount of THM compounds in drinking water. One way to prevent THM formation is to make sure that the chlorine is added to the water only after clarification and the removal of most of the organics. Also, alternative methods of disinfection are available that do not use chlorine. These are discussed later in this section.

Chlorination chemistry When chlorine is dissolved in pure water, it reacts with the H^+ ions and the OH^- ions in the water. Two of the products of this reaction are hypochlorous acid, HOCl, and the hypochlorite ion, OCl^-. These are the actual disinfecting agents. If microorganisms are present in the water, HOCl and OCl^- penetrate the microbe cells and react with certain enzymes. This reaction disrupts the organisms' metabolism and kills them.

Hypochlorous acid is a more effective disinfectant than the hypochlorite ion because it diffuses faster through the microbe cell wall. The relative concentrations of HOCl and OCl^- depend on the pH of the water. The lower the pH, the more HOCl there is relative to the OCl^-. In general, then, the lower the pH of the water, the more effective is the chlorination-disinfection process.

When chlorine is first added to water containing some impurities, the chlorine immediately reacts with the dissolved inorganic or organic substances and is then unavailable for disinfection. [3] The amount of chlorine used up in this initial reaction is called the chlorine demand of the water. If dissolved ammonia, NH_3, is present in the water, the chlorine reacts with it to form compounds called chloramines. Only after the chlorine demand is satisfied and the reaction with all the dissolved ammonia is complete is the chlorine actually available in the form of HOCl and OCl^-.

Chlorine in the form of HOCl and OCl^- is called free available chlorine, whereas chloramines are referred to as combined chlorine. [4] Free chlorine is often the preferred form for disinfection of drinking water. It works faster than combined chlorine, and it does not cause objectionable tastes and odors. Combined chlorine is also effective as a disinfectant, but it is slower acting and it may cause the typical swimming-pool odor of chlorinated water. Its advantage is that it lasts longer and can maintain sanitary protection throughout the water distribution system.

A process called breakpoint chlorination is sometimes used to ensure the presence of free chlorine in public water supplies. To do this, it is necessary to add enough chlorine to the water to satisfy the chlorine demand and to react with all the dissolved ammonia. When this occurs, it is said that the chlorine breakpoint has been reached. Chlorine added beyond the breakpoint will be available as a free chlorine residual in direct proportion to the amount of chlorine added. This is illustrated in Figure 11.1. The chlorine demand and the breakpoint dose vary, depending on the water quality. Sometimes, chlorine doses up to 10 mg/L are needed to obtain a free chlorine residual of 0.5 mg/L.

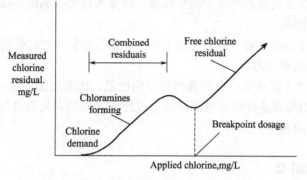

Figure 11.1 Breakpoint chlorination curve

Other Methods of Disinfection

Chlorine dioxide Another very strong oxidant is chlorine dioxide. Chlorine Dioxide (ClO_2) must be generated onsite by combining chlorine and sodium chlorite. Chlorine Dioxide is often used as a primary disinfectant, inactivating the bacteria and cysts. Chloramine is then used as a secondary disinfectant to provide a residual in the distribution system because chlorine dioxide does not maintain a residual long enough to be useful as a distribution system disinfectant. The advantage of chlorine dioxide over chlorine is that chlorine dioxide does not react with naturally occurring organic matter to form THMs. The major disadvantage of chlorine dioxide is the potential formation of chlorite and chlorate, which are potential human carcinogens.

Ozonation Ozone is a sweet-smelling, unstable gas. It is a form of oxygen in which three atoms of oxygen are combined to form the molecule O_3. Because of its instability, it is generated at the point of use. Ozone is widely used in drinking water treatment in Europe and is continuing to gain popularity in the United States. It is a powerful oxidant, more powerful even than hypochlorous acid. It has been reported to be more effective than chlorine in destroying viruses and cysts. In addition to being a strong oxidant, ozone has the advantage of not forming THMs or any of the chlorinated DBPs. As with chlorine dioxide, ozone does not persist in the water, decaying back to oxygen in minutes. Therefore, a typical flow schematic adds ozone either to the raw water or between the sedimentation basins and filter for primary disinfection, then adds chloramine after the filters as the distribution system disinfectant. [5]

Ultraviolet radiation Ultraviolet (UV) radiation has the potential to inactivate pathogens. It is employed by submerging UV lamps into the water to be treated. Multiple lamps are used to provide greater coverage. The major factor in achieving good microorganism kill is the ability of the UV light to pass through the water to get to the target organism. Thus, the lamps must be kept free of slime and precipitates, and the water must be free of turbidity. UV performs very well against both bacteria and viruses. Its major disadvantages are that it leaves no residual protection for the distribution system and is very expensive.

Notes

[1] 但是，溶解在清水中的低浓度氯气却是无害的，只要应用得当，氯气及其副产物引起的不良味道和气味通常不会引起人们的注意。

[2] 尽管余氯可以有效地杀死水中的致病菌，避免水传染疾病的传播，但是加氯消毒会间接引发非传染性健康问题。

[3] 当氯气首次投加在含有一些杂质的水中时，氯气会立即与这些溶解性有机物或无机物发生反应，从而丧失消毒能力。

[4] 以 HOCl 和 OCl$^-$ 的形式存在的氯称作自由性氯，而氯胺称为化合性氯。

[5] 所以，典型的流程是在原水或沉淀池与过滤池之间加入臭氧进行初级消毒，然后再加入氯胺作为配水系统的消毒剂。

Reading Material B

Advanced Oxidation

Advanced oxidation processes (AOPs) are processes to produce hydroxyl free radical (HO·). Hydroxyl free radicals are highly reactive, nonselective oxidants able to decompose many organic compounds. Two AOPs are the combinations of ozone and hydrogen peroxide and ozone and UV radiation. AOPs are most commonly used for the oxidation of chemicals that cannot be removed by other means.

Theory of Advanced Oxidation

Advanced oxidation processes typically involve the generation and use of the hydroxyl free radical (HO·) as a strong oxidant to destroy compounds that cannot be oxidized by conventional oxidants such as oxygen, ozone, and chlorine.[1] With the exception of fluorine, the hydroxyl radical is one of the most active oxidants known. The hydroxyl radical reacts with the dissolved constituents, initiating a series of oxidation reactions until the constituents are completely mineralized. Nonselective in their mode of attack and able to operate at normal temperature and pressures, hydroxyl radicals are capable of oxidizing almost all reduced materials present without restriction to specific classes or groups of compounds, as compared to other oxidants.

Advanced oxidation processes differ from the other treatment processes discussed (such as ion exchange or stripping) because wastewater compounds are degraded rather than concentrated or transferred into a different phase.[2] Because secondary waste materials are not generated, there is no need to dispose of or regenerate materials.

Technologies Used to Produce Hydroxyl Radicals (HO·)

At the present time, a variety of technologies are available to produce HO in the aqueous phase. Of the technologies, only ozone/UV, ozone/hydrogen peroxide, ozone/UV/hydrogen peroxide, and hydrogen peroxide/UV are being used on a commercial scale.

Ozone/UV Production of the free radical HO· with UV light can be illustrated by the following reactions for the photolysis of ozone:

$$O_3 + UV \text{ (or } h\nu, \lambda < 310 \text{ nm)} \longrightarrow O_2 + O(^1D) \qquad (11\text{-}14)$$

$$O(^1D) + H_2O \longrightarrow HO \cdot + HO \cdot \text{ (in wet air)} \qquad (11\text{-}15)$$

$$O(^1D) + H_2O \longrightarrow HO \cdot + HO \cdot \longrightarrow H_2O_2 \text{(in water)} \qquad (11\text{-}16)$$

where O_3 = ozone

UV = ultraviolet radiation (or $h\nu$ = energy)

O_2 = oxygen

O (^{1}D) = excited oxygen atom. The symbol (^{1}D) is a spectroscopic notation used to specify the atomic and molecular configuration (also known as a singlet oxygen)

HO • = hydroxyl radical. The dot (•) that appears next to the hydroxyl and other radicals is used to denote the fact that these species have an unpaired electron.

As shown in Eq(11-15), the photolysis of ozone in wet air results in the formation of hydroxyl radicals. In water, the photolysis of ozone leads to the formation of hydrogen peroxide [see Eq(11-16)]. Because the photolysis of ozone in water leads to the formation of hydrogen peroxide, which is subsequently photolyzed to form hydroxyl radicals, the use of ozone in this application is generally not cost-effective. [3] In air, the ozone/UV process can degrade compounds through direct ozonation, photolysis, or reaction with the hydroxyl radical. The ozone/UV process is more effective when the compounds of interest can be degraded through the absorption of the UV irradiation as well as through the reaction with the hydroxyl radicals. A schematic flow diagram of the processes is illustrated on Figure 11.2.

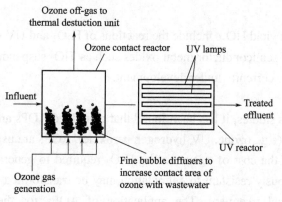

Figure 11.2　Schematic representation of advanced oxidation process involving the use of ozone and UV radiation

Ozone/Hydrogen peroxide　For compounds that do not adsorb UV, AOPs involving ozone/H_2O_2 may be more effective. A schematic flow diagram of the processes is illustrated on Figure 11.3. Compounds in water such as trichloroethylene (TCE) and perchloroethylene (PCE) have been reduced significantly with AOPs using hydrogen peroxide and ozone to generate HO •. The overall reaction for the production of hydroxyl radicals using hydrogen peroxide and ozone is as follows:

$$H_2O_2 + 2O_3 \longrightarrow HO \cdot + HO \cdot + 3O_2 \qquad (11\text{-}17)$$

Hydrogen peroxide/UV　Hydroxyl radicals are also formed when water containing H_2O_2 is exposed to UV light (200 to 280nm). The following reaction can be used to describe the photolysis of H_2O_2:

$$H_2O_2 + UV \text{ (or } h\nu, \lambda \approx 200\text{-}280 \text{ nm)} \longrightarrow HO \cdot + HO \cdot \qquad (11\text{-}18)$$

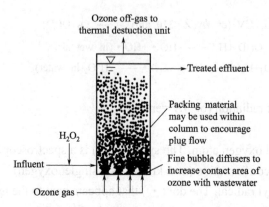

Figure 11.3　Schematic representation of advanced oxidation process involving the use of ozone and hydrogen peroxide

In some cases the use of the hydrogen peroxide/UV process has not been feasible because H_2O_2 has a small molar extinction coefficient, requiring high concentrations of H_2O_2 and not using the UV energy efficiently.

Most recently, the hydrogen peroxide/UV process has been applied to the oxidation of trace constituents found in treated water. The process has been studied for the removal of N-Nitrosodimethylamine (NDMA) and other compounds of concern in treated water including(l) sex and steroidal hormones, (2) human prescription and nonprescription drugs, (3)veterinary and human antibiotics, and(4)industrial and household wastewater products.

Other Processes

Other reactions that yield HO· include the reactions of H_2O_2 and UV with Fenton's reagent and the adsorption of UV by semiconductor metal oxides such as TiO_2 suspended in water, which acts as a catalyst. Still others are currently under development.

Applications

Based on numerous studies, it has been found that combined AOPs are more effective than any of the individual agents (e.g., ozone, UV, hydrogen peroxide). AOPs are usually applied to low COD wastewaters because of the cost of ozone and/or H_2O_2 required to generate the hydroxyl radicals. Material that was previously resistant to degradation may be transformed into compounds that will require further biological treatment. The application of AOPs for the disinfection of treated wastewater and for the treatment of refractory organic compounds is considered below.

Disinfection　Because it was recognized that free radicals generated from ozone were more powerful oxidants than ozone alone, it was reasoned that the hydroxyl free radicals could be used effectively to oxidize microorganisms and refractory organic materials in water.[4] Unfortunately, because the half-life of the hydroxyl free radicals is short, on the order of microseconds, it is not possible to develop high concentrations. With extremely low concentrations, the required detention times for microorganism disinfection are prohibitive.

Oxidation of refractory organic compounds　For the reasons cited above hydroxyl radicals are not used for conventional disinfection; instead they are used more commonly for the oxidation of trace amounts of refractory organic compounds found in highly treated effluents. The hydroxyl radicals, once generated, can attack organic molecules by radical addition, hydrogen abstraction, electron transfer, and radical combination.

Notes

[1] 高级氧化工艺一般涉及产生和利用羟基自由基(HO·)作为强氧化剂破坏常规氧化剂比如氧、臭氧和氯不能氧化的化合物。

[2] 高级氧化工艺与其他处理工艺（比如离子交换或汽提）不同，因为废水中的化合物被降解而并非浓缩或转移到其他相中。

[3] 因为臭氧在水中通过光解作用会生成过氧化氢，随后过氧化氢被光解生成羟基，臭氧用于此工艺中时，其费用一般非常昂贵。

[4] 因为已经认识到由臭氧产生的游离基团与单独臭氧相比是一些更强的氧化剂，所以有理由认为可用羟基自由基有效氧化微生物及水中的难处理有机物。

Unit 12 Adsorption

Adsorption is a mass transfer process wherein a substance is transferred from the liquid phase to the surface of a solid where it is bound by chemical or physical forces. The adsorbate is the substance that is being removed from the liquid phase at the interface. The adsorbent is the solid, liquid, or gas phase onto which the adsorbate accumulates. Although adsorption is used at the air-liquid interface in the flotation process, only the case of adsorption at the liquid-solid interface will be considered in this discussion.

At present, the applications of adsorption in water treatment in the United States are predominately for taste and odor removal. However, adsorption is increasingly being considered for removal of SOCs, VOCs, and naturally occurring organic matter, such as THM precursors and DBPs. The adsorption process has not been used extensively in wastewater treatment, but demands for a better quality of treated wastewater effluent, including toxicity reduction, have led to an intensive examination and use of the process of adsorption on activated carbon.[1] Activated carbon treatment of wastewater is usually thought of as a polishing process for water that has already received normal biological treatment. The carbon in this case is used to remove a portion of the remaining dissolved organic matter.

Types of Adsorbents

The principal types of adsorbents include activated carbon, synthetic polymeric, and silica-based adsorbents, although synthetic polymeric and silica-based adsorbents are seldom used for water adsorption because of their high cost.[2] Because activated carbon is used most commonly in water-treatment applications, the focus of the following discussion is on activated carbon. The two size classifications are powdered activated carbon (PAC), which typically has a diameter of less than 0.074 mm (200 sieve), and granular activated carbon (GAC), which has a diameter greater than 0.1 mm (~140 sieve). The characteristics of granular and powdered activated carbon are summarized in Table 12.1.

Fundamentals of Adsorption

The adsorption process takes place in four more or less definable steps: (1) bulk solution transport, (2) film diffusion transport, (3) pore transport, and (4) adsorption (or sorption). Bulk

Table 12.1　Comparison of granular and powdered activated carbon

Parameter	Unit	Type of activated carbon[a]	
		GAC	PAC
Total surface area	m^2/g	700～1300	800～1800
Bulk density	kg/m^3	400～500	360～740
Particle density, wetted in water	kg/L	1.0～1.5	1.3～1.4
Particle size range	mm(μm)	0.1～2.36	(5～50)
Effective size	mm	0.6～0.9	na
Uniformity coefficient	UC	≤1.9	na
Mean pore radius		16～30	20～40
Iodine number		600～1100	800～1200
Abrasion number	minimum	75～85	70～80
Ash	%	≤8	≤6
Moisture as packed	%	2～8	3～10

[a] Specitfic values will depend on the source material used for the production of the activated carbon.

solution transport involves the movement of the organic material to be adsorbed through the bulk liquid to the boundary layer of fixed film of liquid surrounding the adsorbent, typically by advection and dispersion in carbon contactors.[3] Film diffusion transport involves the transport by diffusion of the organic material through the stagnant liquid film to the entrance of the pores of the adsorbent. Pore transport involves the transport of the material to be adsorbed through the pores by a combination of molecular diffusion through the pore liquid and/or by diffusion along the surface of the adsorbent. Adsorption involves the attachment of the material to be adsorbed to adsorbent at an available adsorption site. Adsorption can occur on the outer surface of the adsorbent and in the macropores, mesopores, micropores, and submicropores, but the surface area of the macro- and mesopores is small compared with the surface area of the micropores and submicropores and the amount of material adsorbed there is usually considered negligible. Because it is difficult to differentiate between chemical and physical adsorption, the term sorption is often used to describe the attachment of the organic material to the activated carbon.

Because the adsorption process occurs in a series of steps, the slowest step in the series is identified as the rate limiting step. In general, if physical adsorption is the principal method of adsorption, one of the diffusion transport steps will be the rate limiting, because the rate of physical adsorption is rapid. Where chemical adsorption is the principal method of adsorption, the adsorption step has often been observed to be rate limiting. When the rate of sorption equals the rate of desorption, equilibrium has been achieved and the capacity of the carbon has been reached. The theoretical adsorption capacity of the carbon for a particular contaminant can be determined by developing its adsorption isotherm as described below.

Development of adsorption isotherms　The quantity of adsorbate that can be taken up by an adsorbent is a function of both the characteristics and concentration of adsorbate and the temperature. The characteristics of the adsorbate that are of importance include: solubility, molecular structure, molecular weight, polarity, and hydrocarbon saturation. Generally, the amount of material adsorbed is determined as a function of the concentration at a content temperature, and the resulting function is called an adsorption isotherm. Adsorption isotherms are developed by exposing a given amount of absorbate in a fixed volume of liquid to varying amounts of activated carbon. Typically, more than ten containers are used, and the minimum time allowed for the samples to equilibrate where powdered activated carbon is used is seven days. If granular activated carbon is used, it is usually powdered to minimize adsorption times. At the end of the test period, the amount of absorbate remaining in solution is measured. The absorbent phase concentration after equilibrium is computed using Eq.(12-1). The absorbent phase concentration data computed using Eq.(12-1) are then used to develop adsorption isotherms as described below.

$$q_e = \frac{(C_0 - C_e)V}{m} \tag{12-1}$$

Where

q_e = adsorbent (i.e., solid) phase concentration after equilibrium, mg adsorbate/g adsorbent

C_0 = initial concentration of adsorbate, mg/L

C_e = final equilibrium concentration of adsorbate after absorption has occurred, mg/L

V = volume of liquid in the reactor, L

m = mass of adsorbent, g

Freundlich isotherm Equations that are often used to describe the experimental isotherm data were developed by Freundlich, Langmuir, and Brunauer, Emmet, and Teller (BET isotherm) (Shaw, 1966). Of the three, the Freundlich isotherm is used most commonly to describe the adsorption characteristics of the activated carbon used in water and wastewater treatment. Derived empirically in 1912, the Freundlich isotherm is defined as follows:

$$\frac{x}{m} = K_f C_e^{1/n} \tag{12-2}$$

where

x/m = mass of adsorbate adsorbed per unit mass of adsorbent, mg adsorbate/g activated carbon

K_f = Freundlich capacity factor, (mg absorbate/g activated carbon) (L water/mg adsorbate)$^{1/n}$

C_e = equilibrium concentration of adsorbate in solution after adsorption, mg/L

1/n = Freundlich intensity parameter

The constants in the Freundlich isotherm can be determined by plotting log (x/m) versus log C_e and making use of Eq.(12-3) rewritten as:

$$\log\left(\frac{x}{m}\right) = \log K_f + \frac{1}{n}\log C_e \tag{12-3}$$

Langmuir isotherm Derived from rational considerations, the Langmuir adsorption isotherm is defined as:

$$\frac{x}{m} = \frac{abC_e}{1+bC_e} \tag{12-4}$$

where x/m = mass of adsorbate adsorbed per unit mass of adsorbent, mg adsorbate/g activated carbon a, b = empirical constants

C_e = equilibrium concentration of adsorbate in solution after adsorption, mg/L

The Langmuir adsorption isotherm was developed by assuming: (1) a fixed number of accessible sites are available on the adsorbent surface, all of which have the same energy, and (2) adsorption is reversible. Equilibrium is reached when the rate of adsorption of molecules onto the surface is the same as the rate of desorption of molecules from the surface. The rate at which adsorption proceeds is proportional to the driving force, which is the difference between the amount adsorbed at a particular concentration and the amount that can be adsorbed at that concentration.[4] At the equilibrium concentration, this difference is zero.

Correspondence of experimental data to the Langmuir equation does not mean that the stated assumptions are valid for the particular system being studied, because departures from the assumptions can have a canceling effect.[5] The constants in the Langmuir isotherm can be determined by plotting $C_e/(x/m)$ versus C_e and making use of Eq.(12-5) rewritten as:

$$\frac{C_e}{(x/m)} = \frac{1}{ab} + \frac{1}{a}C_e \qquad (12\text{-}5)$$

Important Words and Expressions

adsorption [æd'sɔ:pʃən] n. 吸附
adsorbate [æd'sɔ:beit] n. 被吸附物
adsorbent [æd'sɔ:bənt] adj. 吸附的 n. 吸附剂
SOCs（synthetical organic chemicals）人工合成有机物
VOCs（volatile organic compounds）挥发性有机化合物
THM（trihalomethane）三卤甲烷
DBPs（disinfection by-products）消毒副产物
flotation process 浮选过程
activated carbon 活性炭
polishing process 精处理法
synthetic polymeric 合成聚合物
silica-based adsorbent 硅系吸附剂
powdered activated carbon（PAC）粉末活性炭
granular activated carbon（GAC）粒状活性炭
bulk solution 本体溶液，总体溶液
diffusion [di'fju:ʒən] n. 扩散
sorption ['sɔ:pʃən] n. 吸附作用
advection [əd'vekʃən] n. 水平对流
dispersion [dis'pə:ʃən] n. 散布,驱散,传播,散射
stagnant ['stægnənt] adj. 不流动的，停滞的
macropore ['mækrəupɔ:] n. 大孔
mesopore ['mesəupɔ:] n. 中孔
micropore ['maikrəpɔ:] n. 微孔
submicropore ['sʌb'maikrəpɔ:] n. 亚微孔

desorption [di'sɔ:pʃən]   n. 解吸附作用
adsorption isotherm   吸附等温线
solubility [ˌsɔlju'biliti]   n. 溶解度
polarity [pəu'læriti:]   n. 极性
hydrocarbon saturation   烃饱和度
reversible [ri'və:səbl]   adj. 可逆的

Notes

[1] 迄今为止，吸附工艺在废水处理中并未得到普遍应用，但是为了进一步改善二级处理出水的水质，降低其毒性，在必须加强水质检验的同时还应采用活性炭吸附工艺进一步处理。

[2] 吸附剂主要包括三类，即活性炭、合成聚合物及硅系吸附剂，不过合成聚合物及硅系吸附剂由于其成本昂贵，所以很少用于废水处理。

[3] 总体溶液内迁移是指被吸附的有机物通过总体溶液向着吸附剂周围固定液体膜的运动。在炭接触反应器中，一般可以通过平流和分散作用实现这一迁移过程。

[4] 吸附过程进行的速率与在某一特定浓度条件下被吸附的量与在此浓度下可吸附的量之差产生的吸附推动力成正比。

[5] 与 Langmuir 方程式相应的实验数据并非意味着上述假定适用于拟研究的特殊系统，因为相对于假设条件的偏离可能具有一种补偿效果。

Exercises

1. Answering the following questions in English according to the text:

(1) What is the definition of adsorption?

(2) How to define Freundlich Isotherm and Langmuir Isotherm?

2. Using the following each word to make up the sentences, respectively:

(1) adsorption

(2) diffusion

(3) transport

(4) isotherm

(5) adsorbent

3. Put the following English into Chinese:

(1) Economical application of activated carbon depends on an efficient means of regenerating and reactivating the carbon after its adsorptive capacity has been reached. Regeneration is the term used to describe all of the processes that are used to recover the adsorptive capacity of the spent carbon, exclusive of reactivation, including: (1)chemicals to oxidize the adsorbed material, (2)steam to drive off the adsorbed material, (3)solvents, and (4)biological conversion processes. Typically some of the adsorptive capacity of the carbon (about 4 to 10 percent) is also lost in the regeneration process, depending on the compounds been adsorbed and the regeneration method used.

(2) Reactivation of granular carbon involves essentially the same process used to create the activated carbon from virgin material. Spent carbon is reactivated in a furnace by oxidizing the adsorbed organic material and, thus, removing it from the carbon surface. The following series of events occur in the reactivation of spent activated carbon: (1) the carbon is heated to drive off the

absorbed organic material (i.e., absorbate), (2) in the process of driving off the absorbed material some new compounds are formed that remain on the surface of the carbon, and (3) the final step in the reactivation process is to burn off the new compounds that were formed when the absorbed material was burned off. With effective process control, the adsorptive capacity of reactivated carbon will be essentially the same as that of the virgin carbon. For planning purposes, it is often assumed that a loss of 2 to 5 percent will occur in the reactivation process.

4. Put the following Chinese into English：

(1) 活性炭

(2) 吸附等温线

(3) 膜扩散迁移

(4) 吸附是一种传质过程，物质从液相转移到固体表面，通过物理或化学作用相结合。

(5) 当吸着速率等于解吸速率时，则吸附达到平衡，这时的吸附质量即为炭的吸附容量。

Reading Material A

Adsorption Kinetics

Because activated carbon is used most commonly in water-treatment applications, the focus of the following discussion is on activated carbon. As noted previously, both granular carbon (in downflow and upflow columns) and powdered activated carbon are used for water and wastewater treatment. The analysis procedures for both types are described briefly in the following discussion.

Mass Transfer Zone

The area of the GAC bed in which sorption is occurring is called the mass transfer zone (MTZ) (see Figure 12.1).After the water containing the constituent to be removed passes through a region of the bed whose depth is equal to the MTZ, the concentration of the contaminant in the water will have been reduced to its minimum value. [1] No further adsorption will occur within the bed below the

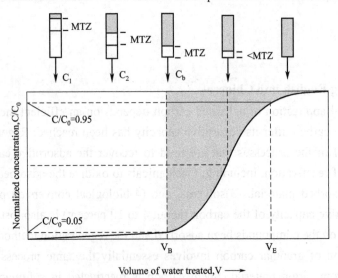

Figure 12.1   Typical breakthrough curve activated carbon showing movement
of mass transfer zone (MTZ) with throughput volume

MTZ. As the top layers of carbon granules become saturated with organic material, the MTZ will move down in the bed until breakthrough occurs. Typically, breakthrough is said to have occurred when the effluent concentration reaches 5 percent of the influent value. Exhaustion of the adsorption bed is assumed to have occurred when the effluent concentration is equal to 95 percent of the influent concentration. The length of the MTZ is typically a function of the hydraulic loading rate applied to the column and the characteristics of the activated carbon. In the extreme, if the loading rate is too great the height of the MTZ will be larger than the GAC bed depth, and the adsorbable constituent will not be removed completely by the carbon. [2] At complete exhaustion, the effluent concentration is equal to the influent concentration.

In addition to the applied hydraulic loading rate, the shape of the breakthrough curve will also depend on whether the applied liquid contains nonadsorbable and biodegradable constituents. The impact of the presence of nonadsorbable and biodegradable organic constituents on the shape of the breakthrough curve is illustrated on Figure 12.2. As shown on Figure 12.2, if the liquid contains nonadsorbable constituents, the nonadasorbable constituents will appear in the effluent as soon as the carbon column is put into operation. If adsorbable and biodegradable constituents are present in the applied liquid, the breakthrough curve will not reach a C/C_0 value of 1.0, but will be depressed, and the observed C/C_0 value will depend on the biodegradability of the influent constituents, because biological activity continues even though the adsorption capacity has been utilized. If the liquid contains nonadsorbable and biodegradable constituents, the observed breakthrough curve will not start at zero and will not terminate at a value of 1.0. The above effects are observed quite commonly in wastewater adsorption applications, especially with respect to the removal of COD.

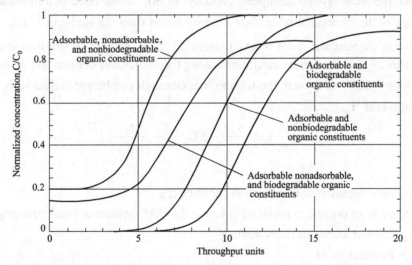

Figure 12.2 Impact of the presence of adsorbable, nonadsorbable, and biodegradable organic constituents on the shape of the activated carbon

Carbon Adsorption Capacity

The adsorptive capacity of a given carbon is estimated from isotherm data as follows. If isotherm data are plotted, the resulting isotherm will be as shown on Figure 12.3. Referring to Figure 12.3, the adsorptive capacity of the carbon can be estimated by extending a vertical line from the point on the horizontal axis corresponding to the initial concentration C_0, and extrapolating the

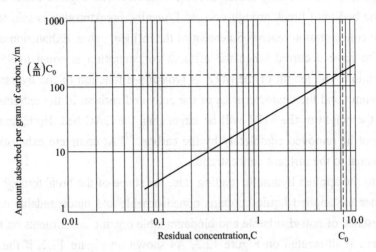

Figure 12.3　Typical activated carbon adsorption isotherm

isotherm to intersect this line. The $q_e=(x/m)_{C_0}$ value at the point of intersection can be read from the vertical axis. The $(q_e)_{C_0}$ value represents the amount of constituent adsorbed per unit weight of carbon when the carbon is at equilibrium with the initial concentration of constituent C_0. The equilibrium condition generally exists in the upper section of a carbon bed during column treatment, and it therefore represents the ultimate capacity of the carbon for a particular waste.

Breakthrough Adsorption Capacity

In the field, the breakthrough adsorption capacity $(x/m)_b$ of the GAC in a full-scale column is some percentage of the theoretical adsorption capacity found from the isotherm.[3] The $(x/m)_b$ of a single column can be assumed to be approximately 25 to 50 percent of the theoretical capacity, $(x/m)_o$. The value of $(x/m)_b$ can be determined using the small-scale column test described later in this section. Once $(x/m)_b$ is known, the time to breakthrough can be approximated by solving the following equation for t_b.

$$(\frac{x}{m})_b = \frac{x_b}{m_{GAC}} = Q(C_0 - \frac{C_b}{2})\frac{t_b}{m_{GAC}} \tag{12-6}$$

Where
　　　　$(x/m)_b$=field breakthrough adsorption capacity, g/g
　　　x_b=mass of organic material adsorbed in the GAC column at breakthrough, g
　m_{GAC}=mass of carbon in the column, g
　　　Q=flowrate, m^3/d
　　　C_0=influent organic concentration, g/m^3
　　　C_b=breakthrough organic concentration, g/m^3
　　　t_b=time to breakthrough, d

Eq.(12-6) was developed assuming that C_0 is constant and that the effluent concentration increases linearly with time from o to C_b (see Figure 12.1). The term $(C_0 - C_b/2)$ represents the average concentration of the organic matter adsorbed up to the breakthrough point. Rearranging Eq.(12-6), the time to breakthrough can be calculated using the following relationship:

$$t_b = \frac{(x/m)_b m_{GAC}}{Q(C_0 - C_b/2)} \tag{12-7}$$

However, as noted previously, because of the breakthrough phenomenon (see Figure 12.3), the usual practice is either to use two or more columns in series and rotate them as they become exhausted, or to use multiple columns in parallel so that breakthrough in a single column will not significantly affect the effluent quality.[4] With proper sampling from points within the column, constituent (e.g., TOC) breakthrough can be anticipated.

Notes

[1] 含有待去除组分的废水通过深度等于 MTZ 的层床后，水中的污染物浓度将降低至最低值。

[2] 在极端情况下，如果水力负荷太大，MTZ 的高度就会大于 GAC 床的深度，可吸附的组分就不会被炭完全去除。

[3] 在一个大型吸附柱的操作现场，颗粒活性炭的穿透吸附容量是吸附等温线上找出的理论吸附容量的某一百分比。

[4] 然而，如前所述，由于穿透现象的存在（见图 12.3），普遍采用的方法是即可用两台或多台活性炭柱串联并伴随着耗尽而切换操作，亦可用多个活性炭柱并联操作，从而当一个炭柱穿透时不会明显影响出水水质。

Reading Material B

Applications of Activated Carbon Adsorption

Carbon adsorption is used principally for the removal of refractory organic compounds, as well as residual amounts of inorganic compounds such as nitrogen, sulfides, and heavy metals. The removal of taste and odor compounds from wastewater is another important application, especially in reuse applications. Both powdered and granular activated carbon is used and appears to have a low adsorption affinity for low molecular weight polar organic species. If biological activity is low in the carbon contactor or in other biological unit processes, these species are difficult to remove with activated carbon. Under normal conditions, after treatment with carbon, the effluent BOD ranges from 2 to 7 mg/L, and the effluent COD ranges from 10 to 20 mg/L. Under optimum conditions, it appears that the effluent COD can be reduced to less than 10 mg/L.

Treatment with Granular Activated Carbon (GAC)

Treatment with GAC involves passing a liquid to be treated through a bed of activated carbon held in a reactor (sometimes called a contactor). Several types of activated carbon contactors are used for advanced water treatment. Typical systems may be either pressure or gravity type, and may be downflow or upflow fixed-bed units having two or three columns in series, or expanded bed upflow-countercurrent type.[1] Typical schematic diagrams of carbon contactors are shown on Figure 12.4.

Fixed-bed A fixed-bed column is used most commonly for contacting water with GAC. Fixed-bed columns can be operated singly, in series, or in parallel. Granular-medium filters are commonly used upstream of the activated carbon contactors to remove the organics associated with the suspended solids present in secondary effluent.[2] The water to be treated is applied to the top of the column and withdrawn at the bottom. The carbon is held in place with an underdrain system at

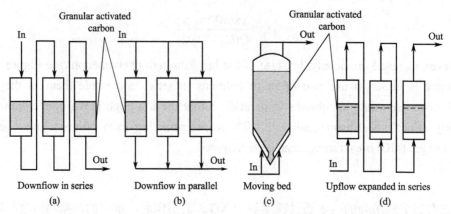

Figure 12.4 Types of activated carbon contactors
(a)downflow in series, (b)downflow in parallel
(c)moving bed, and (d)upflow expended in series

the bottom of the column. Provision for backwashing and surface washing is often provided in water applications to limit the headloss buildup due to the removal of particulate suspended solids within the carbon column. Unfortunately, backwashing has the effect of destroying the adsorption front as discussed later.

The advantage of a downflow design is that adsorption of organics and filtration of suspended solids is accomplished in a single step. Although upflow fixed-bed reactors have been used, downflow beds are used more commonly to lessen the chance of accumulating particulate material in the bottom of the bed, where the particulate material would be difficult to remove by backwashing.[3] If soluble organic removal is not maintained at a high level, more frequent regeneration of the carbon may be required. Lack of consistency in pH, temperature, and flowrate may also affect performance of carbon contactors.

Expanded-bed Expanded-bed, moving-bed and pulsed-bed carbon contactors have also been developed to overcome the problems associated with headloss buildup. In the expanded-bed system, the influent is introduced at the bottom of the column and the activated carbon is allowed to expand, much as a filter bed expands during backwash. When the adsorptive capacity of the carbon at the bottom of the column is exhausted, the bottom portion of carbon is removed, and an equivalent amount of regenerated or virgin carbon is added to the top of the column. In such a system, headloss does not build up with time after the operating point has been reached. In general, expanded-bed upflow contactors may have more carbon fines in the effluent than downflow contactors because bed expansion leads to the creation of fines as the carbon particles collide and abrade, and allows the fines to escape through passageways created by the expanded bed. At present, few, if any, expanded bed contactors are used for the treatment of wastewater.

Treatment with Powdered Activated Carbon (PAC)

An alternative means of achieving adsorption is through the application of powdered activated carbon (PAC). Powdered activated carbon can be applied to the effluent from biological treatment processes, directly to the various biological treatment processes, and in physical-chemical treatment process flow diagrams.[4] In the case of biological treatment plant effluent, PAC is added to the effluent in a contacting basin. After a certain amount of time for contact, the carbon is allowed to settle to the bottom of the tank, and the treated water is then removed from the tank. Because carbon is very fine, a coagulant, such as a polyelectrolyte, may be needed to aid the removal of the carbon particles, or filtration through rapid sand filters may be required. The addition of PAC directly to the aeration basin of an activated-sludge treatment process has proved to be effective in the removal of a number of soluble refractory organics. In physical-chemical treatment processes, PAC is used in conjunction with chemicals used for the precipitation of specific constituents.

Activated Sludge with Powdered Activated Carbon Treatment

A proprietary process, "PACT", combines the use of powdered activated carbon with the activated-sludge process (see Figure 12.5). In this process, when the activated carbon is added directly to the aeration tank, biological oxidation and physical adsorption occur simultaneously. A feature of this process is that it can be integrated into existing activated sludge systems at nominal capital cost. The addition of powdered activated carbon has several process advantages, including(1)system stability during shock loads,(2)reduction of refractory priority pollutants, (3)color and ammonia removal, and(4)improved sludge settleability. In some industrial waste applications, where nitrification is inhibited by toxic organics, the application of powdered activated carbon may reduce or limit this inhibition.

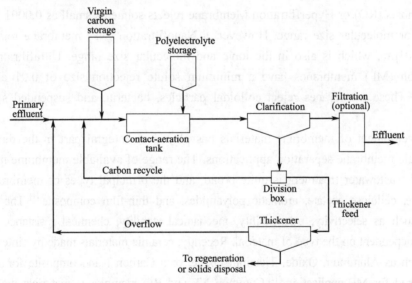

Figure 12.5 Difinition sketch for the application of powdered activated carbon

Carbon dosages typically range from 20 to 200 mg/L. With higher SRT values, the organic removal per unit of carbon is enhanced, thereby improving the process efficiency. Reasons cited for this phenomenon include (1)additional biodegradation due to decreased toxicity, (2)degradation of normally nondegradable substances due to increased exposure time to the biomass through adsorption on the carbon, and (3) replacement of low-molecular-weight compounds with high-molecular-weight compounds, resulting in improved adsorption efficiency and lower toxicity.

Notes

[1] 典型系统既可为压力式，亦可为重力式，可为下流式固体床单元，亦可为上流式固体床单元，每个单元设有两三个活性炭柱，串联操作，或者采用上流式逆流膨胀床。

[2] 活性炭接触器上游常用颗粒滤料过滤器去除二次沉淀池出水中与悬浮固体密切相关的有机物。

[3] 尽管上流式固定床反应器已经开始应用，但在颗粒物通过反洗难以去除的系统中，为了减轻炭床底部颗粒物质的积累概率，下流式炭床应用更为普遍。

[4] 粉末活性炭可加入各种生物处理工艺的出水中，也可直接加入生物处理工艺流程及物理化学处理流程中。

Unit 13　Membrane Filtration Processes

Membrane Filtration represents a very efficient and economical way of separating components that are suspended or dissolved in a liquid. The membrane plays the role of a selective barrier that allows certain compounds to pass through and retains other compounds in the liquid. The liquid passes through the semipermeable membranes which represents the permeameter, which of it containing the retained constituents is the retentate (also known as concentrate).

Membranes are classified by solute exclusion size that is sometimes referred to as pore size. A Reverse Osmosis (RO) or Hyperfiltration Membrane rejects solute as small as 0.0001 μm, which is in the ionic or molecular size range. However, a Nanofiltration (NF) membrane rejects solute as small as 0.001μm, which is also in the ionic and molecular size range. Ultrafiltration (UF) and Microfiltration (MF) membranes have a minimum solute rejection size of 0.01 and 0.10 μm, respectively. These membranes reject colloidal particles, bacteria, and suspended solids by size exclusion.

The development of membrane materials has played an integral part in the development of industrial-scale membrane separation applications. The range of available membrane materials used in water and wastewater treatment is quite broad, and the principal types of membranes used are polypropylene, cellulose acetate, aromatic polyamides, and thin-film composite.[1] The properties of membrane, such as selectivity, permeability, mechanical stability, chemical resistance, and thermal stability, are dependent on the type of material. Recently, ceramic materials made by sintering inorganic materials, such as Aluminum Oxide, Titanium Oxide, or a Carbon Nanocomposite formulation, have been considered for MF applications.[2] Common NF and RO membranes materials include aromatic polyamide and polyamide for spiral-wound configurations, and cellulose triacetate for RO hollow fine fiber membranes.

According to the driving force of the operation, the membrane processes can be classified as：

(1) Pressure gradient driven operations：such as RO, NF, UF, MF, gas separation (GS), or partial pressure driven processes, such as pervaporation (PV).

(2) Concentration gradient driven operations，such as dialysis and osmosis.

(3) Electrical potential gradient driven operations, such as elctrodialysis (ED).

(4) Temperature gradient driven operations，such as membrane distillation (MD).

Membrane modules are the core elements in membrane-based separation and purification system. Typical membrane modules are classified into four types：plate and frame, spiral wound, tubular and hollow fiber.

Plate and frame

In the plate and frame module, membranes are attached to both sides of a rigid plate. The plate may be constructed of solid plastic with grooved channels on the surface, porous fiberglass materials. This type of module is simple and the membrane replacement is easy. But because of its complexity, it is very expensive to operate for large-scale operations.

Spiral wound module

This consists of large consecutive layers of membrane and support material rolled up around a tube. The membranes are glued along three edges with the fourth side left open which is attached to a perforated pipe. Spiral systems are usually staged with three to six membrane elements connected in series in a pressure tube. The feed stream from the first element becomes the feed to the following element, and so on, for each element within the pressure tube. The feed flows axial through the cylindrical module parallel to the central pipe and the permeate flows are radically towards the central pipe. The spiral configuration makes better use of space and is less expensive. However, extensive pretreatment is necessary because it is more sensitive to pollution.

Tubular membrane

In this type of module, the membrane is either cast on the inner surface of, or placed within, a porous tube and sealed into place. The feed solution always flows through the centre of the tubes and the permeameter is collected in the tubular housing. Generally it is used for viscous or bad quality fluids and can be cleaned either mechanically or hydraulically with ease. The system is not very compact and has a high cost per membrane area installed when compared with either the spiral or the hollow fine fiber for water treatment applications.

Hollow fibers membrane

Hollow fiber module consists of a large number of hollow fibers assembled together in a module. The ends of the fibers are epoxy sealed to form a sheet-like permeate tube. The feed solution flows through the open cores of the fibers and then the permeate is collected in the cartridge area surrounding the fibers. The filtration can be carried out either 'inside-out' (the feed solution passes through the bore of the fiber and the permeameter is collected on the outside of the fiber) or 'outside-in' (the feed solution enters the module on the shell side of the fibers and the permeate passes into the fiber bore). The characteristics of this configuration are its extremely high packing density and self-supporting.

Typical operational modes for membrane filtration processes are dead-end and cross flow. In dead-end filtration the direction of the fluid flow is perpendicular to the membrane surface so that the retained particles and other components accumulate and deposit on the membrane surface.[3] In cross-flow filtration the feed flow is parallel to the membrane surface, retentate is removed from the same side further downstream, whereas the permeate flow is tracked on the other side. Moving the feed flow tangentially to the membrane surface can result in much higher permeation fluxes as the stream continuously removes retained material. Comparing to cross flow, (1) the dead-end membranes are relatively easy to fabricate which reduces the cost of the separation process, (2) the dead-end membrane separation process is easy to implement and the process is usually cheaper than cross-flow membrane filtration, and (3) a dead-end filtration is the extensive membrane fouling and concentration polarization.

Membrane fouling refers to a long term flux decline caused by the deposition of retained particles onto the membrane surface and/or within the pores of the membrane, deteriorating the performance of the membranes.[4] Membrane fouling is a widespread problem limiting the performance and application of synthetic membrane processes and, as such, is an important consideration in the design and operation of a membrane system because cleaning frequency, pretreatment requirement, operating condition, cost, and performance are affected by membrane fouling. Fouling of the membrane can occur in three general forms: (1) a buildup of the constituents in the feedwater on the membrane surface, (2) the formation of chemical precipitates due to the chemistry of the feedwater, and (3) the damage to the membrane due to the presence of chemical substances that can react with the membrane or biological agents that can colonize the membrane.[5] In general, there are two approaches to control membrane fouling: (1) pretreatment of the feedwater, and (2) physical and chemical cleaning of the membranes.

Important Words and Expressions

semipermeable ['semi'pə:miəbl]　adj. 半透性的
retentate [ri'tenteit]　n. 保留物，滞留物
exclusion [ik'sklu:ʒ(ə)n]　n. 排除，除外，被排除在外的事物
osmosis [ɔz'məusis]　n. 渗透(作用)，渗透性
selectivity [silek'tiviti]　n. 选择性
permeability [,pə:miə'biliti]　n. 渗透性
ceramic [si'ræmik]　adj. 陶器的
aluminum [ə'lju:minəm]　n. 铝
titanium [tai'teini:əm]　n. 钛
configuration [kən,figju'reiʃən]　n. 构造，结构，配置，外形
module ['mɔdju:l]　n. 模数，模块，登月舱，指令舱
perforate ['pə:fə,reit]　v. 打孔
hyperfiltration [,haipəfil'treiʃən]　n. 超(过)滤
ultrafiltration [,ʌltrəfil'treiʃən]　n. 超滤(作用)
polypropylene [,pɔli'prəupili:n]　n. 聚丙烯
cellulose ['seljə,ləus]　n. 纤维素
acetate ['æsiteit]　n. 醋酸盐，醋酸纤维素及其制成的产品
triacetate [trai'æsi,teit]　adj. 分子中含有三个醋酸基的，三醋酸基的
aromatic [,ærə'mætik]　adj.（芬芳的）芳香的，芳香族的
polyamide [,pɔli'æmaid]　n. 聚酰胺
pervaporation [pəveipə'reiʃən]　n. 全蒸发，过蒸汽化
sintering ['sintəriŋ]　v. 烧结
perpendicular [,pə:pən'dikjələ]　adj. 垂直的，正交的
rigid ['ridʒid]　adj. 刚硬的，刚性的，严格的
axial ['æksiəl]　adj. 轴的，轴向的
dialysis [dai'ælisis]　n. 透析，分离
groove [gru:v]　vt. 开槽于
consecutive [kən'sekjutiv]　adj. 连续的，连贯的
flux [flʌks]　n. 流量，通量
fouling ['fauliŋ]　n. 污垢

precipitate [pri'sipiteit] n. 沉淀物
polarization [,pəuləraiˈzeiʃən] n. 极化(作用)，两极化，分化

Notes

[1] 用于水处理和污水处理的膜材料范围非常广泛，主要的膜材料有聚丙烯、醋酸纤维素、聚芳酰胺以及薄膜复合材料。

[2] 最近，由烧结无机材料如三氧化二铝、二氧化钛或碳纳米复合制剂而制成的陶瓷材料已被考虑应用于微过滤。

[3] 在死端过滤操作过程中，原料液流动方向与膜表面垂直，这样颗粒及其他组分在膜表面积聚沉积。

[4] 膜污染是指长期的流量下降，这是由于被滞留的物质在膜表面和/或膜孔内部沉积所引起的，它会导致膜性能的恶化。

[5] 膜污染一般存在三种形式：（1）进水中的成分在膜表面的累积；（2）由于进水的化学性质形成化学沉淀物；（3）由于化学物质与膜存在反应以及生物制剂的侵蚀，导致膜的损害。

Exercises

1. Answering the following questions in English according to the text：

(1) How to control membrane fouling?

(2) What are the types of membrane modules?

2. Using the following each word to make up the sentences, respectively：

(1) permeate

(2) retentate

(3) configuration

(4) flux

(5) selectivity

3. Put the following English into Chinese：

(1) Both polymeric and inorganic materials are used to produce membranes, which might have a homogeneous or composite structure with both a dense layer and a skin layer which have different porosities and compositions. Also dense or porous membranes might be produced depending on their uses and applications. Further research is related to the production of functionalized membranes or coated membranes, also depending on the field of application.

(2) Concentration polarization and membrane fouling are typical phenomena affecting the performance of MF and UF processes. The general effect of these phenomena is a reduction in the permeate flux through the formation of an additional barrier caused by the retention of feed solution compounds with a consequent increase in the mass transfer resistance. When a feed solution contains a solvent and a solute or a suspended solid is filtered through a porous membrane, some components permeate the membrane under a given driving force while others are retained. This results in a higher local concentration of the rejected solute at the membrane surface, compared to the bulk, with formation of a viscous or gelatinous cake layer. This phenomenon is referred to as concentration polarization. It is not to be confused with the membrane fouling phenomenon that is essentially

caused by deposition of retained particles onto the membrane surface or in the membrane pore.

4. Put the following Chinese into English:

(1) 膜污染

(2) 渗透通量

(3) 死端过滤

(4) 膜组件的清洗大致分为化学清洗和物理清洗两大类型。

(5) 微滤和超滤都是在静压差的推动力作用下进行的液相分离过程。

5. Put the following abbr. into full phrases:

RO； NF； UF； MF； GS； PV； ED； MD

Reading Material A

Ultrafiltration

Today, Ultrafiltration (UF) technology is being used worldwide for treating various waters. It is reported that 50% of the UF membrane plants have been applied on surface waters, including river, reservoir and lake waters. This technology has been used in municipal drinking water application for more than 10 years.

UF is a membrane filtration technique in which small particles and dissolved molecules are separated from fluids by pressure driven. UF is not fundamentally different from MF, except in terms of the size of the molecules which is able to retain. [1] The separation depends on molecular size: suspended solids and solutes with a high molecular weight retained, while water and low molecular weight solutes pass through the membrane. It is possible to retain molecules of 300–500,000 Da of molecular weight by UF, with pore sizes ranging from 0.001 to 0.1 μm. Typical rejected species include sugars, biomolecules, polymers and colloidal particles. Although these high molecular weight solutes can produce an osmotic pressure, they are usually only a few bars. Thus, the hydrostatic pressure difference used as driving force in UF is in the range of 1–10 bars, although in some cases up to 25-30 bars can be used.

Most UF membrane materials are CA and polymeric materials. Because of the low chemical and thermal stabilities, a relatively narrow range of pH tolerance, highly biodegradable of CA membrane, and polymers or polymer blends are employed to produce UF membranes,[2] such as polysulphone, polypropylene, nylon 6, PTFE, polyvinyl chloride and acrylic copolymer. Also some manufactures prepare UF membranes with inorganic materials such as ceramic, carbon-based membrane and zirconia. The properties of membrane materials such as porosity, morphology, surface properties, mechanical strength and chemical resistance should be considered as preparing membranes. The membrane is tested with dilute solutions of well-characterized macromolecules, such as protein, polysaccharide and surfactant of known molecular weight and size, to determine the molecular weight cut off (MWCO).

Typical UF membrane modules are tubular, spiral wound and hollow fiber. The tubular module is often used for small-scale, high-value applications. The tubular module is the choice for cases involving severe fouling because it is easy to mechanical cleaning. While the spiral wound module is more vulnerable to fouling and mechanical cleaning is difficult. Comparing to other modules, hollow fiber modules have much larger ratio of membrane area to unit volume, which are self-supporting. [3] Today, the hollow fiber module in UF is widely used.

There are two basic configurations for UF membrane processes: pressure vessels configuration and vacuum systems. Pressure vessels configuration refers to the membranes with thousands of fibers housed in pressure vessels. The latter are systems where the membranes are submerged or immersed in nonpressurized tanks. The configuration of membranes affects mass transport or performance and design and layout of different configurations differing significantly so that the configuration type should be determined prior to commencement of facility design.

The flow in UF processes can run from inside-out or outside-in through hollow fibers. UF inner and outer diameters vary between manufacturers; however, typical membrane fibers' inner and outer diameter approximates 90 and 1900mm, respectively. In a conventional UF process, the driving force to produce filtrate can work in two ways: positive pressure moving fluid through the fibers, usually at a rating lower than 241 kPa, and negative pressure moving fluid through fibers under vacuum pressure. Combining the two different flow regimes and the two driving forces allows three different processes.

- Inside-out flow with positive pressure
- Outside-in flow with positive pressure
- Outside-in flow with negative pressure

Both inside-out and outside-in flow patterns can be further characterized as either dead-end or cross flow operations. In a dead-end operation, the feedwater perpendicularly pass through the membrane which can cause serious membrane fouling. But the dead-end operation has advantages of low energy consumption and high water recovery. In a cross flow operation, only a portion of the flow passes through the membranes and only a portion of the retained solutes accumulate at the membrane surface. The cross flow regime also incorporates a tangential flow that shears the cake and minimizes the accumulation of solids on the membrane surface.

Comparing to conventional procedures, UF processes have certain advantages. Typically, UF is energy efficient; do not require the addition of chemical compounds or phase changes which often denature labile species; is modular and easy to scale up and down; yields a higher quality product; offers the possibility of carrying out the separation continuously. In addition, UF can be performed either at room temperature or in a cold room. However, in many UF applications, extensive pretreatments are needed in order to limit concentration polarization and membrane fouling phenomena. The low mechanical resistance of the membrane, in some cases, is an additional drawback which can lead to the membrane breaking when there are uncorrected operating procedures.

Notes

[1] 超滤和微滤本质上没有差别，只是它们截留的分子大小不同。

[2] 由于醋酸纤维膜化学稳定性和热稳定性差、允许 pH 值范围窄并且生物降解性高，所以现在多使用聚合物或者聚合物混合物来生产超滤膜。

[3] 与其他膜组件相比，中空纤维组件有很大的比表面积，并且不需外加支撑材料。

Reading Material B

Reverse Osmosis

Osmosis is the phenomenon of water flow through a semipermeable membrane that blocks the transport of salts or other solutes through the membrane. When two solutions having different solute concentration are separated by a semipermeable membrane, water will flow from the side of low solute concentration to the side of high solute concentration. The flow continues until the pressure difference between the two sides of the membrane equals to osmotic pressure of the solution. If imposing a pressure greater than the osmotic pressure across the membrane, pure water flows from the high solute concentration side to the low solute concentration side which is termed reverse osmosis (RO).[1]

Osmosis and RO have been studied over two centuries; however, it was not until the early 1960s the use of RO as a feasible separation process was demonstrated. The RO process can eliminate the dissolved solids, bacteria, viruses and other germs contained in the water. Generally, there are two types of RO membranes: CA (an integral membrane) and thin film (TF, a composite membrane). The support material is commonly polysulphone. A typical efficient RO process is designed to achieve higher water flux with relatively lower energy expenditure. In addition to the membrane materials, the packaging of membranes is also a very important factor in the feasibility of the RO process. The industrially available membrane modules are plate and frame, tubular, spiral wound and hollow fiber elements.[2]

To gain effective operation of RO, feed pretreatment must be done to gain a high quality feed which reduces the potential fouling of RO membrane. In the development of a pretreatment program, the focus is on removing as many fouling constituents in the feed water as possible. The following pretreatment options have been used singly and/or combination.

(1) Pretreatment of a secondary effluent by chemical clarification and multimedia filtration or by multimedia filtration and ultrafiltration is usually necessary to remove colloidal material.

(2) Cartridge filters with a pore size of 5-10 μm have also been used to reduce residual suspended solids.

(3) To limit bacterial activity it may be necessary to disinfect the feedwater using chlorine, ozone, or UV radiation.

(4) The exclusion of oxygen may be necessary to prevent oxidation of iron, manganese, and hydrogen sulfide.

(5) Depending on the type of membrane, removal of chlorine and ozone may be necessary.

(6) The removal of iron and manganese may also be necessary to decrease scaling potential.

(7) To inhibit scale formation, the pH of the feed should be adjusted within the range from 4.0 to 7.5.

RO systems are used in different fields, such as desalination of sea water, separating oil from oily wastewater, treating groundwater for production of pharmaceutical-grade water, boiler feed water and cooling tower blow down recycle for utilities and power generation, cleaning of contaminated surface water and groundwater, ultra-pure water for food processing and electronic industries, water for chemical, pulp and paper industry.

RO is used primarily for desalination of seawater. The first RO water treatment plant was constructed in 1970s in Florida. In the desalination industry of the United States, RO membrane technology is most popular. A typical RO plant configuration generally includes raw water pumps, pretreatments, membrane units, disinfection units, storages, and distribution elements. For desalination application, membrane units are often configured into a multistage continuous process.[3] In such a system, the concentration of the feed stream increases gradually along the length of several stages of membrane modules arranged in series. The feed only reaches its final concentration at the last stage.

RO processing of contaminated aquifers is usually similar to the conventional brackish RO application. Since this type of raw water usually contains low concentrations of suspended solids and low levels of biological activity, it requires a relatively simple pretreatment process. The application to municipal wastewater treatment requires extensive pretreatment prior to the RO process. A typical process for municipal wastewater consists of primary, secondary and tertiary treatments. This process produces an effluent with low turbidity that can be disinfected for discharge. However, the effluent still contains dissolved solids such as colloids, organic matter and bacterial activity. As a result, the water is not generally suitable for reuse. RO membranes are able to produce water with a quality much higher than tertiary effluent.

About 70% of the operating cost of seawater RO desalination is the energy cost. On the contrary, energy is as important as water and is becoming scarce. Therefore, energy recovery devices and alternative energy sources receive the attention of the scientific community. Application of a pressure exchanger can be used to win back energy from the concentrate flow released under high pressure. The concentrate flow from the membranes is directed through the pressure exchanger, where it directly transfers energy to part of the incoming feed water with maximum affectivity. In an RO system that uses a pressure exchanger, it not only saves more than half the total energy but also saves purchase costs of high-pressure pumps.

Notes

[1] 如果在膜一侧施加的压力大于渗透压，水将从高浓度的一侧流向低浓度一侧，这就是反渗透。

[2] 工业用膜组件主要有板框式、管式、卷式、中空纤维式等。

[3] 用于海水淡化的膜单元通常被布置成多段式连续操作系统。

Part Four
Biological Treatment Process

Unit 14 Activated Sludge Process

The activated sludge process is now the most widely used biological process for treatment of municipal and industrial wastewaters. Activated sludge process was developed in England in 1914 and was so named because it involved the production of an activated mass of microorganisms capable of aerobic stabilization of the organic content of wastewater.

The basic activated sludge process is illustrated by Figure 14.1. The mixture of influent wastewater commonly coming from primary clarifier and returning activated sludge is known as mixed liquor. In activated sludge process, the mixed liquor flows to aeration tank in which the microorganisms responsible for treatment are kept in suspension and aerated. In the aeration tank, contact time is provided for mixing and aerating influent wastewater. Aeration serves at least three important functions: (1) mixing the mixed liquor, (2) keeping the activated sludge in suspension, and (3) supplying the oxygen to the biochemical reactions necessary for the stabilization of the wastewater. Once the mixed liquor has received sufficient treatment, excess mixed liquor is discharged into secondary clarifier. The function of the secondary clarifier is to separate the activated sludge solids from the mixed liquor. These solids represent the colloidal and dissolved solids that were originally present in the wastewater. In the aeration unit they were incorporated into the activated sludge floc, which are settleable solids. The separation of these solids, a critical step in the activated sludge process, is accomplished in the secondary or final settling tanks. A part of this settled biomass, described as activated sludge, is returned to the aeration tank which is important to maintain a sufficient concentration of activated sludge in the aeration tank for the desired degree of treatment.[1] The excess sludge must be removed before it loses its activity because of the death of the aerobic organisms resulting from lack of oxygen at the bottom of the tank. The most common

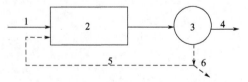

Figure 14.1 Basic activated sludge process
1 influent, 2 aeration tank, 3 secondary clarifier ,4 effluent ,5 return activated sludge ,6 sludge

practice is to waste from the sludge return line. Sometimes waste sludge is removed by withdrawing mixed liquor directly from the aeration tank. The wasted mixed liquor can then be discharged to a thickening tank or to the primary tanks where the sludge settles and mixes with the raw primary sludge. The waste sludge is further thickened by final sedimentation, centrifuging, or flotation thickening and then treated by biological or chemical means.

Since the activated sludge process came into common use, a number of modifications of the conventional activated sludge process have been developed to meet specific treatment objectives:

(1) Complete-mix activated sludge process: A completely mixed system can allow a more uniform aeration of the wastewater in the aeration tank. This process has been applied to handle a variety of wastewaters with great success, especially because the process can sustain shocks and toxic loads.

(2) Step-aeration activated sludge process: In this modified system, influent wastewater is introduced at several points along the aeration tank length. This leads to a relatively homogenous load distribution along the length of the aeration tank resulting in a more efficient use of dissolved oxygen.

(3) Contact-stabilization activated sludge: The influent contacts with a high concentration of biomass in a small contact tank for a short period of time (20 to 40 min). The mixture that flows to the secondary clarifier where it gets settled and the resulting biosolids are returned to a stabilization tank with a hydraulic retention time of 4 to 8 h.[2] In this contact tank, a rapid biosorption of organic compounds is expected followed by the oxidation of the organics. This system would need smaller tankage and produce smaller amounts of biosolids.

(4) Tapered aeration process: In the basic activated sludge process, organic influent is one-point loaded to the head of aeration tank, thus the oxygen demand is extremely high at the head of the aeration tank but very low at the exit end. To overcome this problem, in tapered aeration process, the air supply tapers off with distance along the aeration tank so that supply and demand can be balanced throughout the tank. [3]

(5) Pure oxygen activated sludge process: The pure oxygen activated sludge process is based on such a simple idea that the rate of oxygen transfer in water is proportional to the partial pressure of oxygen, that is, the rate of oxygen transfer is higher for pure oxygen than for atmospheric oxygen.[4] Higher availability of oxygen for microorganisms leads to improved treatment efficiency and reduced production of biosolids and reactor volume.

To ensure high levels of treatment performance with the activated sludge process, several control measures must be considered such as (1) ensuring that there is sufficient level of dissolved oxygen in the aeration tanks, (2) adjusting the amount of return activated sludge, and (3) controlling the waste sludge. Basically there are several parameters one can refer to as a guideline to find out whether the whole process is operating at peak performance. The parameter used most commonly for controlling the process is solids retention time (SRT, the SRT represents the average period of time during which the sludge has remained in the system). Mixed liquor suspended solids (MLSS) concentration may also be used to determine whether the sludge is healthy or whether it is too old or too young. MLSS concentration can be controlled based on the amount of return activated sludge. The food to microorganism ratio (F/M) is commonly used to characterize operating conditions. Oxygen uptake rates (OURs) are also used to monitor and control the activated sludge process.

Sludge volume index (SVI) is the measure of the settle ability and compatibility of sludge and is made from a laboratory column settling test (the sludge volume index is defined as 'the volume occupied by 1g of sludge after it has settled for a specified period of time' generally ranging from 20 min to 1 or 2 h in a 1 or 2 L cylinder. Half an hour is most common settling time).[5]

Important Words and Expressions

  incorporate [in'kɔːpəreit] vt. 合并
  responsible [ri'spɔnsəbl] adj. 有责任的，可靠的，可依赖的，负责的
  suspension [sə'spenʃən] n. 悬浮，悬浮液
  primary ['praiməri] adj. 第一位的，初级的
  biochemical [baiəu'kemikəl] adj. 生物化学的
  sedimentation [ˌsedimen'teiʃən] n. 沉淀，沉降
  clarifier ['klærifaiə] n. 澄清器
  stabilization [ˌsteibilai'zeiʃən] n. 稳定性
  floc [flɔk] n. 絮状物
  biomass ['baiəumæs] n. 生物量
  colloidal [kə'lɔidl] adj. 胶状的，胶质的
  centrifuging ['sentrifjudʒiŋ] n. 离心法，离心过滤
  flotation [fləu'teiʃən] n. 浮选
  modification [ˌmɔdəfi'keiʃən] n. 更改，修改，修正
  homogenous [hə'mɔdʒinəs] adj. 同质的，纯系的
  hydraulic [hai'drɔːlik] adj. 水力的，水压的
  biosorption [ˌbaiəu'sɔːpʃən] n. 生物吸着(作用)
  index ['indeks] n. 指数，指标

Notes

  [1] 一部分沉淀的生物量，即活性污泥，被返回到曝气池中，这是维持曝气池内活性污泥具有足够浓度的重要过程，以便达到期望的处理程度。

  [2] 混合物流入二级沉淀池，在这里进行沉淀，同时，产生的污泥被返回到稳定池中，其水力停留时间为4～8h。

  [3] 针对这一问题，在渐减曝气活性污泥法中，供氧量沿池长逐步递减使供氧量与需氧量平衡。

  [4] 纯氧活性泥处理是基于这样一个简单的想法，氧气在水中的传输速率正比于氧气的分压，即纯氧比大气中的氧传输速率要高。

  [5] 污泥容积指数是衡量活性污泥沉降性能的指标，它可由沉降试验测得（污泥容积指数指的是"经过一定时间的沉淀后，1g 污泥占的体积"，通常是在1L 或2L 的量筒内沉降20min 到 1h 或 2h。最常用的沉降时间是半小时）。

Exercises

1. Answering the following questions in English according to the text：

  (1) What factors should be considered in controlling activated sludge process?

(2) Summarize conventional activated sludge process.

2. Using the following each word to make up the sentences, respectively:
(1) stabilization
(2) aeration
(3) separation
(4) sedimentation
(5) distribution

3. Put the following English into Chinese:

(1) Generally two types of mixing regimes are of major interest in activated sludge process: plug flow and complete mixing. In the first one, the regime is characterized by orderly flow of mixed liquor through the aeration tank with no element of mixed liquor overtaking or mixing with any other element. There may be lateral mixing of mixed liquor but there must be no mixing along the path of flow. In complete mixing, the contents of aeration tank are well stirred and uniform throughout. Thus, at steady state, the effluent from the aeration tank has the same composition as the aeration tank contents.

The type of mixing regime is very important as it affects (1) oxygen transfer requirements in the aeration tank, (2) local environmental conditions in the aeration tank, and (3) the kinetics governing the treatment process.

(2) In the activated sludge process, waste water flows continuously into an aeration tank where air is injected into the waste water to mix the waste water with the activated sludge, and also to provide the oxygen needed for the microorganisms to break down the organic pollutants. The mixed liquor flows to a secondary clarifier or a secondary settling tank where the activated sludge settles out. A portion of the settled sludge is returned to the aeration tank to maintain an optimum concentration of acclimated microorganisms in the aeration tank to break down the organics. Since more activated sludge is produced than is needed for return sludge, the excess sludge is discarded or wasted. The wasted sludge may be further treated in a sludge digested and dewatered on sludge drying beds prior to disposal. The clarified effluent from the secondary settling tank is discharged on land or into a flowing river.

4. Put the following Chinese into English:
(1) 混合液悬浮固体浓度
(2) 污泥容积指数
(3) 水力停留时间
(4) 活性污泥的比好氧速率是衡量活性污泥生物活性的一个重要指标。
(5) 目前，活性污泥法是城市污水和工业废水处理中常用的工艺。

5. Put the following abbr. into full phrases:
SRT；MLSS；OURs；SVI

Reading Material A

Oxidation Ditch

The oxidation ditch, also named continuous loop reactor, was developed in the Netherlands with the first full scale plant installed in Voorschoten, Holland, in 1954. An oxidation ditch is an extended aeration activated sludge treatment process that has been used in small towns, isolated communities, and institutions.[1] Some oxidation ditches are named according to manufacturer's trade names such as Pasveer, Orbal, or Carrousel. Typical oxidation ditch (Figure 14.2) consists of a single or multichannel of an oval or ring shape equipped with aeration equipment called rotors or brushes for generating a water flow and stirring water in the channel to supply oxygen. The only pretreatment typically used in an oxidation ditch system is the bar screen (primarily settling before an oxidation ditch is sometimes practiced). After passing through the bar screen, wastewater flows directly into the oxidation ditch. Ditches may be constructed of various materials, such as concrete, gunite, asphalt, and impervious membranes. Concrete is the most common. L- and horseshoe-shaped configurations have been constructed to maximize land usage. The wastewater moves through the ditch at 0.3 to 0.5 m/s. The cross-sectional area of the ditch is commonly 0.9 to 1.5m deep, which helps to prevent anaerobic conditions from occurring at the bottom of the ditch. Oxidation ditch systems with depths of 2.5m or more with vertical sidewalls and vertical shaft aerators may also be used. Activated sludge is added to the oxidation ditch so that the microorganisms will digest the BOD in the water. Longer retention time within the ditch will allow for a greater amount of organic matter to be broken down by the aerobic bacteria. After treatment, the mixed liquor flows to a secondary clarifier where the sludge and the water are allowed to separate. Some of the sludge is returned to the oxidation ditch to maintain a desirable MLSS concentration. The MLSS concentration in the oxidation ditch generally ranges from 1500 to 5000 mg/ L. The rest of the sludge is sent to waste.

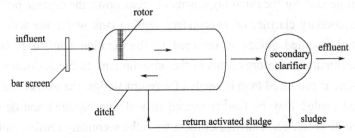

Figure 14.2   Typical oxidation ditch flow diagram

The quality of the mixed liquor in oxidation ditches is almost uniform, in a sense, oxidation ditches are typically complete mixing systems, but they can be modified to approach plug flow conditions.[2] The design criteria are affected by the influent wastewater parameters and the required effluent characteristics, including the decision or requirement to achieve nitrification, denitrification, and/or biological phosphorus removal. Specific design parameters for oxidation ditches include SRT, BOD loading and hydraulic retention time.[3] BOD loading rates vary from less than 160 mg/L/d to more than 800 mg/L/d. A BOD loading rate of 240 mg/L/d is commonly used as a design loading rate. Oxidation ditch volume is sized based on the required SRT to meet effluent quality requirements. The SRT is selected as a function of nitrification requirements and the minimum mixed liquor temperature. Design SRT values vary from 4 to 48 or more days. Typical SRT required for nitrification ranges from 12 to 24 days. Although rarely used as a basis for oxidation ditch design, hydraulic retention time within the oxidation ditch ranges from 6 to 30 hours for most municipal wastewater treatment plants.

Surface aerators, such as brush rotors, disc aerators, draft tube aerators, and fine bubble diffusers, are used to circulate the mixed liquor. The mixing process entrains oxygen into the mixed liquor to foster microbial growth and the motive velocity ensures contact of microorganisms with the incoming wastewater. The aeration sharply increases the dissolved oxygen concentration but decreases as biomass uptakes oxygen as the mixed liquor travels through the ditch. Solids are maintained in suspension as the mixed liquor circulates around the ditch. If design SRT is selected for nitrification, a high degree of nitrification will occur.

Several manufacturers have developed modifications to the oxidation ditch design to remove nutrients in condition cycled or phased between the anoxic and aerobic states. Although the mechanics of operation differ by manufacturer, in general, the process consists of two separate basins, the first anoxic and the second aerobic. Wastewater and return activated sludge are introduced into the first reactor which operates under anoxic conditions. Mixed liquor then flows into the second reactor operating under aerobic conditions. The process is then reversed and the second reactor begins to operate under anoxic condition.

The greatest advantage of the oxidation ditch is the efficiency of removal performance objectives with low operational requirements and operations and maintenance costs. Other advantages of oxidation ditches include (1) produces less sludge than other biological treatment processes owing to extended biological activity during the activated sludge process, (2) it is hard to be affected by load fluctuations, (3) it requires relatively little energy as the rotor is operated efficiently, and(4) it can be easily maintained. Disadvantages of the oxidation ditch include: (1) as the tank is large and the depth is small it requires a large area, and (2) effluent suspended solids concentration is relatively high compared to other modifications of the activated sludge process.

Notes

[1] 氧化沟是延时曝气活性污泥法的一种特殊形式，已应用于一些小的城镇、社区及机构。

[2] 氧化沟内混合液的水质几乎是一致的，从这个意义来说，氧化沟内的流态是完全混合式的，但又具有某些推流式的特征。

[3] 氧化沟的设计参量包括固体停留时间、BOD 负荷及水力停留时间。

Reading Material B

Nutrient Removal

Nutrient removal refers to the removal of nitrogen and phosphorous from wastewater. Nutrient removal in wastewater treatment is (1) to control eutrophication, and (2) to provide nitrogen and phosphorous control for water reuse applications including groundwater recharge.

Nitrogen removal from wastewater can be accomplished through a variety of alternative processes. The popular approach is by biological nitrogen removal. All of biological nitrogen removal processes include aerobic nitrification and anoxic denitrification which has the additional advantage of returning nitrogen to the atmosphere in its natural form. In the first step of nitrification, ammonia (NH_4-N) is oxidized to nitrite (NO_2-N). In the second step, nitrite is oxidized to nitrate (NO_3-N). In anoxic denitrification, nitrite and nitrate are reduced to nitrogen gas. Almost all operating biological nitrogen removal processes can be classified into three groups: combined carbon oxidation/nitrification/denitrification, combined carbon oxidation/nitrification and separate-stage denitrification, and separate-stage carbon oxidation, nitrification and denitrification.[1] The types of suspended growth biological nitrogen removal processes can be classified into single-sludge and two-sludge. The term single-sludge means only one solid separation device is used in the process. In the two-sludge system, the most common system consists of an aerobic nitrification process followed by an anoxic denitrification process, each with its own clarifier, thus producing two sludges. The single-sludge biological nitrogen removal processes are classified into to three groups: preanoxic (the anoxic zone is located before aerobic nitrification zone), postanoxic (the anoxic zone is located after aerobic nitrification zone), and simultaneous nitrification-denitrification (nitrification and denitrification occur in the same tank). In the preanoxic configuration, nitrate being produced in the aerobic zone is recycled to the preanoxic compartment.[2] Postanoxic designs may be operated with or without an exogenous carbon source. The simultaneous nitrification- denitrification applications require DO control or other types of control methods to assure that both nitrification and denitrification occur in a single tank.

Biological phosphorus removal from wastewaters is based on the enrichment of activated sludge with phosphate accumulating organisms, namely PAOs. These PAOs are able to accumulate P in bacterial cells in the form of polyphosphate granules in excess levels normally required to satisfy the metabolic demands of growth;[3] such a storage process is commonly referred to as enhanced biological phosphorus removal. To date, all biological phosphorus removal processes developed are based on alternative aerobic and anaerobic cycle operation. Biological phosphorus removal processes introduced here are the PhoStrip process, the A/O process, and the A^2/O process. The PhoStrip process was first reported in 1965, which combines biological and chemical processes for phosphorus removal. The PhoStrip process has been referred to as a side-stream process since a portion of the return activated sludge flow is diverted for phosphorus stripping and subsequent precipitation with lime. Control of the side-stream permits phosphorus removal to be divided between supernatant from the stripper and waste activated sludge, i.e., phosphorus removal is carried out by chemical precipitation or in the waste biological sludge. A large percentage of the phosphorus removal is tied up as lime sludge, which causes less concern than handling a phosphorus-rich waste biological sludge. The A/O process is generally designed as a high-rate activated sludge system. The key features of the A/O process are its relatively short design sludge retention time and high design organic loading rates which results in greater sludge production and more phosphorus removal per unit of BOD removed in the system. However, the use of further sludge stabilization methods, such as anaerobic, aerobic digestion, must consider the amount of phosphorus released during stabilization and the effect of recycle streams from the stabilization units on facility performance. The modified flow scheme incorporates an anoxic stage for denitrification between the anaerobic and aerobic stages and is called the A^2/O process. The A^2/O process is an activated sludge process specially designed to accomplish biological phosphorus and nitrogen removal. Mixed liquor is recycled from the end of the nitrification stage to feed nitrate nitrogen into the anoxic stage for denitrification. Internal recycle flows of 100–300% have been used. Nitrate nitrogen removals of 40%–70% can be accomplished this way.

Phosphorus removal can also be achieved by chemical precipitation, usually with salts of iron, aluminum, or lime. Chemical phosphorus removal requires significantly smaller equipment footprint than biological removal, and is easier to operate and is often more reliable than biological phosphorus removal. But chemical treatment may lead to excessive sludge production as hydroxides precipitates and the added chemicals can be expensive.

Notes

[1] 几乎所有的生物脱氮工艺可分成三类：碳氧化、硝化和反硝化工艺合并处理；碳氧化和硝化在一个构筑物中完成，然后单独进行反硝化脱氮；碳氧化、硝化、反硝化在不同的构筑物中依次完成。

[2] 在前置反硝化系统中，好氧区产生的硝化液一部分回流至缺氧池。

[3] 聚磷菌能够过量地、超过其生理需要地摄取磷，并将磷以聚合磷酸盐的形态储存于体内。

Unit 15 Attached Growth Biological Treatment Process

Sewage treatment, or domestic wastewater treatment, is the process of removing contaminants from wastewater and household sewage. It includes physical, chemical, and biological processes to remove physical, chemical and biological contaminants. Its objective is to produce a waste stream (or treated effluent) and a solid waste or sludge suitable for discharge or reuse back into the environment. [1]

In 1869, Sir Edward Frankland began his groundbreaking study of filtration performance on raw London sewage by packing laboratory columns with various combinations of coarse gravel and peaty soil. This experiment was the first scientific proof that intermittent sand filtration is an effective treatment for wastewater. The concept of flowing wastewater across some natural material for treatment is the basis of attached growth processes, also referred to as fixed film. Generally, these processes are low maintenance, have low energy requirements, and ,overall, are "low tech"-making them good wastewater treatment technology for small communities, as well as individual homes.

In contrast to activated sludge processes where the waste-consuming bacteria grow in suspension in water tanks, the active bacteria in attached growth processes cling to some surface, natural or manmade, to form the membrane sludge-biofilm and perform the cleaning. [2]

Attached growth technologies work on the principle that organic matter is removed from wastewater by microorganisms. These microorganisms are primarily aerobic, meaning they must have oxygen to live. They grow on the filter media (materials such as gravel, sand, peat, or specially woven fabric or plastic), essentially recycling the dissolved organic material into a film that develops on the media as nutrient. [3] See Figure 15.1.

In all cases, attached growth filters act as secondary treatment devices following a septic tank or other primary treatment. Raw wastewater must be treated first to remove the larger solids and floating debris, because these solids can plug the filter.

There are two basic designs of attached growth or fixed film systems: those that hold the media in place, allowing the wastewater to flow over the bed (such as trickling filters), or those where the

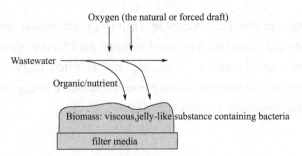

Figure 15.1 Cross-section of an attached growth biomass film

media is in motion relative to the wastewater (e.g. rotating biological disks). In most cases, drains under the media collect the effluent and either send if back through the filter or send it on for further treatment. The main advantages of attached growth processes over the activated sludge process are lower energy requirements, simpler operation, no bulking problems, less maintenance, and better recovery from shock loads. Attached growth processes in wastewater treatment are very effective for biochemical oxygen demand (BOD) removal, nitrification, and denitrification. Disadvantages are a larger land requirement, poor operation in cold weather, and potential odor problems. See Figure 15.2.

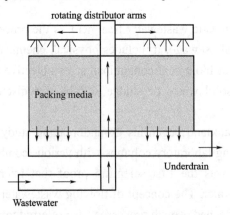

Figure 15.2 Trickling filter-side view

Many small communities, housing developments, and individual homeowners are discovering that the use of filters or rotating biological contactors (RBCs), either alone or in some combination with other technologies, provides low-cost, low-maintenance wastewater treatment.[4]

There are many variations and combinations of these processes, sometimes referred to as hybrids that use the attached growth process in combination with other technologies such as types of attached growth filters: sand, peat, and textile filters; trickling filters and rotating biological contactors; and subsurface flow wetlands.

Sand and peat filters

Treatment filters using sand or peat as media make effective attached growth systems. They can be designed as either single-pass or recirculating filters, meaning that the wastewater is run across the media more than one time. Regardless of the media, the process is generally the same— wastewater from the septic tank is allowed to run through a bed of media and collected from underneath. Treatment occurs as the bacteria grow on the media. Sand filters are constructed beds of sand or other suitable granular material usually 2 to 3 feet deep (See Figure 15.3). Peat filters use a

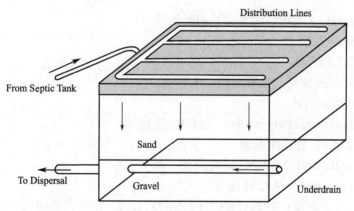

Figure 15.3 Sand filter

two-foot-thick layer of sphagnum peat moss for wastewater treatment. Unsterilized peat is home to a number of different microorganisms, including bacteria, fungi, and tiny plants, making peat a reactive and effective filter.

Textile filters

The use of manmade textiles for wastewater treatment is a fairly recent development. The textile is a synthetic fiber and is durable and resistant to biodegradation. The engineered fabric is packed into a water-tight fiberglass basin, providing a large surface area for biological breakdown, but taking up a much smaller space. The footprint area for a textile filter serving a four-bed-room, single-family home is only about 20 square feet. Textile systems are capable of high removal rates for BOD, total suspended solids (TSS), fecal coliforms, ammonia, and nitrate concentrations comparable to municipal treatment plants.

We will also explain how these systems work and advantages and disadvantages of using them in the following reading materials.

Important Words and Expressions

groundbreaking ['graund,breikiŋ]   adj. 开创性的，突破性的
coarse gravel   粗砂砾
peaty ['pi:ti]   adj. 泥煤似的，多泥煤的
peaty soil   泥炭土
intermittent [,intə'mitənt]   adj. 间歇的，断断续续的；不持续的，不稳定的
intermittent sand filtration   间歇砂滤层
natural material   天然材料
attached growth processes/ fixed film   生物膜法
activated sludge processes   活性污泥法
filter media   过滤介质
natural draft   自然通风
forced draft   强迫通风
biomass ['baiəumæs]（单位面积或体积内）生物的数量
secondary treatment （对污水的）二次处理
septic tank   化粪池

primary treatment （下水道污水的）初级处理
raw wastewater 原废水
floating debris 漂浮物
in place 在适当的位置，已确定的，未移动
in motion 移动；运转
packing medium(pl. packing media) 填料[填密]介质
rotating distributor 旋转配流器
underdrain [ˌʌndəˈdreɪn] n. /v. 暗渠,阴沟；暗渠排水
rotating biological disk 生物转盘
shock loads 冲击荷重；突加载荷[生]（不利）负荷（指有害基因的存在）
biochemical oxygen demand (BOD) 生化需氧量
nitrification [ˌnaɪtrəfəˈkeɪʃən] n. （化）（使）硝化
denitrification [diːnaɪtrɪfɪˈkeɪʃən] n. （多指细菌）使（土壤，空气，水）脱氮（或脱硝）
hybrid [ˈhaɪbrɪd] n. 结合体；混合物
subsurface flow 地下水流；潜流
wetland 塘地

Notes

[1] 废水或生活污水处理，是指去除污水废水中污染物的过程。它包括物理、化学和生物过程，作用是去除物理、化学和生物污染物。其目的是集中产生废物流（或经处理的污水）以及固体废物或污泥进行处理或再进入环境。

[2] 与活性污泥法中降解废物的细菌在水池中悬浮生长相比，生物膜法中的活性细菌吸附在天然或人造滤料表面，并在其上形成膜状污泥——生物膜，使污水得到净化。

[3] 生物膜法工作原理是利用微生物除去污水中的有机物质，这些微生物主要是好氧生物——在有氧环境下生存的微生物，它们附着在滤料（如砾石、沙子或者泥煤）上生长，本质是污水与生物膜接触，污水中的有机污染物作为营养物质被生物膜上的微生物所摄取。

[4] 许多小型社区和私房屋主发现，单独使用滤池、生物转盘或者使其结合其他技术进行污水处理是低成本、较易维护的方法。

Exercises

1. Answering the following questions in English according to the text：

(1) What principle does the attached growth processes work on?

(2) To describe two basic designs of attached growth or fixed film systems according to the text.

2. Using the following each word to make up the the sentences respectively：

(1) filter

(2) microorganism

(3) nutrient

(4) aerobic

(5) organics

3. Put the following English into Chinese：

(1)There are two basic designs of attached growth or fixed film systems: those that hold the media in place, allowing the wastewater to flow over the bed (such as trickling filters), or those where the media is in motion relative to the wastewater (e.g. rotating biological disks).

(2)There are many variations and combinations of these processes, sometimes referred to as hybrids, which use the attached growth process in combination with other technologies such as types of attached growth filters: sand, peat, and textile filters; trickling filters and rotating biological contactors; and subsurface flow wetlands.

4. Put the following Chinese into English:

(1) 生物膜法

(2) 活性泥法

(3) 滴滤池

(4) 生物膜处理法的处理流程包括生物滤池和生物转盘，它们提供生物生长的媒体以使污水流过时进行处理。

(5) 因为生物膜过厚将会导致介质堵塞和滤池上表面积水。

5. Put the following abbr. into full phrases:

RBC；BOD

Reading Material A

Biological Contact Oxidation Process

The 19th century, Germany began to make biological contact oxidation method used for waste water treatment, but limited to the industrial level at that time, without the proper packing, failed to widely used. By the 1970s synthetic plastic industry developing quickly, light honeycomb of packing coming out, Japan and the United States, and began to research and application of biological contact oxidation. China in the 1970s began to study in this way the urban sewage and industrial waste water treatment, and has set up a file in the production application.

Features

Biological contact oxidation method is the basic characteristics of biological membrane method, and general biological membrane law is not the same. On the one hand, this method is used for microbial habitat of packing all dip in with the waste so biological contact oxidation pool and says submerged type ponds. On the other hand, it is the mechanical equipment to the waste oxygen filling, and different from the general bio-filter by natural ventilation for oxygen, which is equivalent to adding aeration for microbial habitat attached packing, can also be called aeration circular ponds or contact aeration pool.[1] The third characteristics is existing in the waste water in the pool about 2 to 5% of the state of suspension activated sludge, wastewater purification also play. And the biological contact oxidation is one kind has the characteristics of activated sludge biological membrane law, with biological membrane method and the advantages of activated sludge process.

Biological contact oxidation of purifying the wastewater basic principle and general biological membrane law the same, it is the biological film adsorption wastewater of organic matter, in aerobic conditions, by microbial organic oxidative decomposition, waste water and introspection.

The biological membrane in the Biological contact oxidation pool is made of filamentous fungi, fungi, protozoa and metazoan composition. In the activated sludge process, filamentous fungi are often affect the normal biological purification factor; And in the biological contact oxidation pool, filamentous fungi in packing space in between stereoscopic structure, greatly add to the Moluccas wastewater biological contact surface, at the same time as filamentous fungi for most organic matter has strong oxidation ability, to the water quality load change have larger adaptability, so is to improve the ability of purification powerful factors.

Processing device

According to the structure is divided into tap type and direct type two kinds, split type of aeration device in one side of the pool, packing into another side, rely on the ascension of the air pump or function, make water flow in packing layer inner circulation, the biological membrane to packing for oxygen. The advantages of this method are the wastewater compartment oxygen filling, oxygen supply full, on biological film growing favor. Defect is the utilization rate of oxygen is low, power consumption is bigger; for smaller hydraulic flushing action, the aging biological membrane is not easy to fall off, with a long cycle metabolism, biological activity small; at the same time in biological membrane off not easily and cause packing jam.[2]

Direct type is in the oxidation ponds packing bottom direct drum wind aeration. Biological membrane directly affected by the updraft strong disturbance, update the faster, keep the higher activity; At the same time in the water load stable, biological membrane can maintain certain thickness, not easy the clogging phenomenon.[3] General biological film thickness control in 1 mm or so is advisable.

Choose the proper packing to increase biofilm and wastewater biological membrane surface area is to improve the contact purifying the wastewater ability, the importance of the measures. General cell-shaped packing, honeycomb of packing shall be according to the wastewater quality aperture (BOD_5 namely BOD, five days of suspended solids concentration), BOD load, oxygen filling choose conditions and so on. Be in usually, BOD_5 concentration for 100-300 milligrams/litre, aperture can choose 32 mm; BOD_5 for 50-100 milligrams/litre can choose 15-20 mm; As in 50 mg/l the following, can choose 10-15 mm diameter of packing.

Packing to light quality, good intensity, strong corrosion resistance to oxidation, don't bring new poison. The currently used more have glass cloth, plastic honeycomb of packing, in addition, also can use rope, synthetic fiber, zeolite, coke and so on. Packing types have honeycomb, mesh, the ripple plate, etc.

Biological contact oxidation of BOD load and wastewater matrix of the concentration, the low BOD concentration (50-300 mg/L) wastewater each cubic meters of filler used daily 2-5 kg (BOD_5), waste water retention time of 0.5-1.5 hours, oxidation ponds oxygen internal friction of about 1-3 mg/L. By oxidation in the pool larger biomass, processing load is high, which can control the oxygen dissolved higher, general requirement oxidation ponds out the water dissolved oxygen remaining for 2-3 mg/L.

Biological contact oxidation method advantage is: purification efficiency; the time needed for processing short; to fill the change of organic load good adaptability; without return sludge, and no sludge inflation problem; Operation management convenient. The existing problem largely in the pool of biological membrane between packing which can appear sometimes jam phenomenon, is yet to be improved. The direction of the research in the light of different water load control aeration strength, in order to eliminate blocked; second is the study of the oxidation pond type and reasonable shape, size and material appropriate packing.[4]

Notes

[1] 二是采用机械设备向废水中充氧，而不同于一般生物滤池靠自然通风供氧，相当于在曝气池中添加供微生物栖附的填料，也可称为曝气循环型滤池或接触曝气池。

[2] 此法的优点是废水在隔间充氧，氧的供应充分，对生物膜生长有利。缺点是氧的利用率较低，动力消耗较大；因为水力冲刷作用较小，老化的生物膜不易脱落，新陈代谢周期较长，生物膜活性较小；同时还会因生物膜不易脱落而引起填料堵塞。

[3] 生物膜直接受到上升气流的强烈扰动，更新较快，保持较高的活性；同时在进水负荷稳定的情况下，生物膜能维持一定的厚度，不易发生堵塞现象。

[4] 研究的方向是针对不同的进水负荷控制曝气强度，以消除堵塞；其次是研究合理的氧化池池型和形状、尺寸和材质合适的填料。

Reading Material B

Trickling Filters

Trickling filters are by far the oldest attached growth process. This simple technology has been used for nearly 100 years to provide low-cost, low-maintenance, biological wastewater treatment. Trickling filters were developed from attempts at filtering municipal wastewater.

In older plants and those receiving variable loadings, trickling filter beds are used where the settled sewage liquor is spread onto the surface of a bed made up of coke (carbonized coal), limestone chips or specially fabricated plastic media. Such media must have large surface areas to support the biofilms that form. The liquor is typically distributed through perforated spray arms. The distributed liquor trickles through the bed and is collected in drains at the base. These drains also provide a source of air which percolates up through the bed, keeping it aerobic. Biological films of bacteria, protozoa and fungi form on the media's surfaces and eat or otherwise reduce the organic content. This biofilm is often grazed by insect larvae, snails, and worms which help maintain an optimal thickness. Overloading of beds increases the thickness of the film leading to clogging of the filter media and ponding on the surface. Recent advances in media and process micro-biology design overcome many issues with trickling filter designs.

How trickling filters work

A trickling filter are used where the settled effluent is spread onto the surface of a deep bed made up of rocks, lava, coke, gravel, slag, polyurethane foam, sphagnum peat moss, ceramic, or plastic media. Such media must have high surface areas to support the biolfilms that form. The effluent is distributed through perforated rotating arms radiating from a central pivot. The distributed effluent trickles through this bed and is collected in drains at the base. These drains also provide a source of air which percolates up through the bed, keeping it aerobic. [1] Biological films of bacteria, protozoa and fungi form on the media's surfaces and digest or otherwise reduce the organic content. This biofilm is grazed by insect larvae and worms which help maintain an optimal thickness. Overloading of beds increases the thickness of the film leading to clogging of the filter media and ponding on the surface.

The wastewater is applied to the surface of the filter (a bed of rocks, gravel or plastic). The wastewater percolates down through the bed to a drain where it collects and discharges, or sent for further cleaning (see Figure 15.4).

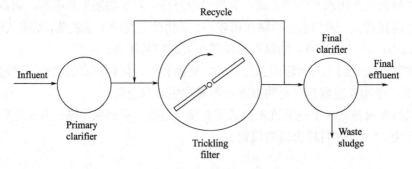

Figure 15.4 Flow diagram for trickling filters

A jelly-like biological film forms on the gravel or plastic where the bacteria break down the organic matter. The film becomes very thick and eventually falls off the supporting surface, and a new slime layer begins to grow in its place. This dropping off is called "sloughing" and should be a continuous process if the system is managed properly. Without the sloughing action, the media will clog and develop anaerobic conditions. The collected liquid is passed to a sedimentation tank where the solids are separated from the treated wastewater. The bacteria clumps that drop off must be treated as suspended solids.

Trickling filter design

Beds of conventional trickling filters are made up of crushed rock, slag, or gravel about 2 to 3 inches in size. The bed is commonly 6 to 10 feet deep, held in place by a reinforced concrete basin. When the media is made up of plastic tubes, which are very light weight, the height can be much greater-these systems can be as tall as 30 feet. These systems are sometimes called tower trickling filters or biotowers. Most newer trickling filters use plastic packing as the working media.

Conventional trickling filters are round in shape with centrally mounted rotating arms for distribution of the wastewater (see Figure 15.5). Nozzles on the arms spray the wastewater evenly across the media. Natural drafts are created by temperature differences between the outside air and air inside the filter. Deep tower filters sometimes require an additional air supply. The temperature of

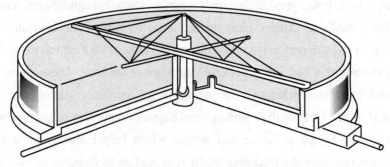

Figure 15.5 Cross-section of a trickling filter

the wastewater is more important to the success of the process than the air temperature.

Trickling filters show a high degree of reliability if operating conditions remain steady and the wastewater temperature does not fall below 55°F for prolonged periods. Sloughing tends to occur during seasonal temperature changes. Since the process is simple to operate, mechanical reliability is high. [2]

The trickling filter process is effective for removing suspended materials but is less effective for removing soluble organics. Figure 15.6 is overall layout including a trickling filter.

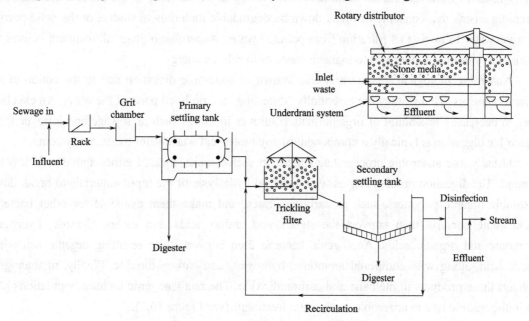

Figure 15.6 Overall layout including a trickling filter

Configurations and components

All sewage trickling filter systems share the same fundamental components:

- a septic tank for fermentation and primary settling of solids
- a filter medium upon which beneficial microbes are promoted and developed
- a container which houses the filter medium
- a distribution system for applying wastewater to be treated to the filter medium
- a distribution system for disposal of the treated effluent or percolation ponds[3]

Notes

[1] 滴滤池被用来解决在岩石、火山岩、焦炭、砂砾、矿渣、聚氨基甲酸乙酯泡沫材料、泥炭藓块或者塑料介质上漫流的污水。这种介质必须有足够的表面积以支持生物膜的形成。污水是由中心枢纽发出，通过旋转臂上的穿孔扩散的。扩散的污水穿过滤池，并在池底通过管道被收集。这些管道同时也让空气进入滤池，以保持其氧气的充足。

[2] 如果操作环境稳定并且污水温度不低于55°F，滴滤池会呈现出高度的安全性及稳定性。随着季节温度的变化，滴滤池会发生有机物剥落的现象。这个方法易操作，且机械可靠性高。

[3] 污水滴滤池有共同的基本部分：用于发酵和固体初级处理的化粪池；微生物介质；容纳介质的装置；将污水分洒到过滤介质上的分布系统；排污的分布系统。

Unit 16 Anaerobic Biological Treatment

Anaerobic biological treatment is a series of processes in which microorganisms break down biodegradable material in the absence of oxygen. After undergoing such a treatment, water can be safely released back into the environment. The biological agents used in the process are anaerobic microorganisms that consume or break down biodegradable materials in sludge, or the solid portion of wastewater following its filtration from polluted water. Anaerobic biological treatment is used for industrial or domestic purposes to manage waste or to release energy.

Anaerobic biological treatment is also known as anaerobic digestion due to the action of the microorganisms. That is, they are essentially "digesting" the polluted parts of the water. An excellent way to decrease the amount of organic matter leftover in things such as sewage and leftover food, anaerobic digestion is typically a component of any biological wastewater treatment system.

Usually, the anaerobic process takes place in sealed tanks, located either above or below the ground. The digestion process begins with bacterial hydrolysis of the input materials to break down insoluble organic polymers, such as carbonhydrates, and make them available for other bacteria. Acidogenic bacteria then convert the sugars and amino acids into carbon dioxide, hydrogen, ammonia and organic acids. Acetogenic bacteria then convert these resulting organic acids into acetic acid, along with additional ammonia, hydrogen, and carbon dioxide. Finally, methanogens convert these products to methane and carbon dioxide. The methanogenic archaea populations play an indispensable role in anaerobic wastewater treatments(see Figure 16.1).

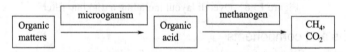

Figure 16.1 The anaerobic biological treatment process

There are four key biological and chemical stages of anaerobic biological treatment:
(1) Hydrolysis
(2) Acidogenesis
(3) Acetogenesis
(4) Methanogenesis

In most cases, biomass is made up of large organic polymers. For the bacteria in anaerobic digesters to access the energy potential of the material, these chains must first be broken down into their smaller constituent parts. These constituent parts, or monomers, such as sugars, are readily available to other bacteria. The process of breaking these chains and dissolving the smaller molecules into solution is called hydrolysis. Therefore, hydrolysis of these high-molecular-weight polymeric components is the necessary first step in anaerobic digestion. Through hydrolysis the complex organic molecules are broken down into simple sugars, amino acids, and fatty acids.

Acetate and hydrogen produced in the first stages can be used directly by methanogens. Other molecules, such as volatile fatty acids (VFAs) with a chain length greater than that of acetate must first be catabolised into compounds that can be directly used by methanogens.

The biological process of acidogenesis results in further breakdown of the remaining components by acidogenic (fermentative) bacteria. Here, VFAs are created, along with ammonia, carbon dioxide, and hydrogen sulfide, as well as other byproducts. The process of acidogenesis is similar to the way milk sours.

The third stage of anaerobic digestion is acetogenesis. Here, simple molecules created through the acidogenesis phase are further digested by acetogens to produce largely acetic acid, as well as carbon dioxide and hydrogen.

The terminal stage of anaerobic digestion is the biological process of methanogenesis. Here, methanogens use the intermediate products of the preceding stages and convert them into methane, carbon dioxide, and water. These components make up the majority of the biogas emitted from the system. Methanogenesis is sensitive to both high and low pHs and occurs between pH 6.5 and pH 8. The remaining, indigestible material the microbes cannot use and any dead bacterial remains constitute the digestate.

A simplified generic chemical equation for the overall processes outlined above is as follows:

$$C_6H_{12}O_6 \longrightarrow 3CO_2 + 3CH_4 \text{(see Figure 16.2)}$$

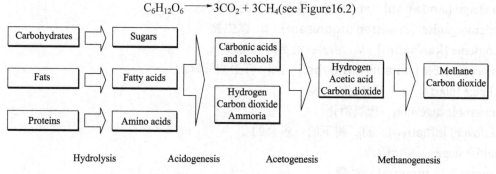

Figure 16.2 The key process stages of anaerobic digestion

We can get from the Figure 16.1 that during the initial stages of the sludge breakdown, the microorganisms, which are mostly bacteria, convert the waste into organic acids, ammonia, hydrogen and carbon dioxide. In the final stages of anaerobic wastewater treatment, the remains of the sludge are converted, by a single-celled microorganism known as a methanogen, into a biogas consisting of methane and carbon dioxide. Many in the scientific community believe that high concentrations of methane and carbon dioxide, also known as greenhouse gases, in Earth's atmosphere, contribute to the process of global warming. This theory, known as the greenhouse effect, postulates that these gases trap heat from the sun in the atmosphere, thereby increasing global temperature. While the theory has led to some controversy, using biogas as an alternative to fossil fuels has some practical applications. Anaerobic biological treatment is widely used as a source of renewable energy. The process produces a biogas, consisting of methane, carbon dioxide and traces of other contaminant gas. This biogas can be utilized directly as cooking fuel, in combined heat and power gas engines or upgraded to natural gas-quality biomethane. The use of biogas as a fuel helps to replace fossil fuels. The nutrient-rich digestate produced also can be used as fertilizer.[1]

An additional benefit of anaerobic biological treatment is its reduction of gas emissions. The biogas that results from the anaerobic wastewater treatment may actually be harnessed and used as an alternative power source for cooking, lighting, heating and engine fuel. In other words, by capturing and utilizing the methane and carbon dioxide produced by anaerobic digestion, the biogas is not released into the atmosphere. [2]

Compared with aerobic biological treatment, anaerobic biological treatment has the advantages of low energy consumption, low sludge production and recoverable gas energy. [3]

In developing countries, government-funded programs are available to help power single homes and farms with the biogas produced by on-site anaerobic digestion. [4] The United Nations also offers funding to anaerobic digestion programs in the developing world, provided proof of reduced gas emissions is available.

In the United States, anaerobic biological treatment is usually part of a municipal wastewater treatment plant. Still, anaerobic digestion is also used by single-family homes in areas not connected to a municipal system and by businesses with on-site wastewater treatment facilities.

Important Words and Expressions

oxygen-free   adj. 无氧气的
undergo [ˌʌndəˈɡəu]   vt. 经受；遭受；忍受
microorganism [ˌmaikrəuˈɔːɡənizəm]   n. 微生物
consume [kənˈsjuːm]   vt. 消耗，消费，耗尽
biodegradable [ˌbaiəudiˈɡreidəbəl]   adj. 可生物降解的
sludge [slʌdʒ]   n. 下水道的污泥
anaerobic digestion   厌氧消化
leftover [ˈleftˌəuvə]   adj. 剩下的，多余的
initial stages   初级阶段
ammonia [əˈməunjə]   n. 氨
hydrogen [ˈhaidrədʒen]   n. 氢，氢气
carbon dioxide   二氧化碳
methanogen [məˈθænəˌdʒen]   n. 产烷生物
biogas [ˈbaiəuɡæs]   n. 生物气，沼气
methane [ˈmeθˌein]   n. 甲烷
greenhouse gas   温室气体
postulate [ˈpɔstʃəˌleit]   vt. 假定，假设
controversy [ˈkɔntrəvəːsi]   n. 争议
fossil fuel   矿物燃料
carbohydrate   碳水化合物
fat   脂肪
protein [ˈprəutiːn]   adj. 蛋白质
fatty acid   脂肪酸
amino acid   氨基酸
carbonic acid   碳酸
acetic acid   乙酸
hydrolysis [haiˈdrɔlisis]   n. 水解作用
acidogenesis [əˈsidədʒenəsis]   n. 酸化

acetogenesis [ˈeisiteudʒiːnəsis] n.（乙）酸化
methanogenesis [meθənəuˈdʒenisis] n. 甲烷生成

Notes

[1] 厌氧生物处理被广泛用作可再生能源的来源,此过程产生沼气,包括甲烷、二氧化碳和微量的废气。这种沼气可直接用于燃料,热电联产和电力燃气发动机,或提炼成天然气。它可产生出沼气作为燃料取代化石燃料,也可产生营养丰富的沼肥可以用作肥料。

[2] 厌氧生物处理的另一个优点是减少气体的排放。厌氧生物处理产生的沼气可以转化为烹饪、照明、加热等能量燃料。换言之,收集并利用厌氧消化产生的甲烷和二氧化碳,生物气体就不会释放到大气中。

[3] 厌氧生物处理与好氧生物处理相比,具有能耗少、污泥产生量低、可回收沼气能源等优点。

[4] 在发展中国家,政府资金扶持项目用于帮助给家庭、农场供给厌氧消化产生的沼气能量。

Exercises

1. Answering the following questions in English according to the text:

(1) What is the anaerobic biological treatment?

(2) To describe the process of the anaerobic biological treatment.

2. Using the following each word to make up the the sentences respectively:

(1) biodegradable

(2) anaerobic

(3) ammonia

(4) methaogen

(5) greenhouse gas

3. Put the following English into Chinese:

(1) An excellent way to decrease the amount of organic matter leftover in things such as sewage and leftover food, anaerobic digestion is typically a component of any biological wastewater treatment system.

(2) Anaerobic digestion is also used by single-family homes in areas not connected to a municipal system and by businesses with on-site wastewater treatment facilities.

4. Put the following Chinese into English:

(1) 厌氧生物处理

(2) 厌氧消化

(3) 二氧化碳

(4) 废水厌氧生物处理是指在无氧条件下通过厌氧微生物的作用,将废水中的各种复杂有机物分解转化成甲烷和二氧化碳等物质的过程,也成为厌氧消化。

(5) 厌氧生物处理发展的初级阶段主要用于自动净化器、化粪池等废水粪便处理过程。

5. Put the following Chem. formula into full phrases:

NH_3; CO_2; CH_4; H_2

Reading Material A
Histories of Anaerobic Biological Treatment

Evidence indicates that biogas was used for heating bath water in Assyria during the 10th century BC and in Persia during the 16th century. Scientific interest in the manufacturing of gas produced by the natural decomposition of organic matter was first reported in the 17th century. Jan Baptita Van Helmont first determined in 17th century that flammable gases could evolve from decaying organic matter. Count Alessandro Volta concluded in 1776 that there was a direct correlation between the amount of decaying organic matter and the amount of flammable gas produced. In 1808, Sir Humphry Davy determined that methane was present in the gases produced by cattle manure. The first anaerobic biological treatment plant was built by a leper colony in Bombay, India, in 1859. In 1895, the technology was developed in Exeter, England, where a septic tank was used to generate gas for the sewer gas destructor lamp, a type of gas lighting. Also in England, in 1904, the first dual-purpose tank for both sedimentation and sludge treatment was installed in Hampton. In 1907, in Germany, a patent was issued for the Imhoff tank, an early form of digest. [1]

Through scientific research, anaerobic biological treatment gained academic recognition in the 1930s. This research led to the discovery of anaerobic bacteria, the microorganisms that facilitate the process. Further research was carried out to investigate the conditions under which methanogenic bacteria were able to grow and reproduce. [2]

In the world of anaerobic biological treatment technology, farm-based facilities are perhaps the most common. Six to eight million family-sized, low-technology digesters are used to provide biogas for cooking and lighting fuels with varying degrees of success. In China and India, there is a trend toward using larger, more sophisticated systems with better process control that generate electricity.

This work was developed during World War II, during which in both Germany and France, there was an increase in the application of anaerobic biological treatment for the treatment of manure. Some anaerobic biological treatment facilities in Europe have been in operation for more than 20 years. More than 600 farm-based digesters operate in Europe, where the key factor found in the successful facilities is their design simplicity. Around 250 of these systems have been installed in Germany alone in the past 5 years. Other factors influencing success have been local environmental regulations and other policies governing land use and waste disposal. Because of these environmental pressures, many nations have implemented or are considering methods to reduce the environmental impacts of waste disposal.

The country with the greatest experience using large-scale anaerobic biological treatment facilities has been Denmark, where 18 large centralized plants are now in operation. In many cases these facilities codigest manure, clean organic industrial wastes, and source separated municipal solid waste (MSW). The anaerobic biological treatment in Denmark increased with an energy initiative that doubled biogas production by the year 2000, and tripled it by the year 2005.

The use of the anaerobic biological treatment for treating industrial wastewaters has grown tremendously during the past decade. Worldwide, more than 1000 vendor-supplied systems now operate or are under construction. It is estimated that European plants comprise 44% of the installed base. Only 14% of the systems are located in North America. A considerable number of the systems are located in South America, primarily Brazil, where they are used to treat the vinasse coproduct from sugar cane-based ethanol production.

More than 35 example industries that use anaerobic biological treatment have been identified, including processors of chemicals, fiber, food, meat, milk, and pharmaceuticals. Many use anaerobic biological treatment as pretreatment step that lowers sludge disposal costs, controls odors, and reduces the costs of final treatment at a municipal wastewater treatment facility. [3]From the perspective of the municipal facility, pretreatment effectively expands treatment capacity.

Although the first digester to use MSW as a feedstock operated in the United States from 1939-1974, it is receiving renewed interest. MSW processing facilities have made significant progress towards commercial use in recent years, with several in operation for more than 15 years. A number of types of systems have been developed; each has its own special benefits.

Technology for MSW is commercially available and in use, but its further application is limited mainly by environmental aspects and process economics. Anaerobic biological treatment is a net energy-producing process, with around 75-150 kWh of electricity created per ton of MSW input. MSW digestion technology is now being demonstrated and fully commercialized.

MSW digestion poses many technical problems. High-solid digestion (HSD) systems have been developed with the potential to improve the economic performance of MSW systems by reducing digester volume and the parasitic energy required for the anaerobic biological treatment process. Several alternative HSD designs have been developed that operate with total solids (TS) concentrations greater than 30%. These designs employ either external or internal mixing, using biogas or mechanical stirrers. In general, all HSD systems have equivalent performance.

Notes

[1] 1859 年，第一个厌氧生物处理厂建于印度孟买的一家麻风病人隔离区。1895 年，此项技术在英国埃克塞特得到发展,这里的一家化粪池产生气体用于路灯照明。而且在英格兰,1904 年，第一座既用于沉淀池又用于污泥处理池的双重功能池在汉普顿建立。1907 年，一项专利——依姆荷夫槽(双层污水处理装置)在德国审批，这是厌氧消化的雏形。

[2] 经过科学研究，厌氧生物处理于 19 世纪 30 年代得到学术认可。这项研究导致了厌氧细菌的发现，这种微生物也推动了处理过程。更进一步的研究用于调查产烷细菌的生长及再生环境。

[3] 已查明有 35 余种工业使用厌氧生物处理，这些工业有化工、纤维、食品、肉类、奶类和制药类等工业。大多数人把厌氧生物处理作为城市污水厂的预处理，它可以降低污泥处理费用，减少气味和降低最终处理费用。

Reading Material B

Upflow Anaerobic Sludge Blanket Reactor

In developing countries, few reliable figures exist on the share of the wastewater collected in sewers that is being treated in the world. In many developing countries the bulk of domestic and industrial wastewater is discharged without any treatment or after primary treatment only. In Latin America about 15% of collected wastewater passes through treatment plants (with varying levels of actual treatment). In Venezuela, a below average country in South America with respect to wastewater treatment, 97 percent of the country's sewage is discharged raw into the environment. In a relatively developed Middle Eastern country such as Iran, the majority of Tehran's population has totally untreated sewage injected to the city's groundwater. However now the construction of major parts of the sewage system, collection and treatment, in Tehran is almost completed, and under development, due to be fully completed by the end of 2012. In Isfahan, Iran's third largest city, sewage treatment was started more than 100 years ago.In Israel, about 50 percent of agricultural water usage (total use was 1 billion cubic metres in 2008) is provided through reclaimed sewer water. Future plans call for increased use of treated sewer water as well as more desalination plants. Most of sub-Saharan Africa is without wastewater treatment.

Industrialization is vital to a nation's economy because it serves as a vehicle for development. However, there are associated problems resulting from the introduction of industrial waste products into the environment. For example, textile industry, which is one the largest water consumer in the world, produces the effluents that contain several types of chemicals such as dispersants, leveling agents, acids, alkalis, carriers and various dyes. Color is one of the most obvious indicators of water pollution and discharge of highly colored synthetic dye effluents can be damaging the receiving water bodies. The release of colored compounds into water bodies is undesirable not only because of their impact on photosynthesis of aquatic plants but also due to the carcinogenic nature of many of these dyes and their break-down products. Therefore, it is necessary to treat completely these types of wastewater before releasing to environment. Upflow anaerobic sludge blanket reactor with anaerobic digester sludge treating starch wastewater has been used to investigate the removal efficiency of chemical oxygen demand(COD) and color of textile dye wastewater.

Upflow anaerobic sludge blanket (UASB) technology, normally referred to as UASB reactor, is a form of anaerobic digester that is used in the treatment of wastewater. [1]

The UASB reactor is a methanogenic (methane-producing) digester that evolved from the anaerobic digester. A similar but variant technology to UASB is the expanded granular sludge bed (EGSB) digester.

UASB uses an anaerobic process whilst forming a blanket of granular sludge which suspends in the tank. Wastewater flows upwards through the blanket and is processed (degraded) by the anaerobic microorganisms. The upward flow combined with the settling action of gravity suspends the blanket with the aid of flocculants. [2] The blanket begins to reach maturity at around 3 months. Small sludge granules begin to form whose surface area is covered in aggregations of bacteria. In the absence of any support matrix, the flow conditions create a selective environment in which only those microorganisms, capable of attaching to each other, survive and proliferate. Eventually the aggregates form into dense compact biofilms referred to as "granules". A picture of anaerobic sludge granules can be found here.

Biogas with a high concentration of methane is produced as a by-product, and this may be captured and used as an energy source, to generate electricity for export and to cover its own running power.[3] The technology needs constant monitoring when put into use to ensure that the sludge blanket is maintained, and not washed out (thereby losing the effect). The heat produced as a by-product of electricity generation can be reused to heat the digestion tanks.

The blanketing of the sludge enables a dual solid and hydraulic (liquid) retention time in the digesters. Solids requiring a high degree of digestion can remain in the reactors for periods up to 90 days. Sugars dissolved in the liquid waste stream can be converted into gas quickly in the liquid phase which can exit the system in less than a day.

UASB reactors are typically suited to dilute waste water streams (3% TSS with particle size >0.75mm).

Conventional treatment settles sludge which is then digested, and then aerates the remaining liquids which use bacteria to oxidise the potential digester fuel, and uses up energy to drive the compressors. The result is that on a standard western treatment works the energy produced from settled sludge digestion is all used by the aeration process, with little power export.

With UASB the aeration the whole process of settlement and digestion occurs in one or more large tank(s). Only the UASB liquids, with reduced BOD, needs to be aerated.

This leads to a halving of the aeration energy and a doubling of the power generated from digestion, leading over all to a tripling of power generated.

UASB has many features in the aspect of treating wastewater.

UASB solves air, liquid and solid problems during different kinds of reactors. The treatment effect is reliable in treating industrial or domestic wastewater and it currently has been extensively applied for food, beer and beverage, paper making, chemical, municipal and other industries.

Notes

[1] 上流式厌氧污泥床技术，即 UASB 反应器，是污水处理过程中厌氧消化的一种形式。

[2] 上流式厌氧污泥床利用厌氧环境同时形成悬浮在池中的颗粒污泥区。污水向上流动经过厌氧细菌附着的污泥床并且被厌氧微生物降解。向上流和重力沉淀作用在絮凝剂的协助下使污泥层处于悬浮状态。

[3] 沼气副产品中具有高浓度的甲烷，沼气被收集并作为发电的能源弥补自身运行能耗。

Part Five

Sludge Treatment, Reuse and Disposal

Unit 17 Thickening

The solids content of primary, activated, trickling filter, or mixed sludge(i.e., primary plus activated) varies considerably, depending on the characteristics of the sludge, the sludge-removal and-pumping facilities, and the method of operation. Thickening is a procedure used to increase the solids content of slude by removing a portion of the liquid fraction. To illustrate, if waste activated sludge, which is typically pumped from secondary settling tanks with a content of 0.8 percent solids, can be thickened to a content of 4 percent solids, then a fivefold decrease in sludge volume is achieved. Thickening is generally accomplished by physical means, including gravity settling, flotation, and centrifugation. Some of the possibilities for separate sludge thickening are presented in Table 17.1.

Table 17.1 Occurrence of thickening methods in sludge processing

Method	Type of sludge	Frequency of use and relative success
Gravity	Untreated primary	Increasing; excellent results
Gravity	Untreated primary and waste activated sludge	Often used, especially for small plants; satisfactory results with sludge concentrations in the range of 4 to 6 percent
Gravity	Untreated primary and waste activated sludge	Some new installation; marginal results
Gravity	Waste activated sludge	Essentially never used; poor results
Gravity	Digested primary and waste activated sludge mixture	Used to a lesser extent in new plants; used to reduce the amount of conditioning chemicals prior to mechanical dewatering
Dissolved-air flotation	Untreated primary and waste activated sludge	Some limited use
Dissolved-air flotation	Waste activated sludge	Increasing; good results
Solid-bowl conveyor centrifuge	Waste activated sludge	Some limited use; solids capture problem
Disk centrifuge	Waste activated sludge	Some limited use; data now being accumulated

Application

The volume reduction obtained by sludge concentration is beneficial to subsequent treatment processes, such as digestion, dewatering, drying, and combustion, from the following standpoints: (1) capacity of tanks and equipment required, (2) quantity of chemicals required for sludge conditioning, and (3) amount of heat required by digesters and amount of auxiliary fuel required for heat drying or incineration, or both.

On large projects when sludge must be transported a significant distance, such as to a separate plant for processing, a reduction in sludge volume may result in a reduction of pipe size and pumping costs. On small projects, the requirements of a minimum practicable pipe size and minimum velocity may necessitate the pumping of significant volumes of wastewater in addition to sludge, which diminishes the value of volume reduction. [1] Volume reduction is very desirable when liquid sludge is transported by tank trucks for direct application to land as a solid conditioner.

Sludge Thickening Equipment

Mechanical type sludge thickening equipment uses physical process to concentrate the sludge by removing the water portion thus leading to increased amount of the solid percentage. There are different methods to achieve this and generally taking out the average of all the available options, usually the sludge content can be increased by 4-5 folds depending on how well the equipment is operated. [2] Let us study some of the options available which are commonly used in the industries' wastewater treatment systems.

Gravity Thickening

Method relying on gravity principle can be applied to both untreated primary and even waste activated sludge. It is normally done in a circular tank similar in design compared with a typical plant sedimentation tank. Flow of sludge coming from the aeration system is directed to the center well and the design is such that there is sufficient detention time enough for good settling to take place. Waste that is collected at the bottom of the tank is allowed to settle, become compact and then pumped out from the bottom effluent outlet pipe going to either a digester or secondary dewatering equipment. Usually there is a weir and channel for the clarified water to overflow out and the rotating raking arm with blade will turn in circular motion in order to create a slow stirring effect. [3] What result is that by doing this, it will ensure that compactness will take place and get the sludge to travel to the bottom. Occasionally process can be improved by slowing down the feed rate while the design must be properly planned out to allow sufficient detention time.

Flotation Thickening

Flotation thickening is considered an improved process of the gravity method and basically it uses similar principle as mentioned before like the DAF system. To recap back, what it does is that compressed air is introduced to the incoming feed channel and then these are diverted to a pressure vessel in order to force air to dissolve in the water. After that, the flow will be slowly released so that when exposed to atmospheric pressure, dissolved air will become finely dispersed bubbles, carrying together with them the sludge floating to the top. Flotation method is normally applied to waste activated sludge and the efficiency of the system normally takes into account the air to solid ratio and sometimes addition of coagulant or polymer is used to aid in the separation process. [4] Other parameters that need to be taken into consideration are mainly the loading rate on how the incoming flow can be adjusted or lowered down so that air to solid ratio is improved. Apart from that, settling characteristics of the solid waste measured in SVI value is also another factor that determines the efficiency of the unit. Obviously the lower the SVI (below 50), the better it gets and this is the most ideal condition to get a good separation.

Centrifugal Thickening

This method is often applied to waste solids coming from suspended growth biological treatment process. Generally it can be used in tandem along with the gravity thickener to further concentrate and increase the solid content.[5] As mentioned earlier, not only does it play the role and function to thicken the sludge but it helps in dewatering process as well. For more information, refer to the solid bowl centrifuge and the imperforated basket design which are two of the main and most commonly used technology in most industrial effluent treatment plants.

Important Words and Expressions

trickling filter　滴滤池
centrifugation [sen,trifju'geiʃən]　n. 离心法；离心过滤
conveyor [kən'veiə]　n. 传送带；传送装置
disk centrifuge　盘式离心机
auxiliary [ɔːg'ziljəri]　adj. 辅助的
desirable [di'zaiərəbl]　adj. 可取的，合意的
compactness [kəm'pæktnis]　n. 紧密，坚实
recap back　扼要重述；概括
coagulant [kəu'ægjələnt]　n. 絮凝剂
polymer ['pɔləmə]　n. 聚合物（体）
tandem ['tændəm]　n. 串联
imperforate [im'pəːfərit]　adj. 无洞的，无孔的

Notes

[1] 在小工程中，满足最小可用的管径和最小速度的要求就能够抽提大量的污水和污泥，这降低了污泥量减少的价值。

[2] 有很多方法能够达到这种效果，而且通常情况下，根据设备运行的情况，各种可行的方法都能将污泥固体含量提高4～5倍。

[3] 通常澄清水通过堰板和渠道实现溢流，同时一个带有叶片的耙臂做圆周运动以此产生缓慢搅拌的作用。

[4] 气浮浓缩方法通常应用于活性污泥，系统的效率通常需要考虑气固比，有时投加混凝剂或聚合物来帮助分离过程。

[5] 一般离心分离串联在重力浓缩机之后，进一步浓缩和增加固体含量。

Exercises

1. Answering the following questions in English according to the text:

(1) The volume reduction obtained by sludge concentration is beneficial to subsequent treatment processes, why?

(2) what thickening equipments are commonly used in the industries' wastewater treatment systems?

2. Using the following each word to make up the sentences, respectively:
   (1) illustrate
   (2) obtain
   (3) operate
   (4) commonly
   (5) rely on …

3. Put the following English into Chinese:

(1) In addition to the physical and chemical characteristics, the biological parameters of sludge can also be important. The volatile solids parameter is in fact often interpreted as a biological characteristic; the assumption being the VSS is a gross measure of viable biomass. Another important parameter, especially in regard to ultimate disposal, is the concentration of pathogens, both bacteriological and viral. The primary clarifier seems to act like a viral and bacteriological concentrator, with a substantial fraction of these microorganisms existing in the sludge instead of the liquid effluent.

(2) Reuse of composted sludge as a soil conditioner in agriculture and horticulture returns carbon, nitrogen, phosphorus and elements essential for plant growth back to the soil. Less chemical fertilisers are required and the organic carbon helps to improve soil structure for soil aeration, water percolation and root growth. The nitrogen and phosphorus are also released gradually for plant uptake compared to the more soluble chemical fertilisers. The potential of leaching of the nutrients to ground or surface water by rainfall run-off is much reduced. Pathogens and heavy metals can, however, limit the reuse of sludge.

4. Put the following Chinese into English:
   (1) 活性污泥的固体含量
   (2) 重力沉降
   (3) 离心分离
   (4) 如果二沉池的活性污泥的固体含量从0.8%浓缩到4%，这样污泥的体积能够减少5倍。
   (5) 浮选浓缩被认为是重力法的改善方法。

Reading Material A

Sources and Characteristics of Solids and Sludge

To design sludge-processing, -treatment, and –disposal facilities properly, the sources, characteristics, and quantities of the solids and sludge to be handled must be known. Therefore, the purpose of this section is to present background data and information on these topics, which will serve as a basis for the material to be presented in the subsequent sections of this chapter.

Sources

The sources of solids in a treatment plant vary according to the type of plant and its method of operation. The principal sources of solids and sludge and the types generated are reported in Table 17.2. For example, in a continuous-flow stirred-tank activated-sludge process, if sludge wasting is accomplished from the mixed-liquor line or aeration chamber, the activated-sludge settling tank is not a source of sludge. On the other hand, if wasting is accomplished from the solids return line, the activated-sludge settling tank constitutes a sludge sources. If the sludge from the mixed-liquor line or aeration chamber is returned to the primary settling tank for thickening, this obviates the need for a thickener and therefore reduces by one the number of independent sludge sources in the treatment plant. [1] Processes used for thickening, digesting, conditioning, and filtering the sludge produced from primary and activated-sludge settling tanks also constitute sludge sources.

Table 17.2 Sources of solids and sludge from a conventional wastewater-treatment facility

Unit operation or process	Type of solids or sludge	Remarks
Screening	Coarse solids	Coarse solids are often comminuted and returned to the wastewater for removal in subsequent treatment facilities
Grit removal	Grit and scum	Scum removal facilities are often omitted on grit removal facilities
Preaeration	Scum	In some plants, scum removal facilities are not provided in preaeration tanks
Primary sedimentation	Primary sludge and scum	The quantities of both sludge and scum depend on the nature of the collection system and whether industrial wastes are discharged to the system
Aeration tank	Suspended solids	Suspended solids are produced from the conversion of BOD. If wasting is from the aeration tank, flotation thickening is normally used to thicken the waste activated sludge
Secondary sedimentation	Secondary sludge and scum	Provision for scum removal on secondary settling tanks is now a requirement of the U.S. Environmental Protection Agency
Sludge-processing facilities	Sludge and ashes	The characteristics and moisture content of the sludge and ashes depend on the operations and processes that are used

Characteristics

To treat and dispose of the sludge produced from wastewater-treatment plants in the most effective manner, it is important to know the characteristics of the solids and sludge that will be processed. The characteristics vary depending on the origin of the solids and sludge, the amount of aging that has taken place, and the type of processing to which they have been subjected.[2] Some of the physical characteristics are summarized in Table 17.3.

Table 17.3 Characteristics of sludge produced during wastewater treatment

Solids or sludge	Description
Screening	Screenings include all type of organic and inorganic materials large enough to be removed on bar racks. The organic content varies, depending on the nature of the system and the season of the year
Grit	Grit is usually made up of the heavier inorganic solids that settle with relatively high velocities. Depending on the operating velocities, grit may also contain significant amounts of organic matter, specially fats and grease
Scum	Scum consists of the floatable materials skimmed from the surface of primary and secondary settling tanks. It may include grease, vegetable and mineral oils, animal fats, waxes, soaps, food waste, vegetable, skins, hair, paper and cotton, cigarette tips, plastic suppositories, rubber prophylactics, grit particles, and similar materials. The specific gravity of scum is less than 1.0 and usually around 0.95
Primary sludge	Sludge from primary sedimentation tank is usually gray and slimy and, in most cases, has an extremely offensive odor. It can be readily digested under suitable conditions of operation
Chemical-precipitation sludge	Sludge from chemical precipitation tank is usually dark in color, though its surface may be red if it contains much iron. Its odor may be objectionable, but not as bad as odor from primary sedimentation sludge. While it is somewhat slimy, the hydrate of iron or aluminum in it makes it gelatinous. If it is left in the tank, it undergoes decomposition like the sludge from primary sedimentation but at a slower rate. It gives off gas in substantial quantities and its density is increased by standing

Solids or sludge	Description
Activated sludge	Activated sludge generally has a brown flocculant appearance. If the color is quite dark, it may be approaching a septic condition. If the color is lighter than usual, there may have been unde raeration with a tendency for the solids to settle slowly. Sludge in good condition has an inoffensive characteristic odor. It tends to become septic rather rapidly and then has a disagreeable odor of putrefaction. It will digest readily alone or mixed with fresh wastewater solids
Trickling-filter sludge	Trickling-filter humus is brownish, flocculant, and relatively inoffensive when fresh. It generally undergoes decomposition more slowly than other undigested sludge, but when it contains many worms it may become offensive quickly. It is readily digested
Digested sludge (aerobic)	Aerobically digested sludge is brown to dark and has a flocculant appearance. The odor of aerobically digested sludge is not offensive; it is often characterized as musty. Well-digested aerobic sludge dewaters easily, and the resulting dry solids inoffensive
Digested sludge (anaerobic)	Anaerobically digested sludge is dark brown to dlack and contains an exceptionally large quantity of gas. When thoroughly digested, it is not offensive, its odor being relatively faint and like that of hot tar, burnt rubber, or sealing wax. When drawn off on porous beds in thin layers, the solids first are carried to the surface by the entrained gases, leaving a sheet of comparatively clear water below them which drains off rapidly and allows the solids to sink down slowly on to the bed. [3] As the sludge dries, the gases escape, leaving a well-cracked surface with an odor resembling that of garden loam
Septage	Sludge from septic tanks is black. Unless well digested by long storage, it is offensive because of the hydrogen sulfide and other gases it gives off. The sludge can be dried on porous beds if spread out in thin layers, but objectionable odors are to be expected while it is draining unless it has been well digested

Typical data on the chemical composition of untreated and digested sludges are reported in Table 17.4. Many of the chemical constituents, including nutrients, are important in considering the ultimate disposal of the processed sludge and the liquid removed from the sludge during processing. [4] The fertilizer value of sludge, which should be evaluated where the sludge is to be used as a soil conditioner, is based primarily on the content of nitrogen, phosphorus, and potash. The measurement of pH, alkalinity, and organic acid content is important in process control of anaerobic digestion.

Table 17.4　Typical chemical composition of untreated and digested sludge

Item	Untreated primary sludge		Digested sludge	
	Range	Typical	Range	Typical
Total dry solids(TS), %	2.0-8.0	5.0	6.0-12.0	10.0
Volatile solids (% of TS)	60-80	65	30-60	40.0
Grease and fats (ether-soluble, % of TS)	6.0-30.0	—	5.0-20.0	—
Protein (% of TS)	20-30	25	15-20	18
Nitrogen (N, % of TS)	1.5-6.0	4.0	1.6-6.0	4.0
Phosphorus (P_2O_5, % of TS)	0.8-3.0	2.0	1.5-4.0	2.5
Potash (K_2O, % of TS)	0-1.0	0.4	0.0-3.0	1.0
Cellulose (% of TS)	8.0-15.0	10.0	8.0-15.0	10.0
Iron (not as sulfide)	2.0-4.0	2.5	3.0-8.0	4.0
Silica (SiO_2, % of TS)	15.0-20.0	—	10.0-20.0	—
pH	5.0-8.0	6.0	6.5-7.5	7.0
Alkalinity (mg/L as $CaCO_3$)	500-1500	600	2500-3500	3000
Organic acids (mg/L as HAc)	200-2000	500	100-600	200
Thermal content (MJ/kg)	14-23	16.5[a]	6-14	9[b]

[a] Based on 65 percent volatile matter.
[b] Based on 40 percent volatile matter.
Note: MJ/kg×429.92 = Btu/lb

Selected from "Syed R.Qasim.Wastewater Treatment Plants:Planning, Design, and Operation. Technomic Publishing Company, 1999."

Notes

[1] 如果来自混合液的污泥或者曝气池中的污泥返回到初沉池中浓缩,就能避免使用浓缩池,因而在污水厂中就可以减少一个独立的污泥来源。

[2] 固体和污泥的特征根据其来源,老化发生时间的长短,以及处理的方法不同而不同。

[3] 当薄层上多孔床中的固体被排走时,这些固体首先被产生的气体托到表层,留下相对较干净的水,这些水迅速被排走,使固体慢慢下沉到多孔床上。

[4] 在考虑污泥的最终处置和污泥处理中分离出的液体时,包括营养物质在内的很多化学物质都起着很重要的作用。

Reading Material B

Introduction of Flotation Thickening

Flotation Processes

Flotation is a solid-liquid separation process. Separation is artificially induced by introducing fine gas bubbles (usually air) into the flotation process system. The gas bubbles become attached to the solid particulates, forming a gas-solid aggregate with an overall bulk density less than the density of the liquid; thus, these aggregates rise to the surface of the fluid.[1] Once the solid particles have been floated to the surface, they can be collected by a skimming operation.

In potable water treatment and wastewater treatment, flotation is used successfully as a clarification process to remove coagulated/flocculated impurities and suspended solids. In sludge treatment, flotation is used as a thickening process to concentrate various types of organic and chemical sludges.

Air flotation systems may be classified as: (1) dispersed air flotation and (2) dissolved air flotation (DAF). In dispersed air flotation, air bubbles are generated by introducing air through a revolving impeller or porous media. This type of flotation system finds some special application in wastewater treatment when wastewater contains surface-active agents or separate suspended particles on the basis of its surface energy. Another chapter of this handbook entitled, "Dispersed Air Flotation and Electroflotation" presents the dispersed air flotation process in detail.

DAF may be subclassified as: (1) pressure flotation and (2) vacuum flotation. Pressure flotation involves air being dissolved in the wastewater under elevated pressures and later released at atmospheric pressure.[2] Vacuum flotation, however, consists of applying a vacuum to wastewater aerated at atmospheric pressure. Dissolved air-pressure flotation, considered herein, is the most commonly used in treatment of potable water, wastewater, and sludge. Since the applications of DAF for water and wastewater treatment are introduced elsewhere, this chapter emphasizes only DAF thickening processes.

Other flotation processes, which can be used for sludge thickening include:
- Electroflotation.
- Biological flotation.
- Sequencing batch flotation.

Electroflotation and sequencing batch flotation are discussed elsewhere in this handbook series in detail. Biological flotation adopts the chemistry of nitrification and denitrification for generation of fine nitrogen and carbon dioxide bubbles in its flotation thickening process reactors for concentration of mainly waste activated sludges (WAS). [3]

DAF Thickener Components

The principal components of a dissolved air-pressure flotation system are a pressurizing pump, air injection facilities, a pressure retention tank, a backpressure- regulating device, usually a throttling valve, and a flotation unit. The primary variables for flotation design are pressure, recycle ratio, feed solid concentration, detention period, air-to-solids ratio, and solids and hydraulic loadings. Optimum design parameters must be obtained from bench scale or pilot plant studies.

DAF Thickener Advantages and Disadvantages

Since the 1957 installation of the first municipal DAF thickener in the Bay Park Sewage treatment plant, Nassau County, New York, about 300 US municipal installations (over 700 units) have been installed. Although the principal use of the DAF thickener has been to thicken WAS, about 20% of the installations handle other sludge types. Table 17.5 lists the types of municipal wastewater sludges currently being thickened by DAF thickeners.

Table 17.5 Design criteria of DAF thickening process based on the types of sludges

Sludge type	Feed solids concentration (%)	Typical loading rate without polymer (lb/ft^2/d)	Typical loading rate with polymer (lb/ft^2/d)	Float solids concentration (%)
Primary + WAS	2	20	60	5.5
Primary +(WAS + FeCl$_3$)	1.5	15	45	3.5
(Primary + FeCl$_3$) +WAS	1.8	15	45	4
WAS	1	10	30	3
WAS + FeCl$_3$	1	10	30	2.54
Digested primary +WAS	20	60	10	4
Digested primary +(WAS + FeCl$_3$)	4	15	45	8
Tertiary (alum)	1	8	24	2

Source: US EPA.

WAS = waste activated sludge.

The following are the advantages and disadvantages of DAF thickeners compared with other major thickening equipment. The advantages of a DAF thickener are:

(1) It provides better solids-liquid separation than a gravity thickener.

(2) For many sludges, it yields a higher concentration of solids than a gravity thickener.

(3) It requires less area than a gravity thickener.

(4) It offers excellent sludge equalization control.

(5) It has less chance of odor problems than a gravity thickener.

(6) It can remove grit from a sludge processing system.

(7) It removes grease.

The disadvantages of a DAF thickener are:

(1) Its operating cost is higher than for a gravity thickener with equal flow capacity.

(2) DAF-thickened sludge concentration is less than in a centrifuge.

(3) It requires more area than a centrifuge.

(4) It has very little sludge storage capacity.

Selected from "Lawrence K. Wang, Nazih K. Shammas, William A. Selke, and Donald B. Aulenbach. BIOSOLIDS TREATMENT PROCESSES, Handbook of Environmental Engineering, 2007, Volume 6, 71-100"

Notes

[1] 气泡附着在固体颗粒表面，形成一个气固聚合体，它的整体密度比水的密度小；因此这些聚合体能够上升到液体的表面。

[2] 溶气气浮法可以细分为（1）加压溶气气浮和（2）真空气浮两种类型。加压溶气气浮是将空气在加压条件下溶解在污水中，在大气压下释放。

[3] 生物浮选采用在气浮浓缩反应器中的硝化和反硝化反应生成的氮气和二氧化碳气泡来浓缩剩余活性污泥。

Unit 18　Anaerobic Digestion

The purpose of digestion is to attain both of the objectives of sludge treatment-a reduction in volume and the decomposition of highly putrescible organic matter to relatively stable or inert organic and inorganic compounds.[1] Additionally, anaerobic sludge digestion produces a valuable by-product in the form of methane gas.

General Description

Sludge digestion is carried out in the absence of free oxygen by anaerobic organisms. It is, therefore, anaerobic decomposition. The solid matter in raw sludge is about 70 percent organic and 30 percent inorganic or mineral. Much of the water in wastewater sludge is "bound" water which will not be separated from the sludge solids. The facultative and anaerobic organisms break down the complex molecular structure of these solids setting free the "bound" water and obtaining oxygen and food for their growth.[2]

Anaerobic digestion involves many complex biochemical reactions and is dependent on many interrelated physical and chemical factors. For purposes of simplification, the anaerobic degradation of domestic sludges occurs in two steps.

In the first step, acid forming bacteria attack the soluble or dissolved solids, such as the sugars. From these reactions organic acids, at times up to several thousand ppm, and gases, such as carbon dioxide and hydrogen sulfide are formed. This is known as the stage of acid fermentation and proceeds rapidly. It is followed by a period of acid digestion in which the organic acids and nitrogenous compounds are attacked and liquefied at a much slower rate.

In the second stage of digestion, known as the period of intensive digestion, stabilization and gasification, the more resistant nitrogenous materials, such as the proteins, amino-acids and others, are attacked.[3] The pH value must be maintained from 6.8 to 7.4. Large volumes of gases with a 65 or higher percentage of methane are produced. Methane is an odorless, highly inflammable gas which can be used as a fuel. The organisms which convert organic acids to methane and carbon dioxide gases are called methane formers. The solids remaining are relatively stable or only slowly putrescible, can be disposed of without creating objectionable conditions and have value in agriculture.

The whole process of sludge digestion may be likened to a factory production line where one group of workers takes the raw material and conditions it for a second group with different "skills" who convert the material to the end products.

In a healthy, well operating digester, both of the above stages are taking place continuously and at the same time. Fresh wastewater solids are being added at frequent intervals with the stabilized solids being removed for further treatment or disposal at less frequent intervals. The supernatant digester liquor, the product of liquefaction and mechanical separation is removed frequently to make room for the added fresh solids and the gas is, of course, being removed continuously.

While all stages of digestion may be proceeding in a tank at the same time with the acids produced in the first stage being neutralized by the ammonia produced in subsequent stages, best and quickest results are obtained when the over-all pH of 6.8 to 7.4 predominates.[4] The first stage of acid formation should be evident only in starting up digestion units. Once good alkaline digestion is established, the acid stage is not apparent unless the normal digestion becomes upset by overloading, poisonous chemicals or for other reasons. It is critical to the overall process to maintain balanced populations of acid formers and methane formers. The methane formers are more sensitive to environmental conditions and slower growing than the acid forming group of bacteria and control the overall reactions.

Process Indicators

The progress of digestion can be measured by the destruction of organic matter (volatile solids), by the volume and composition of gases produced, by the pH, volatile acids, and alkalinity concentration. It is recommended that no parameter or test be used to predict problems or control digesters. Several of the following parameters must be considered together.

Volatile Solids Reduction

The reduction of organic matter as measured by the volatile solids indicates the completeness of digestion. Raw sludge usually contains from 60 to 70 percent volatile solids while a well digested sludge may have as little as 50 percent. This would represent a volatile solids reduction of about 50 percent. Volatile solids reduction should be measured weekly and trended. Downward trends in volatile solids reduction might mean:

(1) Temperature too low and/or poor temperature control.
(2) Digester is overloaded.
(3) Ineffective mixing of digester contents.
(4) Grit and/or scum accumulations are excessive.
(5) Low volatile solids in raw sludge feed.

A well digested sludge should be black in color, have not an unpleasant tarry odor and, when collected in a glass cylinder, should appear granular in structure and show definite channels caused by water rising to the top as the solids settle to the bottom.[5]

Volume and Composition of Digester Gases For domestic wastewater in a normally operating digestion tank, gas production should be in the vicinity of 12 cu.ft. of gas per day per pound of volatile matter destroyed. This would indicate that for a 50 percent reduction of volatile matter, a gas yield of six cu.ft. per pound of volatile matter added should be attained. The quantity of gases produced should be relatively constant if the feed rate is constant. Sharp decreases in total gas production may indicate toxicity in the digester. A popular figure for sludge from average domestic sewage is an expected gas yield of one cu.ft. per capita per day. Industrial wastes, depending on their character may raise or lower this figure materially. The gas is usually about 70 percent methane, about 30 percent carbon dioxide and inert gases such as nitrogen. An increasing percentage of carbon dioxide may be an indication that the digestion process is not proceeding properly.

In plants with primary and secondary digester, raw sludge is pumped to the primary digester displacing partially digested sludge. The major portion of the digestion with the greatest gas yield is in the primary digester.

pH pH measures the hydrogen ion concentration of the sludge and indicates if the sludge is acid or alkaline. Generally, the pH must be maintained between 6.5 to 7.5 to promote methane gas formation. Decreases in pH mean possible digester upset. Normally, however, the decreases in pH occur very rapidly and hence pH gives little advance notice of trouble. A low pH indicates that an upset has already occurred.

Volatile Acids and Alkalinity Ratio Volatile acids (mainly acetic acid) are generated by the acid forming bacteria as a result of the initial breakdown of the sludge solids. The volatile acids concentration indicates digestion progress and is probably the best warning sign of trouble. In a well operating digester, the volatile acids concentration should be measured weekly and remain fairly constant. Sudden increases in volatile acids means digester trouble. During periods of digester imbalance, volatile acids should be measured daily.

Bicarbonate Alkalinity indicates the buffering capacity of the sludge, the ability to keep the pH constant, and the ability to neutralize acids. Normally, the bicarbonate alkalinity varies between 1500 and 6000 mg/L (as calcium carbonate).

The ratio between the volatile acids and the bicarbonate alkalinity concentrations is an excellent process indicator. Normally if the digester is operating properly. A rising volatile acids to bicarbonate alkalinity ratio means possible trouble. Sometimes either decreasing the sludge feed to digester or resting the digester will correct the problem.

$$\frac{\text{volatile acids concentration, mg/L}}{\text{bicarbonate alkalinity concentration, mg/L}} \text{ is less than 0.25}$$

Selected from http://water.me.vccs.edu/courses/ENV149/stabilization2.htm

Important Words and Expressions

decomposition [ˌdiːkɔmpəˈziʃən] n. 分解作用
putrescible [pjuːˈtresibl] adj. 易腐烂的
inert [inˈəːt] adj. 惰性的
methane [ˈmeθˌein] n. 甲烷，沼气
facultative [ˈfækəltətiv] adj. 兼性的
molecular [məˈlekjələ] adj. 分子的
hydrogen sulfide 硫化氢

fermentation [ˌfəːmenˈteiʃən]   n. 发酵
liquefied [ˈlikwifaid]   adj. 液化的
gasification [ˌgæsifiˈkeiʃən]   n. 气化
inflammable [inˈflæməbəl]   adj. 易燃的
supernatant [sjuːpəˈneitənt]   n. 上清液
liquefaction [ˌlikwiˈfækʃən]   n. 液化
vicinity [viˈsiniti]   n. 接近，邻近
bicarbonate [baiˈkɑːbənit]   n. 碳酸氢盐

Notes

[1] 消化的目的是实现污泥处理的两个目标——减少污泥体积和分解高度易腐败有机质，成为相对稳定的或惰性的有机和无机化合物。

[2] 兼氧和厌氧微生物分解这些固体的复杂分子结构，释放结合水，并且为它们自身的生长获得氧气和食物。

[3] 消化的第二个阶段，被称作是消化、稳定和气化的强化阶段，抵抗力较强的含氮化合物，如蛋白质、氨基酸等，被进一步分解。

[4] 所有的消化阶段可以在一个池子同一时间进行，在第一阶段产生的酸被随后阶段产生的氨中和，当整个过程的 pH 值控制在 6.8～7.4 之间，就能得到最好和最快的结果。

[5] 消化好的污泥应该是黑色的，没有令人不愉快的柏油气味，当把它们收集在一个玻璃缸时，应该出现粒状结构，并且有明显的通道，这些通道是由于水上升到顶部，而固体沉降到底部造成的。

Exercises

1. Answering the following questions in English according to the text:

(1) What is the purpose of digestion?

(2) What are the two steps of anaerobic digestion?

2. Using the following each word to make up the sentences, respectively:

(1) additionally

(2) putrescible

(3) convert

(4) facultative

(5) critical

3. Put the following English into Chinese:

(1) Final or ultimate disposal of sludge, which cannot be reused, is by landfilling or incineration. Since sludge for landfilling usually contains heavy metals or toxic chemicals, lining of the landfill with clay or plastic liner may be required to prevent contamination of groundwater. Incineration of sludge is by a multiple hearth furnace or fluidised bed furnace. Energy input is required to dry the sludge before combustion is self-sustaining. Combustion flue gases usually need treatment to meet air pollution control standards. Investment and operating costs are high.

(2) How is a frequently wasted renewable source of energy. It is composed of the food scraps and garden waste which most householders dispose of in landfills or, at best, compost; only few

harness the energy which organic waste contains despite being a readily available resource, and its conversion to energy (ie, biogas) through anaerobic digestion being relatively straightforward. Biogas is a flammable gas containing upward of 50% methane which can be burnt to produce heat energy. In addition to providing clean renewable energy, anaerobic digestion of how also produces a residue which is an excellent organic fertiliser that can be used in farming to reduce the amount of waste normally disposed of in landfills.

4. Put the following Chinese into English：
(1) 厌氧消化
(2) 复杂的生化反应
(3) 挥发性酸和碱的比例
(4) 甲烷是一种无味，高度易燃的气体，可做燃料。
(5) 二氧化碳含量的升高是一个迹象，表明消化过程不正常。

Reading Material A

Design of Digestion Tank

Process Design

Ideally, the design of anerobic sludge-digestion processes should be based on an understanding of the fundamental principles of biochemistry and microbiology discussed in biological treatment of wastewater. Because these principles have not been appreciated fully in the past, a number of empirical methods have also been used in the design of digesters. Therefore, the purpose of this discussion is to illustrate the various methods that have been used to design digesters in terms of size. These methods are based on (1) the concept of mean cell residence time, (2) the use of volumetric loading factors, (3) observed volume reduction, and (4) loading factors based on population.[1]

Mean Cell Residence Time

Digester design based on mean cell residence time involves application of the principles. The respiration and oxidation end products of anaerobic digestion are methane gas and carbon dioxide. The quantity of methane gas can be calculated using Eq.(18-1):

$$V_{CH_4} = (0.35 m^3/kg)\{[EQS_0(10^3 g/kg)^{-1}] - 1.42(P_x)\} \quad (18\text{-}1)$$

where V_{CH_4} = volume of methane produced, m^3/d

0.35 = theoretical conversion factor for the amount of methane produced from the conversion of 1kg of BOD_L

E = efficiency of waste utilization

Q = flowrate, m^3/d

S_0 = ultimate BOD_L of influent, g/m^3

1.42 = conversion factor for cell tissue to BOD_L

P_x = net mass of cell tissue produced per day, kg/d

For a continuous-flow stirred-tank high-rate digester without recycle, the mass of biological solids synthesize daily P_x can be estimated using Eq.(18-2).

$$P_x = \frac{YQ(ES_0) \times (10^3 g/kg)^{-1}}{1 + k_d \theta_c} \quad (18\text{-}2)$$

where

P_x = net mass of cell tissue produced, kg/d
Y = yield coefficient, mg/mg or g/g
Q = flowrate, m^3/d
E = efficiency of waste utilization
S_0 = ultimate BOD_L of influent, g/m^3
k_d = endogenous coefficient, d^{-1}
θ_c = mean cell residence time, d

(Note that for a continuous-flow stirred-tank flow-through digester, θ_c is the same as the hydraulic retention time θ_c.) Value for Y and k_d as found for various types of waste are given in Table 18.1. Typical values for θ_c for various temperature are reported in Table18.2.

Table 18.1 Typical kinetic coefficients for the activated-sludge process

Coefficient	Basis	Value	
		Range	Typical
k	d^{-1}	2-10	5.0
k_s	mg/L BOD_5	25-100	60
	mg/L COD	15-70	40
y	mg VSS/mg BOD_5	0.4-0.8	0.6
	mg VSS/mg COD	0.25-0.4	0.4
k_d	d^{-1}	0.04-0.075	0.06

Table 18.2 Suggested mean cell residence times for use in the design of continuou-flow stirred-tank digesters

Operation temperature, ℃	θ_c^M, d	θ_c^d, d
18	11	28
24	8	20
30	6	14
35	4	10
40	4	10

Loading Factors

One of the common methods used to size digesters is to determine the required volume on the basis of a loading factor. Although a number of different factors have been proposed, the two that seem most favored are based on (1) the kilograms of volatile solids added per day per cubic meter of digester capacity and (2) the kilograms of volatile solids added per day per kilogram of volatile solids in the digester.[2] The similarity between these loading factors and the food-to-microorganism ratio is apparent. In applying these loading factors, another factor that should also be checked is the hydraulic detention time, because of its relationship to organism growth and washout and to the type of digester used (for example, only 50 percent or less of the capacity of a conventional standard-rate single-stage digester is effective).

Ideally, the conventional single-stage digestion tank is stratified into three layers with the supernatant at the top, the active digestion zone in the middle, and the thickened sludge at the bottom. Because of the storage requirements for the digested sludge and the supernatant, and the excess capacity provided for daily fluctuations in sludge loading, the volumetric loading for standard-rate digesters is low. [3] Detention times based on cubic meters of untreated sludge pumped vary from 30 to more than 90d for this type of tank. The recommended solids loading for standard-rate digesters are from 0.5 to 1.6 kg/m^3·d (0.03 to 0.10 lb/ft^3·d) of volatile solids.

For high-rate digesters, loading rates of 1.6 to 6.4 kg/m^3·d (0.10 to 0.40 lb/ft^3·d) of volatile solids and hydraulic detention periods of 10 to 20 d are practicable. The six high-rate digestion tanks at the Newtown Creek Plant of New York City are designed for a volatile-solids loading of 3.43 kg/m^3·d (0.214 lb/ft^3·d) and a detention period of 17.6 d with an untreated sludge concentration of 8 percent solids. The tanks are also designed so that four tanks can handle the entire load and the other two can be used for storage and residual gas extraction. Under these conditions, the volatile-solids loading becomes 5.13 kg/m^3·d (0.32 lb/ft^3·d) and the detention period 11.7d. Four draft-tube mixers in each tank are designed to turn over the entire tank contents in 30 min. The effect of sludge concentration and hydraulic detention time on the volatile-solids loading factor is reported in Table 18.3.

Table 18.3 Effect of sludge concentration and hydraulic detention time on volatile-solids loading factor

Sludge concentration %	Volatile-solids loading factor, kg/m^3·d			
	10d	12d	15d	20d
4	3.06	2.55	2.04	1.53
5	3.38	3.19	2.55	1.91
6	4.59	3.83	3.06	2.30
7	5.36	4.46	3.57	2.68
8	6.12	5.10	4.08	3.06
9	6.89	5.74	4.59	3.44
10	7.65	6.38	5.10	3.83

The degree of stabilization obtained is also often measured by the percent reduction in volatile solids. This can be related either to the mean cell residence time or to the detention time based on the untreated sludge feed. Since the untreated sludge feed can be measured easily, this method is more commonly used. In plant operation, this calculation should be made routinely as a matter of record whenever sludge is drawn to processing equipment or drying beds. The results of this calculation can also be used as a guide for scheduling the withdrawal of sludge.

In calculating the volatile-solids reduction, it is assumed that the ash content of the sludge is conservative; that is, the number of pounds of ash going into the digester is equal to that being removed.

Volume Reduction

It has been observed that as digestion proceeds, if the supernatant is withdrawn and returned to the head end of the treatment plant, the volume of the remaining sludge decreases approximately exponentially. [4] If a plot is prepared of the remaining volume versus time, the required volume of the digester os represented by the area under the curve. It can be computed using Eq.(18-3):

$$V = \left[V_f - \frac{2}{3}(V_f - V_d) \right] t \quad (18-3)$$

where   V= volume of digester, m^3 (ft^3)

V_f = volume of fresh sludge added per day, m³/d (ft³/d)

V_d = volume of digested sludge removed per day, m³/d (ft³/d)

t = digestion time, d

Selected from "Syed R. Qasim. Wastewater Treatment Plants: Planning, Design, and Operation. Technomic Publishing Company, 1999."

Notes

[1] 这些方法是基于平均细胞停留时间的概念、容积负荷因素的应用、观察到的体积量的减少以及细菌数的负荷因素。

[2] 尽管提出了很多不同的因素，两个最受青睐的因素是基于（1）每天每立方米的消化容积添加的挥发性固体的千克数和（2）消化池中每日每千克挥发性固体添加的挥发性固体的千克数。

[3] 由于对消化污泥和上清液的存储要求，以及由于污泥负荷每日的波动而提供的反应器富余容量，造成了标准速率消化池的容积负荷很低。

[4] 据观察，随着消化反应的进行，如果上清液被排除并返回到污水处理厂始端，剩余污泥量近似按指数递减。

Reading Material B

Digester Gas Utilization

Gas Utilization Equipment

Digester biogas is often flared to dispose of the gas and remove associated odors by converting reduced sulfur compounds to sulfur dioxide. However biogas represents a significant power source that can be converted to electricity with remaining waste heat used to heat the digesters. The following describes some of the technologies that can be used to convert biogas to more useful forms of energy.

Heating Systems

One application for the digester gas is direct use in a boiler for producing hot water. A hot water heater would have a low capital equipment cost and will operate at about 80% thermal efficiency based on the higher heating value of the fuel. The estimated concentrations of H_2S and NH_3 should not affect operation of a hot water system, other than the need to construct the boiler from materials resistant to acid gas corrosion.[1]

Electric Power Production

Table 18.4 summarizes technologies currently available or being developed for combined heat and power that might be applicable for use with biogas. The technologies that are commercially available or near commercially available in the range of 400 kW are internal combustion reciprocating engine-generator sets and gas turbine-generator sets.

Of the technologies listed in Table 18.5 the reciprocating engine or industrial gas turbine are commercially available as standalone power generators or as combined heat and power units. There are several companies in North America and Europe that supply either gas turbine or reciprocating engine-generator sets with or without recovery of waste heat for combined heat and power units.[2] Table 18.4 compares the reciprocating and gas turbine options. Selection of the best system must

Table 18.4 Comparison of reciprocating engine and gas turbine options at 98.3 GJ/day fuel input

	Reciprocating Engine	Gas Turbine
Capital cost	$800/kW	$1600/kW
Maintenance cost	high	low
Electric Efficiency	35%	25%
Efficiency including waste heat recovery	80%	80%
H_2S tolerance	<200 ppm	<10,000 ppm
NO_x emissions	medium	low
fuel supply pressure	near atmospheric	requires boost compressor
low heating value gas	OK	may need natural gas supplement

Table 18.5 Small combined heat and power options

	Reciprocating Engine	Microturbine	Industrial Turbine	Stirling Engine	Fuel Cell
Current Size Range (kW)	5 to 50,000	30 to 200	500 kW to 150 MW	0.3 to 25	<250 kW
Electric Efficiency (%)	20 to 45	25 to 30	30 to 50	15 to 30	40 to 50
Current Capital Cost ($/kW)	$600 to $1,000	$1,500 to $1,800	$600 to 800	>$1,500	very high
Future Capital Cost ($/kW)	<$500	$200 to $400	$500 to $600	$200 to $300	-

take into consideration the following:

- initial capital cost
- maintenance costs
- relative demand for electricity and heat
- relative prices of electricity and heat (which determines importance of electric conversion efficiency)
- emissions of pollutants
- noise
- tolerance of engine to sulphur and/or nitrogen compounds and to changes in gas composition

Reciprocating Engines

Reciprocating engine based systems are the most developed and most common cogeneration systems. Reciprocating engines fueled by natural gas or hydrocarbon liquid fuels are available in sizes from several kW to 10 MW. The amount of fuel energy converted to electricity generally increases with size, ranging from 30% for small units to 40% for large engines. The amount of fuel converted to thermal energy is from 40 to 50% resulting in overall efficiencies of 80 to 85%. Of the small cogeneration systems available, reciprocating engines offer the highest conversion of fuel energy to electricity.

Operating and maintenance costs can be a significant portion of total electricity cost with reciprocating engine cogeneration plants as discussed above. The engine requires frequent oil changes and minor overhauls. Most engines require a major overhaul about every 5 years. These costs must be factored in during the selection and costing process.

Table 18.6 shows example predicted capital and operating costs for a reciprocating engine combined heat and power unit sized for 300 kW of electricity production. Based on 200 m^3/hr of biogas production with a conservative heat content equivalent to 40% methane the engine generator set would produce 300 kW of electric power. The capital cost shown does not include the synchronizing switch gear that may be required if the generator was to be tied into the electric grid to enable electricity sales to the transmission system. [3]

Table 18.6   Estimated costs for internal combustion engine combined heat and power unit 300 kW

	Biogas H$_2$S Concentration		
	0 ppm	200 ppm	500 ppm
capital	$270,200	$270,200	$270,200
maintenance[$/(kW·h)]	0.0113	0.0134	0.0134
oil change interval (hours)	1,000	360	360

Maintenance costs are a significant portion of the total cost of ownership of a reciprocating engine generator set. Table 18.7 shows an example breakdown of lifecycle costs for a reciprocating engine generator set and the impact of 200 ppm H$_2$S in the feed gas on the relative proportion of maintenance and fuel cost. Some of the cogeneration options under development promise lower maintenance costs. Industrial turbines and microturbines potentially have low maintenance costs but their conversion efficiency to electricity is not as high as reciprocating engines. Stirling cycle engines have totally enclosed moving parts that do not come into contact with combustion gases and also no need for oil changes. Although not yet commercially available, stirling engines should have minimal maintenance costs.

Table 18.7   Predicted operating costs of reciprocating engine combined heat and power unit for two H$_2$S levels

	0 ppm H$_2$S	200 ppm H$_2$S
Life Cycle Costs		
maintenance	15.1%	17.5%
fuel	84.9%	82.5%
Maintenance Costs		
lube oil	16.0%	29.5%
planned service	30.5%	25.6%
top end overhaul	23.4%	19.6%
bottom end overhaul	30.2%	25.3%
oil change interval	1,000 hrs	360 hrs

Gas Turbines

Conventional combustion turbine is a mature technology with several suppliers worldwide. Turbines can be fueled with natural gas or oil. Units range in size from 500 kW to 250 MW. Single cycle turbines have efficiencies from 20 to 45% at full load, with efficiency increasing with size.

Combining a gas turbine with a steam turbine cycle can improve efficiencies further to over 50% for large units. Gas turbine generally has a higher capital cost than reciprocating engine but this is balanced by lower operating costs. [4] For plants above 10 MW, gas turbines are generally less expensive than reciprocating engines.

Gas turbine requires a supply of high pressure feed gas and would require a gas compressor to operate on sewage biogas. This will increase the capital cost and reduce the efficiency of conversion to electricity. Construction of cogeneration plants using gas turbines is well developed commercial technology. Typical turbine exhaust temperature is about 500°C. A Heat Recovery Steam Generator (HRSG) is installed to recover energy from the turbine exhaust and this energy could be used to supply heat demands to the waste treatment system.

Notes

[1] 硫化氢和氨的估计浓度不应影响热水系统的运行，否则需要建造锅炉的材料能够抗酸性气体腐蚀。

[2] 在北美和欧洲有几家公司，他们提供燃气轮机或往复式发动机-发电机组，有的有废热回收的热电机组，有的没有。

[3] 如果发电机是被捆绑到电网，使电力销售到传输系统，那么资本成本显示不包括必需的同步转换装置。

[4] 燃气轮机通常比往复式发动机有较高的资本成本，但是被较低的运营成本平衡。

Unit 19 Dewatering

Many of the methods for dewatering biomass sludges are the same as those used to dewater water treatment plant residuals. The following discussion focuses on the particular considerations in application to dewatering biomass sludge. In the past, vacuum filtration was the predominant dewatering device for municipal sludge. It has been replaced by alternative mechanical dewatering equipment (Metcalf & Eddy, 2003). Vacuum filters, reed beds, and lagoons are not considered in this discussion.

Sludge Drying Beds

The most popular method of sludge dewatering in the past has been the use of sludge drying beds. These beds are especially popular in small plants because of their simplicity of operation and maintenance.[1] In 1979, 77 percent of all United States wastewater treatment plants utilized drying beds; one-half of all the municipal sludge produced in the United States was dewatered by this method (U.S. EPA, 1979). Most of these plants are located in small- and medium-sized communities, with an average flow rate of less than 8,000 m^3/d. Some larger cities, such as Albuquerque, Fort Worth, Texas, Phoenix, and Salt Lake City, use sand drying beds. Although the use of drying beds might be expected in the warmer, sunny regions, they are also used in several large facilities in northern climates.

Sand drying beds for wastewater sludge are constructed in the same manner as water treatment plant sludge-drying beds. Typical loading rates are given in Table 19.1.

Table 19.1 Typical loading rates for open sludge drying beds

Type of biosolids	Sludge loading rate, kg dry solids/m$^2 \cdot$y
Primary, degested	120-150
Primary and waste activated digested	60-100
Source: Metcalf & Eddy, 2003	

Source: Metcalf & Eddy, 2003

Centrifugation

In addition to the solid-bowl centrifuge, a "high-solids" centrifuge is used to dewater biosolids. The high-solids centrifuge is a modification of the solid-bowl configuration. The modification primarily consists of a slightly longer bowl length, a lower differential bowl speed to increase residence time, and a modified scroll.

Dosage rates for polymers range from 0.1 to 7.5 g/kg of sludge measured on a dry solids basis. Higher polymer doses may be required for the high-solids centrifuge. Typical performance data are given in Table 19.2.

Table 19.2 Typical dewatering performance for solid-bowl centrifuges

Type of sludge	Cake solids, %	Solids capture, %	
		Without chemicals	With chemicals
Untreated primary alone	25-35	75-90	95+
with air activated sludge	12-20	55-65	92+
Waste activated sludge	5-15	60-80	92+
Anaerobically digested Primary	25-35	65-80	92+
Primary and activated sludge	15-20	50-65	90+
Aerobically digested Waste activated sludge	8-10	60-75	90+

Source: Metcalf & Eddy, 2003; U.S.EPA,1979

Continuous Belt-Filter Presses

The continuous belt-filter presses (CBFP) used in treating wastewater sludges is the same as that used for water treatment plant sludges. [2] It is one of the predominant dewatering devices used in the United States today. The CBFP is successful with many normal mixed sludges. Typical dewatering results for various types of sludges are given in Table 19.3.

CBFPs are available in belt widths from 0.5 to 3.5 m. The most common size used for municipal applications is 2.0 m. Belt speeds vary from 1.0 to 2.5 m/min. At low feed-solids concentrations, the capacity of the gravity drainage zone usually is limiting and belt speed must be reduced to maximize gravity drainage. As the feed solids concentration increases, a point is reached where the solids loading and thickness of the cake becomes controlling. At this point, the loading rate must be reduced to prevent sludge from being forced out of the edges of the CBFP (Task Committee, 1988).

Typical continuous filter press manufacturer's data are given in Table 19.4.

Filter Press

Both the recessed plate and diaphragm filter presses are used to dewater biosolids sludges. Advantages cited for filter presses include high concentrations of cake solids, good filtrate clarity, and high solids capture. Disadvantages include batch operation, mechanical complexity, high chemical costs, high labor costs, and limited filter cloth life.

Table 19.3 Typical performance data for a belt filter press

Type of sludge	Dry feed Solid, %	Loading per metre belt width		Dry polymer[a], g/kg dry solids	Cake solids, %	
		L/min	kg/h		Typical	Range
Raw primary (P)	3-7	110-190	360-550	1-4	28	26-32
Waste activate sludge (WAS)	1-4	40-150	45-180	3-10	15	12-20
P + WAS(50:50)[b]	3-6	80-190	180-320	2-8	23	20-28
P + WAS(40:60)[b]	3-6	80-190	180-320	2-10	20	18-25
P + trickling filter (TF)	3-6	80-190	180-320	2-8	25	23-30
Anaerobically digested:						
P	3-7	80-190	360-550	2-5	28	24-30
WAS	3-4	40-150	45-135	4-10	15	12-20
P + WAS	3-6	80-190	180-320	3-8	22	20-25
Aerobically digested:						
P + WAS, unthickened	1-3	40-190	135-225	2-8	16	12-20
P + WAS (50:50), thickened	4-8	40-190	135-225	2-8	18	12-25
Oxygen activated WAS	1-3	40-150	90-180	4-10	18	15-23

[a] Polymer needs based on high molecular weight polymer (100% strength, dry basis).
[b] Ratio is based on dry solids for the primary and WAS.
Source: WEF, 1998.

Table 19.4 Typical continuous filter press manufacturer's data

Hydraulic loading m³/h	Solids loading kg/h	Belt with m
1-3	25-120	0.5
3-5	120-200	0.75
5-20	125-510	1.0
20-30	510-815	1.5
30-40	765-1,070	2.0
40-50	1,020-1,275	2.5
50-60	1,275-1,530	3.0

Note: these presses are representative but do not represent actual choices. Actual manufacturers' data must be used for real world design.

Features that should be considered in the design of filter press installations include a sludge grinder ahead of the press, high pressure washing systems, an acid wash to remove calcium scale when lime is used as a conditioner, cake breakers following the press, and equipment such as an overhead crane to facilitate removal and maintenance of the plates.[3]

Inclined Screw Press

The screw conveyor is located inside a stainless steel, wedge-shaped wire screen basket. It is inclined about 20 from horizontal. The lower, wider section of the basket serves as a gravity dewatering stage where free water drains by gravity. The screen openings are about 0.25 mm. The screw rotates at 1 to 4 rpm. As the sludge moves up the rotating screw, the screen narrows. This creates pressure that forces the water to flow out through the screen. The pressure in the pressure zone is controlled by the position of a cone at the discharge end of the basket. The dewatered sludge is driven through the gap between the cone and the basket and drops into a conveyor or dumpster.

A polymer-fed reactor is an essential part of the process. Hydraulic loading rates range from 10 to 20 m^3/h. Solids loading rates range from 275 to 500 kg/h. Polymer consumption ranges from 1 to 6 g/kg of dry solids. Wash water to clear the screen is on the order of 400 L/h. Reported performance data indicates that a solids feed of 2 to 3 percent may be dewatered to 20 to 25 percent cake solids, while a feed of 1 percent may be dewatered to 12 to 15 percent cake solids (Atherton et al., 2006; Newhof, 2009).

Comparison of Mechanical Dewatering

A brief summary of comparative performance of mechanical dewatering processes is given in Table 19.5.

Table 19.5 Comparison of mechanical dewatering performance

Dewatering unit	Cake solids, % TSS[a]	Recovery cost, % TSS	Polymer cost, % Mg dry solids[b]
Belt press	X	90-95[c]	Y
Centrifuge	X±2	90-95[c]	0.8Y
Filter press-low pressure	X+8	98+	1.1Y
Filter press-high pressure	X+10	98+	1.1Y
Filter press-diaphragm	X+12	98+	1.1Y
Screw press	X−2	90+	1.2Y

[a] Relative to belt press, X denotes base level; TSS=total suspended solids.
[b] Relative to belt press, Y denotes base level; %/Mg=percent per megagram.
Source: U.S. EPA, 1979.

Important Words and Expressions

dewater [diːˈwɔːtə] vt. 使脱水；使浓缩；使增稠

vacuum [ˈvækjuəm] n. 真空；空间；真空吸尘器 adj. 真空的；利用真空的；产生真空的 vt. 用真空吸尘器清扫

reed [riːd] n. [作物] 芦苇；簧片；牧笛；不可依靠的人 vt. 用芦苇盖；用芦苇装饰

concentration [ˌkɔnsenˈtreiʃən] n. 浓度；集中；浓缩；专心；集合

centrifuge [ˈsentrifjuːdʒ] vt. 用离心机分离；使…受离心作用 n. 离心机；[机][化工] 离心分离机

dosage [ˈdəusidʒ] n. 剂量，用量

polymer [ˈpɔlimə] n. [高分子] 聚合物

diaphragm [ˈdaiəfræm] n. 隔膜；快门，[摄] 光圈；横隔膜；隔板

grinder [ˈgraində] n. [机] 研磨机；研磨者；磨工；臼齿

hose [həuz] n. 软管 vt. 用软管浇水；痛打

aeration [ˌeiəˈreiʃən] n. [环境] 曝气；通风；充气

Notes

[1] 鉴于污泥干化床运行和维护简单，因而在小型污水处理厂得到广泛应用。

[2] 和用于处理自来水厂产生的剩余污泥相同，带式压滤机亦可用于处理污水处理厂产生

的剩余污泥。

[3] 压滤设备在设计时应考虑的因素包括：压滤前用粉碎机把污泥预处理的系统，与压滤设备配套的高压冲洗系统，当石灰石做调理剂时用于去除钙盐的酸洗系统，压滤设备后的滤饼破碎机，以及为了便于拆卸和维修滤板的设备如吊车。

Exercises

1. Answering the following questions in English according to the text:

    (1) What's the most common size used for municipal applications? What's the belt speeds?

    (2) What's the operation parameters' range of inclined screw press?

2. Using the following each word to make up the sentences, respectively:

    (1) dewater

    (2) concentration

    (3) centrifuge

    (4) dosage

    (5) grinder

3. Put the following English into Chinese:

    (1) Currently, numbers and capacity of WWTPs under construction exceeds those of WWTPs put into use. In the next five years (2011-2015) the capacity of WWTPs in China will increase by 1500×10^4 t/d every year.

    (2) At the same time, sludge management has become a Gordian knot in China as less than 25% of WWTPs have been equipped with stable operating sludge treatment facilities, and less than 10% have relatively efficient working facilities. The current way to deal with sludge is condensing, dewatering and landfilling.

4. Put the following Chinese into English:

    (1) 污泥干化床

    (2) 带式压滤机

    (3) 板框压滤机

    (4) 污泥机械脱水方法有真空吸滤法、压滤法和离心法等。

    (5) 预处理的目的在于改善污泥脱水性能，提高机械脱水效果与机械脱水设备的生产能力。

5. Put the following abbr. into full phrases:

    CBFP；TSS；ThOD；TKN

Reading Material A

Conditioning Methods

Sludge is conditioned to improve dewatering characteristics. Conditioning by the addition of chemicals is the predominant method used in the United States. It is the focus of this discussion. Heat treatment is used to a limited extent. It will be discussed more briefly.

Chemical Conditioning

The use of chemicals to condition sludge and biosolids for dewatering is economical because of the increased yields and greater flexibility obtained. Chemical conditioning can reduce the 90 to 99 percent incoming moisture content to 65 to 85 percent, depending on the nature of the solids to be treated. Chemical conditioning results in coagulation of the solids and release of the absorbed water. Conditioning is used in advance of mechanical dewatering systems such as centrifugation, belt-filter presses, and pressure-filter presses. Chemicals used include ferric chloride, lime, alum, and organic polymers.

Adding conditioning chemicals to sludges and biosolids may increase the dry solids. Polymers do not increase the dry solids while iron salts and lime can increase the dry solids by 20 to 30 percent.

Chemicals are most easily applied and metered in the liquid form. Dissolving tanks are needed if the chemicals are received as dry powder. In most plants, these tanks should be large enough for at least one day's supply of chemicals and should be furnished in duplicated. In large plants, tankage sufficient for one shift is usually adequate. The tanks must be fabricated or lined with corrosion-resistant material. Polyvinyl chloride, polyethylene, and rubber are suitable materials for tank and pipe linings for acid solutions. Metering pumps must be corrosion-resistant. These pumps are generally of the positive-displacement type with variable-speed or variable-stroke drives to control the flowrate.

Factors Affecting Chemical Conditioning

Factors that affect the selection of the type and dosage of the conditioning agents are the properties of the solids and the type of mixing and dewatering devices to be used. Important solids properties include source, solids concentration, age, pH, and alkalinity. Sources such as primary sludge, waste activated sludge, and digested biosolids are good indicators of the range of probable conditioner doses required. Solids concentrations will affect the dosage and the dispersal of the conditioning agent. The pH and alkalinity may affect the performance of the conditioning agents, in particular the inorganic conditioners. When lime is used to maintain a high pH for dewatering, strong ammonia odor and lime scaling problems may occur. The method of dewatering may also affect the selection of the conditioning chemical because of the differences in mixing equipment used by various vendors and the characteristics of particular methods of dewatering. For example, polymers are used commonly in centrifuge and belt-press dewatering but are used less frequently for pressure filtration. Laboratory-or pilot-scale testing is recommended to determine the types of chemical conditioning agents required, particularly for solids and biosolids that may be difficult to dewater.

Dosage

The chemical dosage required for any sludge is determined in the laboratory. Tests used for selecting chemical dosage include the Buchner funnel test for the determination of specific resistance of sludge, capillary suction time test (CST), and the standard jar test.[1] The Buchner funnel test is a method of testing sludge drainability or dewatering characteristics using various conditioning agents. The capillary suction test relies on gravity and the capillary suction of a piece of thick filter paper to draw out water from a small sample of conditioned sludge. The standard jar test, the easiest method to use, consists of testing standard volumes of sludge samples (usually 1 L) with different conditioner concentrations, followed by rapid mixing, flocculation, and settling using standard jar test apparatus. [2] Detailed descriptions of testing procedures are provided in WEF (1988).

In general, it has been observed that the type of sludge has the greatest impact on the quantity of chemical required. Difficult-to-dewater sludges that require larger doses of chemicals, generally do not yield as dry a cake, and have poorer quality of filtrate or centrate.

Chemical Application

Chemicals are most easily applied and metered in liquid form. Dry chemicals are dissolved in day tanks. Polyvinyl chloride, polyethylene, and rubber lined tanks are suitable. Corrosion resistant metering pumps are used. Typically, these are positive displacement; variable speed pumps (Metcalf & Eddy, 2003).

The chemical dosing point may be an important factor in determining the size of the dose. The polymer does not mix and react with the biosolids instantaneously. The provision of polymer addition points 9 to 12 m and 18 to 24 m ahead of the dewatering device provides the operator flexibility in selecting the best option.[3] For centrifuges, internal addition is often the best (LaMontagne and Yevilevich, 2006).

Mixing

Intimate admixing of sludge and coagulant is essential for proper conditioning. The mixing must not break the floc after it has formed, and the detention should be kept to a minimum so that sludge reaches the dewatering unit as soon after conditioning as possible.[4] Mixing requirements vary depending on the dewatering method used. A separate mixing and flocculation tank is usually provided ahead of pressure filters; a separate flocculation tank may be provided for a belt-filter press or the conditioner may be added directly to the sludge feed line of the belt-press unit; and in-line mixers are usually used with a centrifuge. It is generally desirable in design to provide at least two locations for the addition of conditioning chemicals.

Heat Treatment

Another conditioning approach is to heat the sludge at high temperatures (175 ℃ to 230 ℃) and pressures (1,000 to 2,000 kPa). Under these conditions, much like those of a pressure cooker, water that is bound up in the solids is released, improving the dewatering characteristics of the sludge.[5] Heat treatment has the advantage of producing a sludge that dewaters better than chemically conditioned sludge. The process has the disadvantages of relatively complex operation, high maintenance requirements, and the creation of highly polluted cooking liquors (soluble BOD may exceed 5,000 mg/L) that when recycled to the treatment plant impose a significant added treatment burden.[6] In addition, the process has high capital and operating costs. For these reasons, very few new facilities have been built in recent years (Metcalf & Eddy, 2003).

Notes

[1] 用以选择化学药剂投加量的试验包括决定污泥比阻的瓷漏斗试验，毛细吸入时间试验（CST）和标准的大口瓶试验。

[2] 标准大口瓶试验是最容易使用的方法，包括将污泥试样标准体积（通常为1 L）用不同的调理剂浓度在标准大口瓶试验装置中快速搅拌、絮凝和沉淀。

[3] 加药点设置在脱水设备之前9～12 m与18～24 m为脱水设备在最佳工况运行提供了条件。

[4] 在絮体形成后，决不要因为混合而破坏絮体，而且停留时间应保持最短，因此，污泥在调理后尽可能快地到达脱水单元。

[5] 在这些条件下，类似于高压锅的工作原理，污泥中的水释放出来，提高了污泥的脱水性能。

[6] 这种工艺的缺点是操作相对复杂、维护要求高，同时产生的高浓度有机废水（溶解性 BOD 可能超过 5,000 mg/L）回流到污水处理厂进行处理时增加了污水处理厂的负荷。

Reading Material B

Filter Presses

Continuous Belt Filter Press (CBFP)

The belt filter press operates on the principle that bending a sludge cake contained between two filter belts around a roll introduces shear and compressive forces in the cake, allowing water to work its way to the surface and out of the cake, thereby reducing the cake moisture content.[1] The device employs double moving belts to continuously dewater sludges through one or more stages of dewatering (Figure 19.1).

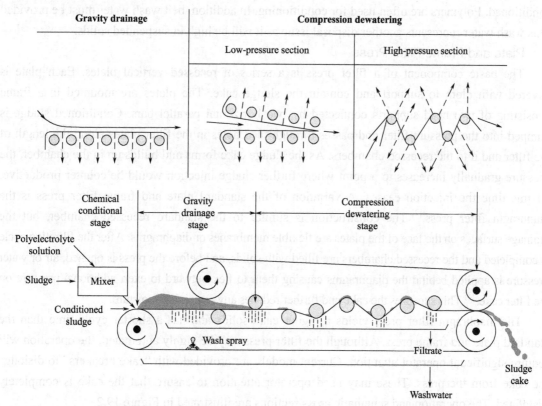

Figure 19.1　Continuous belt filter press (Source: U.S. EPA, 1979.)

Typically the CBFP includes the following stages of treatment:

(1) A reactor/conditioner to remove free-draining water.

(2) A low pressure zone of belts with the top belt being solid and the bottom belt being a sieve; here further water removal occurs, and a sludge mat having significant dimensional stability is formed.

(3) A high pressure zone of belts with a serpentine or sinusoidal configuration to add shear to the pressure dewatering mechanisms.

The design and selection of a belt filter press is often based on the "throughput" of the press. Throughput is the rate at which residuals can be dewatered. The throughput can be either hydraulically or solids limited. A belt press having a particular type and width of belt has a maximum loading capacity for a given type of residual. The solids loading is considered the most critical factor, and throughput is expressed in terms of solids loading: kg/meter of belt width per hour. For coagulant sludges the typical loading rate is about 150 kg/(m·h), but sludges thickened to 4 percent may be loaded at a rate of 400 to 570 kg/(m·h) (Cornwell, 2006).[1] Lime sludges up to 30 percent solids have been dewatered to 60 percent solids (MWH, 2005). Typical belt widths are 1.0, 1.5, 2.0, and 3.0 m.

Discharge from the press may be directly to a truck. Other options include conveyors and hoppers or roll-off boxes.

The belt press has a relatively low energy requirement compared to other mechanical dewatering devices. To achieve acceptable solids concentrations, the sludge fed to the CBFP must be conditioned. Polymers are often used for conditioning. In addition, belt wash water must be provided. This wash water represents another disposal issue as it will be high in suspended solids.

Plate and Frame Filter Press

The basic component of a filter press is a series of recessed vertical plates. Each plate is covered with cloth to support and contain the sludge cake. The plates are mounted in a frame consisting of two head supports connected by two horizontal parallel bars. Conditioned sludge is pumped into the pressure filter and passes through feed holes in the filter plates along the length of the filter and into the recessed chambers. As the sludge cake forms and builds up in the chamber, the pressure gradually increases to a point where further sludge injection would be counter productive. At this time the injection ceases. A variation of the standard plate and frame filter press is the diaphragm filter press.[2] The construction is similar to the standard recessed chamber, but the drainage surfaces on the face of the plates are flexible membranes or diaphragms. After the filtration cycle is completed and the recessed chambers are filled with solids, and before the press is opened, air or water pressure is applied behind the diaphragms causing them to flex outward to exert additional pressure on the filter cake.[3] This squeezes the cake and further reduces any remaining moisture.

The diaphragm filter press yields a higher cake solids and has a shorter cycle time than the standard plate and frame press. Although the filter press may be highly automated, the operation will require significant operator attention. Current models are provided with "cake breakers" to dislodge the cake from the press. These may need operator attention to ensure that the cake is completely dislodged. The operation and schematic cross sections are illustrated in Figure 19.2.

A typical pressure filtration cycle begins with the closing of the press to the position shown on Figure 19.2(a). Sludge is fed for a 20 to 30 minute period until the press is effectively full of cake. The pressure at this point is generally the designed maximum (700 to 1,700 kPa) and is maintained for one to four hours, during which more filtrate is removed and the desired cake solids content is achieved.[4] The filter is then mechanically opened, and the dewatered cake is dropped from the chambers onto a conveyor belt or hopper for removal. Cake breakers are usually required to break up the rigid cake into conveyable form. Because plate pressure filters operate at high pressures and because many units use lime for conditioning, the cloths require routine washing with high-pressure water, as well as periodic washing with acid.

While filter presses work well for lime sludges, they require large quantities of conditioning agents, including lime and fly ash, to produce a dry cake from coagulation sludges. In either case, thickening before filtration is typical.

Alum sludges are conditioned using lime and/or fly ash. Lime dosage is typically in the range of 10 to 15 percent of the sludge solids. Fly ash is applied at dosage of about 100 percent of the sludge solids. Polymers are dosed in the range of 1 to 2 g/kg. While cake solids may be between 45 and 50 percent dry solids, as much as 30 percent of the dry solids may be conditioning chemicals and/or fly ash. To reduce the volume of sludge, only polymer may be used for conditioning. This is an economic issue as well as an operational issue. The cost of polymer, which is very expensive, must be weighed against the cost of disposing of a larger volume of solids.

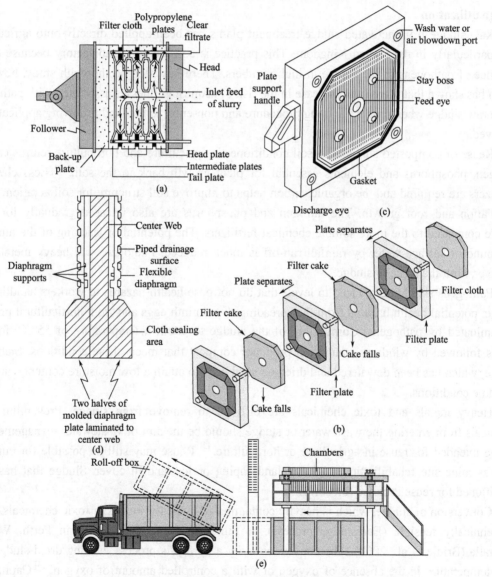

Figure 19.2 Plate and frame filter press
(a) Filling the press, (b) cake breaking, (c) plate details for recessed plate
(d) diaphragm plate details, (e) plate and frame solids off-loading system

Notes

[1] 带式压滤机的工作原理为两条滤带夹带着污泥层通过辊压筒，靠滤带本身的张力形成对污泥层的压榨力和剪切力，把污泥层中的水挤压出来，从而降低泥饼的含水率。

[2] 压滤周期（常规挤压过程）完成后，滤室内充满污泥，在打开板框之前，弹性膜通过充气或充水膨胀，使压滤室内的污泥进一步得到压缩。

[3] 压滤的常规最大设计压力为 700～1700kPa，持续 1～4h，在这个过程中去除了滤液，生成了滤饼。

Unit 20 Sludge Utilization and Disposal

Sludge utilization

Raw sludge from activated sludge treatment plants has been applied directly onto agricultural land particularly in the United Kingdom. This practice is considered unsatisfactory because of the presence of pathogens in the sludge in high numbers. There has been no thorough study, however, which has shown that there is an increase in the risk of acquiring illnesses associated with pathogens in the raw sludge when proper handling procedure and non-entry to the land following application is observed.

Reuse of composted sludge as a soil conditioner in agriculture and horticulture returns carbon, nitrogen, phosphorus and elements essential for plant growth back to the soil. [1] Less chemical fertilizers are required and the organic carbon helps to improve soil structure for soil aeration, water percolation and root growth. The nitrogen and phosphorus are also released gradually for plant uptake compared to the more soluble chemical fertilizers. The potential of leaching of the nutrients to ground or surface water by rainfall run-off is much reduced. Pathogens and heavy metals can, however, limit the reuse of sludge.

Pathogens should be reduced to levels that do not pose health hazards to workers handling the sludge, potential health hazards from the spreading of helminth eggs and from horticultural produce contaminated by pathogens. Composting of the sludge to attain a temperature of 55 ℃ for two weeks followed by windrow maturation produces compost that meets these conditions. Stabilized sludge, which has been dewatered and dried on sand beds to attain a low moisture content, can meet the same conditions.

Heavy metals and toxic chemicals are difficult to remove from sludge. Preventing these chemicals from entering the wastewater or sludge should be the aim of wastewater management for sludge intended for reuse in agriculture or horticulture. [2] Reuse may still be possible for purposes such as mine site rehabilitation, highway landscaping or for landfill cover. Sludge that has been conditioned for reuse is called 'biosolids'.

Conversion of sludge, which is heavily contaminated by heavy metals or toxic chemicals, to oil is technically feasible (Enersludge process). A full-scale plant is operating in Perth, Western Australia (Bridle et al., 2000). The conversion is by a pyrolysis process, heating dried sludge to a high temperature in the absence of oxygen or with a controlled amount of oxygen. [3] Capital and running costs of an oil from sludge process are high.

Thermal depolymerization uses hydrous pyrolysis to convert reduced complex organics to oil.

The premacerated, grit-reduced sludge is heated to 250℃ and compressed to 40 MPa. The hydrogen in the water inserts itself between chemical bonds in natural polymers such as fats, proteins and cellulose. The oxygen of the water combines with carbon, hydrogen and metals. The result is oil, light combustible gases such as methane, propane and butane, water with soluble salts, carbon dioxide, and a small residue of inert insoluble material that resembles powdered rock and char. All organisms and many organic toxins are destroyed. Inorganic salts such as nitrates and phosphates remain in the water after treatment at sufficiently high levels that further treatment is required. The energy from decompressing the material is recovered, and the process heat and pressure is usually powered from the light combustible gases. The oil is usually treated further to make a refined useful light grade of oil, such as no.2 diesel and no.4 heating oil, and then sold. The choice of a wastewater solid treatment method depends on the amount of solids generated and other site-specific conditions. However, in general, composting is most often applied to smaller-scale applications followed by aerobic digestion and then lastly anaerobic digestion for the larger-scale municipal applications.

Sludge Disposal

When a liquid sludge is produced, further treatment may be required to make it suitable for final disposal. Typically, sludges are thickened (dewatered) to reduce the volumes transported off-site for disposal. Processes for reducing water content include lagooning in drying beds to produce a cake that can be applied to land or incinerated; pressing, where sludge is mechanically filtered, often through cloth screens to produce a firm cake; and centrifugation where the sludge is thickened by centrifugally separating the solid and liquid.

Final or ultimate disposal of sludge, which cannot be reused, is by landfilling or incineration. Since sludge for landfilling usually contains heavy metals or toxic chemicals, lining of the landfill with clay or plastic liner may be required to prevent contamination of groundwater. [4] Incineration of sludge is by a multiple hearth furnace or fluidized bed furnace. Energy input is required to dry the sludge before combustion is self-sustaining. Combustion flue gases usually need treatment to meet air pollution control standards. Investment and operating costs are high. There are concerns about sludge incineration because of air pollutants in the emissions, along with the high cost of supplemental fuel, making this a less attractive and less commonly constructed means of sludge treatment and disposal. [5] There is no process which completely eliminates the requirements for disposal of biosolids. In South Australia, after centrifugation, the sludge is then completely dried by sunlight. The nutrient rich biosolids are then provided to farmers free-of-charge to use as a natural fertilizer. This method has reduced the amount of landfill generated by the process each year.

Important Words and Expressions

pathogen ['pæθədʒən]   n. 病原体；病菌
compost ['kɔmpɔst]   n. 堆肥；混合物   vt. 堆肥；施堆肥
horticulture ['hɔːtikʌltʃə]   n. 园艺，园艺学
percolation [ˌpəːkə'leiʃən]   n. 过滤；浸透
helminth ['helminθ]   n. 寄生虫，蛔虫；蠕虫，肠虫
windrow ['windrəu]   n. 料堆；干草列；风积丘   vt. 将…进行排列
rehabilitation [ˌriːhəbili'teiʃən]   n. 复原

pyrolysis [pai'rɔlisis]   n. [化学] 热解；[化学] 高温分解
depolymerization [di:,pɔliməraiˈzeiʃən]   n. [高分子] 解聚（合）作用
premacerate [pri'mæsəreit]   v. 预浸软
cellulose ['seljuləus]   n. 纤维素；（植物的）细胞膜质
combustible [kəmˈbʌstəbl]   adj. 易燃的；易激动的；燃烧性的   n. 可燃物；易燃物
methane ['meθein]   n. [有化] 甲烷；[能源] 沼气
propane ['prəupein]   n. [有化] 丙烷
butane ['bju:tein]   n. [有化] 丁烷
incineration [in,sinəˈreiʃən]   n. 焚化；烧成灰
landfill ['lændfil]   n. 垃圾填埋地；垃圾堆

Notes

[1] 在农业和园艺中作为土壤改良剂回用的堆肥污泥把碳、氮、磷和对植物生长重要的元素返回土壤中。

[2] 为了使（剩余）污泥可回用于农业和园艺中，污水管理的目的是防止化学品进入污水或污泥。

[3] 转化是通过裂解过程，即在无氧或在控制氧量的条件下把干污泥加热到一定的高温实现的。

[4] 由于填埋的污泥中通常含有重金属或有毒化学品，为了防止污染地下水，可能需要黏土或塑料材料的填埋隔层。

[5] 由于焚烧过程产生的气体中含有大气污染物以及需要大量的燃料，使得污泥焚烧在污泥处理和处置中成为一种缺少吸引力而且应用较少的方法。

Exercises

1. Answering the following questions in English according to the text:

(1) What are the reasons that the composting is most often applied to smaller-scale applications followed by aerobic digestion and then lastly anaerobic digestion for the larger-scale municipal applications?

(2) When a liquid sludge is produced, what are the further treatment methods that may be required to make it suitable for final disposal?

2. Using the following each word to make up the sentences, respectively:

(1) biosolids
(2) compost
(3) percolation
(4) pyrolysis
(5) depolymerization
(6) premacerate
(7) landfill

3. Put the following English into Chinese:

(1) Sludge incineration is mainly applied in developed regions because of its high cost. The first sludge incineration project in China, the sludge drying-incineration project of Shidongkou in

Shanghai (213 t/d, 20 % DS), enlightens many tentative projects among cities (China Water Net, 2010). Currently, most sludge incineration projects are located in the Yangtze River Delta, which is one of the most developed regions.

(2) Sludge is not only material resource, but also an energy source in a cement plant. The cement industry can safely handle a great amount of sewage sludge. At present, co-processing of sewage sludge in cement plant has been used in some cities in China, and typical cases are Guangzhou Heidelberg Yuexiu Cement Co., Ltd. (600 t/d, 20 % DS), Beijing Xingbeishui Cement Co., Ltd. (500 t/d 20 % DS), and Chongqing Nanshan Cement Co., Ltd. (150 t/d, 20 % DS) (China Water Net, 2010).

4. Put the following Chinese into English：

(1) 污泥回收利用

(2) 污泥处理

(3) 污泥处置

(4) 最终的处置与利用的主要方法是：作为农肥利用、建筑材料利用、填地与填海造地利用以及排海。

(5) 污泥堆肥一般采用好氧条件下，利用嗜温菌、嗜热菌的作用，分解污泥中有机物质并杀灭传染病菌、寄生虫卵与病毒，提高污泥肥分。

Reading Material A

Incineration

Incineration is complete combustion, which is the rapid exothermic oxidization of combustible elements in sludge. Dewatered sludge will ignite at temperature of 420 to 500 ℃ in the presence of oxygen. Temperatures of 760 to 820 ℃ are required for complete combustion of organic solids. In the incineration of sludge, the organic solids are converted to the oxidized end products, primarily carbon dioxide, water vapor, and ash. Particulates and other gases will also be present in the exhaust, which determines the selection of the treatment scheme for the exhaust gases before venting them to the atmosphere.

Sludge is incinerated if its utilization is impossible or economically infeasible, if storage area is limited or unavailable, and in cases where it is required for hygienic reasons. [1]

One of the principal parameters of sludge incineration is the sludge moisture. Sludge cake with 30 to 50% solids is autogenous; that is, it can be burned without auxiliary fuel. Sludge cake with 20 to 30% solids may require an auxiliary fuel for combustion. Therefore, before incineration, the moisture content of the sludge should be reduced by mechanical dewatering or thermal drying.

Another important parameter of sludge incineration is the heating value of sludge. It represents the quantity of heat released per unit mass of solids. The amount of heat released from sludge is a function of the types and combustible elements present in sludge. The primary combustible elements in sludge are carbon, hydrogen, and sulfur. Carbon burned to carbon dioxide has a heating value of 34 MJ/kg, hydrogen has a heating value of 144 MJ/kg, and sulfur has a heating value of 10 MJ/kg. Consequently, any changes in the carbon, hydrogen, or sulfur content of sludge will raise or lower its heating value.

Methods of Incineration

The process of sludge incineration in furnaces can be divided into the following stages: heating, drying, distillation of volatile matter, combustion of the organic fuel matter, and calcination to burn the residual carbon. [2] Heating the sludge to 100 ℃ and then drying it at about 200 ℃ consume the principal quantity of heat and are generally required for the incineration process. These parameters also affect the selection of the size of the mail and auxiliary equipment and consequently, determine the cost in general. In the course of moisture evaporation in the drying zone, volatile substances are liberated together with the moisture, which sometimes results in objectionable odors.

The combustion of the sludge takes place at temperatures between 200 and 500 ℃, due to the thermal radiation of the flame and the incandescent walls of the combustion chamber, as well as the convection heat transfer from the exhaust gases. The calcination of the ash fraction of the sludge is completed by its cooling to a temperature at which it can be removed from the site. [3]

The design temperature in the furnace should not exceed the melting point of ash and should not be below 700 ℃, thus providing reliable deodorizing of the gases. Systems for sludge incineration should provide complete combustion of the organic fraction of the sludge and utilization of the heat of the exhaust gases. [4]

Furnace selection for combustion of dewatered sludge is determined by sludge moisture content and the noncaking nature of the carbonized residue. The first property excludes the possibility of combusting the sludge directly in a flame or in cyclone furnaces without predrying, and the second property excludes the possibility of combusting the sludge on grates; thus, at the present time, multiple-hearth, fluidized-bed, and rotating drum furnaces are most often used. These furnaces are described in the following sections.

Multiple-Hearth Incineration

The furnace shell is a vertical steel and quality of sludge treated. The furnaces can be installed in the open air. The drawbacks of multiple-hearth furnaces in clued high capital cost, large area required, presence of rotating mechanism in the high-temperature zone, and frequent failure of the rake devices.

Fluidized-Bed Incineration

Fluidized-bed furnaces are well known in drying and roasting technology in various industrial fields. The furnace, a vertical steel cylinder lined internally with refractory brick or heat-resistant concrete, consists of a cylindrical furnace chamber, a lower conical section with an impermeable air distribution grate, and dome-shaped crown. Heat-resistant quartz sand 0.6 to 2.5 mm in size is placed on the grate to a depth of 0.8 to 1 m.

The turbulent bed in the furnace is formed when air is blown through the distribution grate at a rate at which the sand particles move in a turbulent manner and appear to boil in the flow of gas. The air is supplied by a blower to a recuperator, in which it is heated by the exhaust gases leaving the furnace to a temperature of 600 to 700 ℃. The heated air enters under the distribution grate at a pressure of 12 to 15 kPa.

The design of the furnace amounts to determining the material and thermal balances of the sludge combustion process, establishing the geometric dimensions of the furnace elements, and the quantities of auxiliary fuel, air, and exhaust gases. The dimensions of the furnace are determined from the volume of the sludge combusted and the air velocity in the distribution grate. This velocity depends on the hydrodynamic regime of the furnace operation and size of the sand bed as well as the properties of the sludge. The quantity of air required for complete oxidation of the organic matter in sludge is determined from the ultimate composition.

Notes

[1] 如果污泥无用利用或污泥利用在经济上不合理，或污泥存储面积受限甚至无处存储，或基于卫生原因的情况下，污泥采用焚烧处理。

[2] 污泥在炉中焚烧的过程可分成以下步骤：加热、干化、挥发性物质的干馏、有机燃料的燃烧以及残余碳的焙烧。

[3] 污泥中灰分的煅烧可以通过降温完成，即降到可以从中去除的温度。

[4] 污泥焚烧系统应该包括污泥有机成分的完全燃烧和尾气中余热的利用。

Reading Material B

Landfilling

"Ultimate disposition" of biosolids or residue (i.e., ash from incineration) falls into four general categories: landfilling, dedicated land disposal, land application, and utilization.

Landfilling

When there is an acceptable, convenient site, the landfill is typically selected for ultimate disposal of biosolids, grit, screenings and other solids. Landfilling of biosolids and/or ash in a sanitary landfill with municipal solid waste is regulated by the U.S. EPA. Dewatering is typically required and stabilization may be required before the landfill can be used. If methane recovery is practiced at the landfill site, the addition of biosolids may be welcome as it will increase gas production. [1]

Dedicated Land Disposal

Dedicated land disposal means the application of heavy sludge loadings to some finite land area that has limited public access and has been set aside or dedicated "for all time" to the disposal of wastewater sludge. Dedicated land disposal does not mean in-place utilization. No crops may be grown. Dedicated sites typically receive liquid sludges. While application of dewatered sludges is possible, it is not common. In addition, disposal of dewatered sludge in landfills is generally more cost-effective.

One of the common sites for dedicated land disposal is a location where surface mining has taken place. The biosolids improve the recovery of the land by providing organic matter and nutrients for plant growth. [2]

Land Application of Biosolids

One of the methods for disposition of biosolids/wastewater sludge is by land application. Land application is defined as the spreading of biosolids on or just below the soil surface. The application to land for agricultural purposes is beneficial because the organic matter improves soil structure, soil aggregation, water holding capacity, water infiltration, and soil aeration. In addition, macronutrients (such as nitrogen, phosphorus, and potassium) and micronutrients (such as iron, manganese, copper, and zinc) aid plant growth. These contributions also serve as a partial replacement for chemical fertilizers. To qualify for application to agricultural and nonagricultural land, the biosolids must, at a minimum, meet the pollutant ceiling concentrations, Class B requirements for pathogens, and vector attraction requirements. For biosolids processed for application to lawns and gardens, Class A criteria and one of the vector-attraction reduction requirements must be met.

Site Selection

A critical step in land application of biosolids is the identification of a suitable site. Among the factors that must be considered are topography (for erosion potential), soil characteristics, depth to the groundwater, accessibility, proximity to critical areas (such as domestic water supply, property boundaries, public access), and haul distance. The employment of a soil scientist to assist in the assessment is critical. The plan that determines the selection process should involve all the stake holders.

Design Loading Rates

Nitrogen and heavy metals concentrations in the sludge are two of the major concerns in determining the sludge loading rate. [3] The nitrogen limit is typically determined on an annual basis. Heavy-metal loadings are based on long-term averages.

The nitrogen loading rate is typically set to match the available nitrogen provided by commercial fertilizers. It is dependent on the crop and can vary from 120 to 245 kg/(ha·y) for field crops(corn, wheat, and soybeans) and from 175 to 670 kg/(ha·y) for forage crops (alfalfa, and grasses).

Extensive soil testing and analysis by a soil scientist is essential in determining an appropriate loading rate.

Application Methods

The application methods are broadly classified as liquid application and dewatered biosolids application.

Liquid biosolids application This method is attractive because of its simplicity. Dewatering processes are not required. The solids concentrations range from 1 to 10 percent. The application method may be by vehicular application or by irrigation.

Vehicular application may be either surface distribution or subsurface distribution. Special vehicles are used. They have wheels designed to minimize compaction and to improve mobility. For surface distribution, rear-mounted spray manifolds, nozzles, or guns are used. For subsurface injection, two alternatives are commonly used. Injection shanks force the liquid into the ground directly. Alternatively, plows or discs with manifolds apply the biosolids that are then incorporated immediately after injection by covering spoons.

Injection below the soil surface is preferred as it minimizes odors, reduces vector attraction, minimizes ammonia loss, eliminates surface runoff, and minimizes visibility, which leads to better public acceptance. However, this method is not suitable for all crops.

Irrigation may be by sprinkling or furrow irrigation. These methods find application in locations isolated from public view and access. They have the following disadvantages: high power costs for the pumps, contact of all parts of the crop with the biosolids, potential odors, vector attraction, and high visibility to the public.

Dewatered Biosolids Application

Application of dewatered solids is similar to the application of semisolid animal manure. Typical solids concentrations are in the range of 15 to 20 percent. It must be followed by incorporation. This method has the potential to generate dust and odors as well as being an attraction to vectors. Public acceptance of this application method may be difficult to achieve.

Utilization

Wastewater solids may sometimes be used beneficially in ways other than as a soil nutrient. Of the several methods worthy of note, composting and co-firing with municipal solid waste are two that have received increasing amounts of interest in the last few years.[4] The recovery of lime and the use of the sludge to form activated carbon have also been in practice to a lesser extent.

Notes

[1] 由于生物污泥会提高产（甲烷）气率，如果污泥填埋场所具有甲烷回收装置，生物污泥会受欢迎。

[2] 通过提供植物生长需要的有机物质和营养物质，生物污泥提高了土壤的复原程度。

[3] 在确定污泥负荷率时，污泥中的氮和重金属浓度是两个主要因素。

[4] 在污泥处置的几种值得注意的方法中，堆肥和与城市垃圾一起焚烧的方法在过去几年中受到越来越多的关注。

Part Six

Building Water Supply and Drainage

Unit 21　　Cold Water Supply

Drinking water

Under the Water Supply Regulations 1999: every dwelling is required to have a wholesome water supply system, and this should be provided in sufficient quantities for the needs of the user, and at a temperature below 20 ℃. The most important place to provide drinking water in dwellings is at the kitchen sink. However, because there is a likelihood that all taps in dwelling will be used for drinking, they should all be connected in such a way that the water remains in potable condition. This means that all draw-off taps in dwellings should either be connected direct from the mains supply, or from a storage cistern that is protected.

Drinking water supplies should also be provided in suitable and convenient locations in places of work such as offices and commercial buildings, particularly where food and drink are prepared or eaten. [1] If no such location exists, drinking water should be provided near but not in toilet. However, drinking water fountains may be installed on toilet area, provided they are sited well away from WCs and urinals and comply with the requirements of BS 6465: Part 1.

To avoid stagnation, drinking water points are fitted in places of work along with taps for other purposes, all taps should be labelled 'drinking water 'or 'non-drinking water'. [2]

In tall buildings where drinking water is needed above the pressure limit of the mains water supply, it may be necessary for the water to be pumped to the higher level. [3] In such cases any drinking water must be supplied from a 'protected' drinking water cistern or from a drinking water header.

Where a water softener of the base exchange type is installed, it is recommended that connections for drinking water are made upstream of the softener so they do not receive softened water. The Department of Health recommends that unsoftened drinking water should be available for infant feed preparation and to assist recommendation to reduce sodium intake in the general population.

Cold water systems

(1) Systems in buildings

Water may be supplied to cold taps either directly from the mains via the supply pipe or indirectly from a protected cold water storage cistern. In some cases a combination of both methods of supply may be the best arrangement.

A supply 'direct' from the mains is preferred because water quality from storage cannot be guaranteed. However, pressure reliability of the mains supply should be considered especially where connections are made near to the ends of distributing mains. Where constant supply pressure may be a problem, storage should be considered.

Factors to consider when designing a cold water system should be taken into account the available pressure and reliability of supply, particularly where any draw-off point is at the extreme end of a supply pipe or situated near the limit of main pressure.

(2) Systems in buildings other than dwellings

In the case of buildings, the water consumption is likely to be similar to that of a dwelling. For larger buildings, such as office blocks, hostels and factories it will usually be preferable for all water, except drinking water, to be supplied indirectly from cold water storage cisterns. Drinking water should be taken directly from the water supplier's main wherever practicable.

(3) System outside buildings

Pipeline system should conform to national or European standards as appropriate. The system should be designed to ensure that the quality of potable water in system does not deteriorate. Precautions should be taken to prevent risk of contamination through backflow, stagnation, cross connection or any other cause. Systems outside buildings should generally be designed for a life of at least of 50 years although replacement or renovation of components such as pumps, meters and controls may need earlier attention.

Service pipe diameter should be determined by hydraulic calculation after consultation with the consumer and the water supplier. This is particularly important in the case of nondomestic users where design requirements may create greater demands on the available supply. Calculations should also take into account any future supply needs that might be expected. In premises where water for firefighting purposes is required, the local fire service should be consulted and relevant regulations complied with.

Pipelines should be designed to accommodate thermal movement. Particular attention should be given to the difference in temperature during installation compared to the expected temperature when filled and in use. Considerable stress can occur in pipelines where insufficient expansion joints are inserted. This can be a particular problem when plastics pipes are pulled through the ground by mole plough when stresses caused by 'stretching' are combined with those of contraction through cooling.

The design layout for below ground water systems will depend on local circumstances, but in all cases consideration should be given to the following:

1) Adoption of shortest practical route to allow reasonable access for maintenance;

2) Minimum depth of cover for frost penetration and the maximum depth of cover for ease of repair;

3) Location of other services, buildings and structures. Minimum distances should be maintained between water, other services and buildings;

4) Provision and location of valves, air valves, washouts and hydrants where appropriate;

5) Pipe materials and corrosion protection systems in aggressive or contaminated soils;

6) Adverse ground conditions and difficult terrain, earth loads and traffic loads;

7) Risk of damage to and from trees and tree roots;

8) Risk of damage to and from other utilities, works and apparatus.

(4) pumping systems

Where the height of the building lies above satutory level or when the available pressure is insufficient to supply the whole of a building and the water supplier is unable to increase the supply pressure in the supplier's mains, consideration should be given to the provision of a pump. Where the pump delivers 0.12 L/s the water undertake must be notified and written consent obtained before the pump is fitted. It is important that the water supplier is consulted and written consent received before fitting any pump. The water supplier will wish to ensure that Water Regulation are complied with respect of backflow risk, and that any pump will not have adverse effects on the mains and other users.

Important Words and Expressions

dwelling ['dweliŋ]　n. 住处，处所

potable ['pəutəbəl]　adj. 可以喝的，适合饮用的　n.饮料

cistern ['sistən]　n. 蓄水池, 储水箱；地下储水池

softener ['sɔfnə]　n. 软化剂；柔软剂

premises ['premisiz]　n. (包括附属建筑、土地等在内的)房屋或其他建筑物；[律](契约)前言，契据的缘起部分(记述财产的详情、当事人姓名等)

valve [vælv]　n. 阀, 活门；（心脏的）瓣膜；真空管；贝壳；（管乐器的）活栓　vt. 装阀于；以活门调节

hydrant ['haidrənt]　n. 给水栓, 消防龙头

terrain [te'rein]　n. 地形, 地面, 地域, 地带

mains [meinz]　n. 电源, 总输电线, 干线

backflow [bæk,fləu]　n. 逆流, 流向来源

Notes

[1] 还应在诸如办公室和商业楼等工作场所合适且方便的位置提供饮用水供应，特别是准备食品饮料或就餐的地方。

[2] 为了避免淤塞，除其他用途的水龙头外，还将饮用水点设在工作场所，所有的水龙头应标明"饮用水"或"非饮用水"。

[3] 高层建筑中在干线供应压力线以上也需要饮用水，因此用泵将水送至更高楼层是很必要的。

Exercises

1. Answering the following questions in English according to the text：

(1) How should service pipe diameter be determined?

(2) Which factors should be considered for the design layout of below ground water systems?

2. Using the following each word to make up the sentences, respectively：

(1) install

(2) supply
(3) design
(4) calculate
(5) maintain

3. Put the following English into Chinese：

(1) Factors to consider when designing a cold water system should be taken into account the available pressure and reliability of supply, particularly where any draw-off point is at the extreme end of a supply pipe or situated near the limit of main pressure.

(2) Precautions should be taken to prevent the risk of contamination through backflow, stagnation, cross connection or any other cause. Systems outside buildings should generally be designed for a life of at least of 50 years although replacement or renovation of components such as pumps, meters and controls may need earlier attention.

4. Put the following Chinese into English：

(1) 饮用水
(2) 蓄水池
(3) 供水
(4) 可以通过供水管直接由主干线将水供应到冷水水龙头。
(5) 还可以从受保护的冷水蓄水池间接将水供应到冷水水龙头。

Reading Material A

High-Rise Buildings Water Supply System

High-rise building, especially multi-story structural systems mainly apply to office building, large shopping centers and exhibition halls, etc. High-rise buildings are often equipped with water uplifting system, in particularly through equipped intermediate storage tanks or basins.[1] The mentioned tanks are distributed throughout the entire building height at certain intervals. The water is uplifted to the tank, located above, and later it is pumped from it and supplied to another tank, located above, and etc.

Since the very high-rise buildings are using this system, so it is important that the system structure to be relatively light-weight and would not overload the structure of the building with useless weight. The system would also be capable of treating water from the sea or other surface water pools and turn it into potable water or water suitable for daily activities.[2] With the reference to these criteria, a water supply system has been developed for high-rise buildings, which operation principle lies in water evaporation, which is performed at the lower part of the building, while water steam is uplifted in shafts being affected by natural traction. Upon reaching the top of the shaft, water steam gets cool up to the temperature of dew point and condenses. Condensed water is collected and supplied to pipelines. There is also an option to direct surplus water downwards by pipelines, equipped with turbines for power production.

Copper is the most common material for supply pipe; it resists corrosion, so water runs freely and pipes don't leak for many decades. It often be equipped with galvanized steel pipe in an older home, which tends to clog with minerals and rust over time and can develop leaks. Nowadays, many homes have plastic supply pipe, most commonly cross-linked polyethylene (PEX), which installs quickly and is expected to last virtually forever.

Water arrives via a main supply pipe, which is typically 1 inch in diameter or larger. (A pipe is measured by its inside dimension, so a 1-inch copper pipe is about 1 1/8 inches in outside diameter.) In most cases, the pipe runs through at least one main shutoff valve, located outside the house in a "Buffalo box" buried in the yard near the house or just inside the basement or crawl space. It then usually passes through a water meter, and there is likely another main shutoff after the water meter.

The main supply line usually runs to the water heater, where it divides into cold and hot water pipes. From there, supply pipes almost always travel in pairs, hot and cold. [3] Pipes from the water heater are typically 3/4 inch but may be 1/2 inch. Horizontal pairs run to below walls and then vertical pairs, called risers, run up to the various rooms.

In newer homes, there are separate lines running from the water heater to each room, so water use in one area does not affect use in another area. In an older home, a single line may loop throughout the house, meaning, for instance, that if someone flushes a toilet downstairs the cold water supplying a shower upstairs will have lessened pressure, causing the shower water to suddenly become hot.

This water supply system for high-rise and particularly high-rise buildings are used to the ones that located in the regions of hot climate, where solar energy is sufficient for the evaporation of the required amount of water.

Basically, the high-rise building water supply system comprises of a water basin with casing, made of transparent material, the shaft for water steam flow and upper condensation facility, from which the water may flow into the upper tank.[4] The mentioned water basin may be a land-based water tank, which is continually supplied with ground or surface (river, sea, etc.) water. The basin may also be equipped in the shore of a large water body (sea, ocean, river, lake, etc.), if the building is located close to such water body. In both cases, a transparent casing is arranged above the water surface, leaving an air gap. This air gap is used to transfer water steam affected by natural traction, which appears in the shaft due to temperature difference. In order to establish conditions under which a constant one direction steam flow would appear in the mentioned air gap, one side of the casing on the opposite side than the shafts open for environmental air to pass through it. Thus, the casing at one side has an opening, at the other - contraction for water steam flow to pass to the lifting shaft. Casing flanks are closed and directly attached to the walls of the basin. In case the basin is arranged in the shore of a large water pool, the bottom of the basin is made inclined, a water outlet is left at the bottom of the inclination in basin's wall for water outflow, therefore, the remaining water with the major salt and sewage content settles to the bottom and withdraws via the stated outlet. Water change of tide takes place, which ensures prevention of salt and other sewage sediments accumulation in the basin. The walls of the shaft are properly insulated from the outside in order the steam temperature throughout the entire height of the shaft would drop as less as possible. By sustaining approximately constant temperature in one shaft, steam does not condense on the half-way and useless condensate does not accumulate.

Notes

[1] 高层建筑往往配备水的提升系统，特别是通过设置中间储存池或者储存盆。

[2] 该系统还有能力处理从海上或者其他表面水池取的水，将它变成饮用水或者用于其他日常活动的水。

[3] 主供水管经常连接至水加热器，并在那里分为冷水管和热水管。水加热器后的管道几乎是成对铺设，即冷水管和热水管。

[4] 基本上，高层建筑热水供应系统包括一个热水盆系统，由透明材料制成，具有水蒸气流动的上冷凝设备，其中的水可能流入水箱。

Reading Material B

Hydraulic Calculation of Building Water Supply System

Water supply designed for water consumption of dwelling district should be determined according to the following water consumptions: residential domestic water consumptions, public building water consumption, green belt water consumption, water space (amusement facilities) water consumption, road (square) water consumption, public facilities water consumption, unpredictable water consumption and pipe leakage water consumption and fire control water consumption.[1]

The followed are the procedure to size the supply pipes：

(1) Assume a pipe diameter;

(2) Determine the flow rate;

(a) by using loading units;

(b) for continuous flows;

(c) Obtain the design flow rate by adding (a) and (b).

(3) Determine the effective pipe length;

(d) Work out the measured pipe length;

(e) Work out the equivalent pipe length for fittings;

(f) Work out the equivalent pope length for draw-offs;

(g) Obtain the effective pipe length by adding (d), (e) and (f).

(4) Calculate the permissible loss of head;

(h) Determine the available head;

(i) Determine the head loss per meter run through pipes;

(j) Determine the head loss through fittings;

(k) Calculate the permissible head loss.

(5) Determine the pipe diameter;

(6) Decide whether the assumed pipe size will give the designed flow rate in (c) without exceeding the permissible head loss in (k).

1. Design flow of building water supply inlet pipe should comply with following demands:

(1) When building domestic water consumption all are directly supplied by outdoor pipe net, building domestic water consumption design second flow should be taken.

(2) When building domestic water consumption are supplied by self-pressurized, design flow of inlet pipe should be the design replenishing flow may not be exceed building maximum daily maximum hourly domestic water consumption and must not less than building maximum daily average hourly domestic water consumption.

(3) When building domestic water consumption are supplied by both outdoor pipe net and

self-pressurized, the inlet pipe design flow should be the sum of calculated results according to sub clause 1, 2 of this Clause.

2. Design second flow of residential building domestic water supply should comply with following procedures and calculating methods:

(1) Based upon residence plumbing fixture water supply equivalent, number of persons, number of hours and hour variation coefficient, according to Eq.(21-1) to calculate the maximum water consumption of plumbing fixture water supply equivalent average outflow probability:

$$U_0 = q_0 m K_h / 0.2 N_g T * 3600 \qquad (21\text{-}1)$$

Where U_0-Domestic water supply pipe during maximum water consumption plumbing fixture water supply equivalent average outflow probability; q_0 -Maximum water consumption day water consumption rate; m-Each family number of persons; K_h-Hour variation coefficient; T-Water consumption hours (h); 0.2-Each plumbing fixture water supply equivalent rated flow (L/s).

(2) Based upon calculated pipe sections plumbing fixture water supply equivalent total amount, according to Eq.(21-2) to calculate this pipe section plumbing fixture water supply equivalent simultaneous outflow probability:

$$U = [1 + \alpha_c(N_g - 1)0.49] / N_g^{0.5} \qquad (21\text{-}2)$$

Where U-Calculated pipe section plumbing fixture water supply equivalent simultaneous outflow probability (%); α_c-Coefficient corresponds to different U_0, find out from appendix C; N_g-Calculated pipe section plumbing fixture water supply equivalent total amount.

(3) Based upon calculated pipe section plumbing fixture water supply equivalent simultaneous outflow probability, according to Eq.(21-3) to calculate design second flow of this pipe section:

$$Q_g = 0.2 U N_g (L/s) \qquad (21\text{-}3)$$

Where Q_g-Design second flow of calculated pipe section (L/s).

(4) Water supply main with two or more than two different maximum water consumption pluming fixture water supply equivalent average outflow probability water supply branch, this pipe section's maximum hour plumbing fixture water supply equivalent average outflow probability may be calculated according to Eq(21-4):

$$U_0 = \sum U_{oi} N_{gi} / \sum N_{gi} \qquad (21\text{-}4)$$

Where U_0-Water supply main's plumbing fixture water supply equivalent average outflow probability; U_{oi}-Branch pipe's maximum water consumption hour plumbing fixture water supply equivalent average outflow probability; N_{gi}-Correspond branch pipe's plumbing fixture water supply equivalent total amount.

(5) Water flow velocity of domestic water supply may be taken according to Table 21.1.

Table 21.1 Water flow velocity of domestic water supply pipeline

Nominal diameter (mm)	15~20	25~40	50~70	≥80
Water flow velocity (m/s)	≤1.0	≤1.2	≤1.5	≤1.8

(6) Water head loss along water supply pipeline may be calculated according to following Eq(21-5):

$$i = 105 C_h^{-1.85} d_j^{-4.87} q_g^{1.85} \qquad (21\text{-}5)$$

Where i-Water head loss per unit length of pipeline (kPa/m); d_j-Pipe calculated internal diameter of pipe (m); q_g-Water supply design flow (m^3/s); C_h-Coefficient of Hazen-Williams. Various kind of plastic pipe, lining pipe C_h=140; Copper pipe, stainless steel pipe C_h=130; Cement, resin lined cast iron pipe C_h=130; Steel pipe cast iron pipe C_h=100.

(7) The partial head loss of domestic water supply net work may be calculated according to the method of connections, and calculated by pipe fitting equivalent length method. [2] When the method of pipe fitting equivalent length data is insufficient, it may be taken according to following pipefitting connection and head loss along pipe net work percentage:

- Pipe (accessory) fitting internal diameter is the same of pipe diameter, when tee branch is used, take 25%-30%; when manifold is used, take 15%-20%.
- Pipe (accessory) fitting internal diameter is slightly greater than pipe diameter, when tee branch is used, take 50%-60%; when manifold is used, take 30%-35%.
- Pipe (accessory) fitting internal diameter is slightly less than pipe diameter, pipe (accessory) fitting is spigot and socket connection, when tee branch is used, take 70%-80%; when manifold is used, take 35%-40%.

Notes

[1] 住宅区给水的设计用水量可根据以下确定：居民生活用水、公共建筑用水、绿化用水、娱乐设施用水、公路用水、公共设施用水、不可预知耗水和管道泄漏耗水，火灾控制用水。

[2] 国内给水管网的局部水头损失的计算可根据管件的连接方法，或者采用当量长度法。

Unit 22 Building-Drainage System

A building drainage system used for apartment houses, detached houses, etc. generally includes a drainage stack passing through stories;[1] appliance drainage pipes connected to water-service terminal appliances such as a kitchen and a basin provided on each of the stories and extending while being tilted at a slight slope with respect to a floor slab of the story; and a combined joint for connecting the drainage pipes on each story to the stack, the joint being provided on the same story; wherein waste water from the water-service terminal appliances on each story is discharged in the drainage pipes, being introduced to the joint provided on the same story, and is combined to a fluid flowing in the stack. At the joint of such a conventional drainage system, the drainage pipes cross the stack at an angle of 90° or slightly smaller than 90°, and therefore, the joint is required to have a large capacity, particularly, a large horizontal cross-section. As a result, this arise problems that the joint becomes heavy and expensive, and further becomes poor in the degree of freedom in design because the joint requires a wide space.

A drainage apparatus system for a building having a basement floor between walls supported on footings, the drainage apparatus comprising: drain tile disposed about an outer perimeter of the footings to accumulate water adjacent the outer perimeter of the footings; at least one bleeder conduit disposed beneath the basement floor and connected at a first end to the drain tile located exteriorly of the building and at a second end to a discharge pipe to direct water from the drain tile to the discharge pipe; a hollow body having first and second ends and a flow passage extending between the first and second ends, the first and second ends fluidically interposed to the at least one bleeder line in a location spaced from the drain tile beneath and covered by the basement floor, the body having an upper portion with an openable end accessible through the basement floor, allowing a fluid stream to be injected into the hollow body through the openable end into the flow passage; and a one way valve disposed within the hollow body, the valve including a valve member movably mounted in the hollow body for fluid pressure responsive movement between a first position blocking fluid flow through the fluid passage in the hollow body in a first direction from the open end of the upper portion toward the first end of the hollow body and a second position allowing fluid flow from the first end and from the open end of the upper portion only toward the second end of the hollow body in a direction toward a sewer conduit to enable clean out of the bleeder line and the sewer conduit.

A building drainage system includes one or more of an interior located bleeder line cleanout incorporating a one-way flow valve, an exterior drainage and tile cleanout having concentrically disposed pipes with an end accessible from ground surface level, having apertures allowing the ingress of water through the pipes and to the drain tile system, and an exterior drainage system including a horizontal drain member located below soil surface level and spaced from the building foundation wall and a drainage path from the horizontal drain member to a reservoir also located below soil surface level.[2] A discharge path is formed from the reservoir to the surrounding soil or through a pipe to a remote located pop-up discharge valve.[3]

A drainage apparatus for a building drain tile system fluidically connected to bleeder conduits below a foundation floor, the drainage apparatus comprising: a hollow body fluidically interconnected to one bleeder line, the body having an upper portion accessible from the building floor; one way valve means disposed within the body for allowing fluid flow through the body and the one bleeder line in one direction and for blocking fluid flow of a fluid stream injected through the upper portion of the body in a direction opposite from allowed fluid flow direction through the body; a vertically extending interior conduit having first and second ends, the first end fluidically coupled to a building drain tile system, the second end accessible from above soil grade level, the interior conduit having side wall apertures allowing the ingress of water from an exterior of the interior conduit to the interior of the interior conduit; an exterior conduit concentrically disposed about and spaced from the interior conduit; the exterior conduit including a plurality of apertures allowing fluid flow from the exterior to the interior of the exterior conduit; and particulate material disposed between the interior conduit and the exterior conduit allowing fluid flow through the exterior conduit and the interior conduit to the building drain tile system.

The indoor sewage drainage system is consist of: fixture trap, fixture branch, waste stack, building drain, building trap, venting pipe, sewage lifting equipment and so on. A house has at least one main stack, a vertical pipe that runs from above the roof down to the main sewer line. The house's various toilets, faucets, tubs, and appliances have horizontal pipes that run into the main stack. Horizontal pipes must be sloped so water cannot settle in them.

Venting is a sometimes complicated matter, but the principle is straightforward: like that little air hole in a gas can, a vent pipe allows air to come behind the drain water, so it flows smoothly. Without venting, drain water can gurgle, much like water coming out of an upturned thin-necked bottle. Local and national codes have very specific requirements for vent pipes.

The conventional building drainage system has the following problems: namely, when the drainage of waste water flowing in a drainage pipe connected to an appliance in a full-channel manner is completed, air is strongly sucked from the drainage port of the appliance through the drainage pipe by a siphon suction force; and such air interferes with the waste water remaining in the drainage pipe, to cause large suction noise.

Important Words and Expressions

drainage ['dreinidʒ] n. 排水，放水；排水系统，下水道；废水，污水，污物
basin ['beisn] n. 盆，碗；流域
slab [slæb] n. 厚板，平板，厚片
tile [tail] n. 瓦片，瓷砖 vt. 用瓦片、瓷砖等覆盖
perimeter [pə'rimitə] n. 周边；周围；边缘
sewer ['su:ə] n. 污物处理（系统）
aperture ['æpətʃə] n. 孔，隙缝；（照相机的）光圈，孔径
reservoir ['rezəvwɑ:] n. 水库；储藏，汇集
venting ['ventiŋ] n. 消除；泄去；排去；通风
faucet ['fɔ:sit] n. <美> 水龙头
siphon ['saifən] n. 虹吸管
suction ['sʌkʃən] n. 吸，抽吸

Notes

[1] 用于公寓、房屋等的建筑排水系统一般包括贯穿每层楼的排水管。

[2] 建筑排水系统包括一个或多个内置的具有单向阀的泄水管线清扫口、外部排水系统，此外还有陶瓷清扫口，作为终端将各种管线连接起来露出地面，其上有孔口可允许水流通过管线到达排水系统以及建筑物外部排水系统。

[3] 从水库到周边土壤或通过管道输送到远处的弹出式排泄阀形成排放路径。

Exercises

1. Answering the following questions in English according to the text：

(1) Which parts should be comprised in a drainage apparatus system for a building having a basement floor?

(2) What are the problems for the conventional building drainage system?

2. Using the following each word to make up the sentences, respectively：

(1) drainage

(2) discharge

(3) sewer

(4) suction

(5) venting

3. Put the following English into Chinese：

(1) At the joint of such a conventional drainage system, the drainage pipes cross the stack at an angle of 90° or slightly smaller than 90°, and therefore, the joint is required to have a large capacity,

particularly, a large horizontal cross-section.

(2) The joint is required to have a large capacity, particularly, a large horizontal cross-section. As a result, this arise problems that the joint becomes heavy and expensive, and further becomes poor in the degree of freedom in design because the joint requires a wide space.

4. Put the following Chinese into English:

(1) 泄水管

(2) 排水瓦

(3) 建筑排水系统

(4) 通风有时是一件复杂的事，但原理却很简单。

(5) 室内污水排水系统包括卫生器具、器具排水横支管、废水管道、建筑排水管道、排气管、污水提升设备等。

Reading Material A
Home Plumbing System

Home plumbing systems must bring hot and cold water to the kitchen, bathrooms, laundry room and exterior taps at adequate pressures and in the required volumes. [1] They must safely remove waste water while venting waste water odors and gases and keeping them out of the living quarters. For the water supply, there must be shut-off valves for the entire system and for each unit supplied with water so that individual units can be shut down without affecting the entire system. Home plumbing systems are passive recipients of supplied water from the municipal system. A major system is defined as the water mains that bring drinking water to the house while a minor system is the plumbing system, including service line that carries the water within property boundaries. [2] Drainage network and plumbing system are basic provision for buildings all over the world.

Waste water supply

Decide where to place your main stack. The main stack is a large pipe, usually 3 or 4 inches in diameter, that passes through the building from the basement to the roof. The lower part collects waste from toilets, the middle part collects waste water from other fixtures and the top part is used for venting. Venting is needed to equalize the pressure in the system as water pours through the pipes and pushes air in front of it or pulls air in behind it.

Fixtures must be within about 5 feet of the main stack or they will need larger drain pipes or separate venting. If a bathroom is located far from the main stack, it may have its own stack rising through the roof and joining with the lower section of the main stack.

Place your drains and vents. Drain and vent pipes are usually 1 1/2 or 2 inches. Pipes must slant 1/4 inch per foot to drain well. Bends to join the stack or other main drains must be smooth, not angled sharply, to promote smooth water flow. This means using two 45 degree angles for a slow turn rather than one 90 degree angle.

Each fixture (except a toilet) must have a trap, which is a U-shaped bend in the pipe under the fixture. This bend traps water and prevents gases and odors from entering the living quarters. Toilets have their own built-in trap and, therefore, must not have another one in the piping.

Each fixture must be vented. Fixtures located within 5 feet of the main stack and connected with a pipe 2 inches or larger can be "wet" vented, which means that there is enough room in the drain pipe for both waste and air flow simultaneously. If the pipe is longer, water may flow slowly and block the pipe, thus blocking air circulation and venting. For these cases, an additional pipe must be run from the fixture drain pipe up to join the main stack at the venting section.

Prepare a rough-in plumbing diagram. Many jurisdictions require this diagram to get a permit. The diagram shows all drainage pipes, pipe fittings and vents in a three-dimensional perspective drawing. It shows all pipe sizes, traps, vents and angles of connection. The building inspector uses the diagram to make sure the design is acceptable and the proposed installation satisfies the local building codes.

Fresh water supply system

Place the hot water tank in the design. For smaller installations 1/2-inch pipe can be used throughout the house but 3/4-inch pipe is needed for the main pipes of larger homes. The cold water pipe needs a shut-off valve and then is split with one branch attached to the cold water fitting of the hot water tank. [3] The hot water pipe starts from the top of the hot water tank and needs a shut-off valve in order for the cold water/hot water pipe pair to be ready for distribution. [4]

Determine the paths of the cold water/hot water pipe runs. It is possible to run a pair of pipes to each fixture from a manifold in the basement, but it is more common to run a pipe pair to each fixture group and to distribute the water from there.

Run 3/4-inch pipe for runs that will supply more than one grouping of fixtures. Run 1/2-inch pipes to the fixtures. Special fixtures such as spa-type bathtubs and rainhead showers may work better with 3/4-inch pipe all the way to the fixture. The 3/4-inch pipe supplies more water volume at a higher pressure even if the fixture itself has only 1/2-inch fittings. If fixtures in a group can be located along one wall or along two walls, the piping will be considerably easier.

Design the final runs to each fixture for the rough-in supply pipes. Sinks normally have the two pipes coming out of the wall just below the bottom of the sink. Toilets have the cold water pipe coming out of the wall under the tank. Tubs and showers are custom designed depending on the arrangement of taps, temperature controls, faucets and shower heads. Washing machines have the two pipes brought out close to the side or behind the machine and the pipes need shut-off valves. Shut-off valves for the other fixtures are added when the final connections to each unit are done.

Notes

[1] 在足够的压力和需要量下，住宅管道系统必须将热水和冷水接入厨房、浴室、洗衣房以及外部的水龙头。

[2] 一个主要的系统被定义为供水干管，它将饮用水供给住宅，而次要的系统是室内管道系统包括给房屋建造区内供水的给水管道。

[3] 冷水管需要一个截止阀和一个连接到热水箱的冷水拟合器的分管。

[4] 热水管从顶部的热水箱开始和需要一个截止阀，为的是对冷、热水管进行分配。

Reading Material B

Hydraulic Calculation of Building -Drainage System

1. Rated outflow of domestic drainage system of residential district is the 85%-95% of corresponded rated water consumption of domestic water supply system.

2. Rated flow of domestic sewage of public building and hourly variation coefficient is the same of rated domestic water supply water consumption of public building and hourly variation coefficient, it should be determined according to the Present Code.

3. Design flow of domestic sewage of residential district should be determined base upon the sum of residential domestic sewage maximum hourly flow and public building domestic sewage maximum hourly flow. [1]

4. Building domestic sewage design second flow of dwelling, dormitory, hotel, hospital, sanatorium, kindergarten, old age pension, office building, market, expo-center, school building etc. should be calculated according to following Eq.(22-1):

$$q_p = 0.12\alpha N_p^{0.5} + q_{max} \qquad (22\text{-}1)$$

Where q_p-Calculated pipe section drainage design second flow (L/s); N_p-Calculated pipe section plumbing fixture drainage total equivalent; α-Coefficient, which base upon usage of building, is determined according to Table 22.1; q_{max}-Outflow of maximum plumbing fixture at calculated pipe section (L/s).

Table 22.1 Coefficient α determined by usage of building

Name of building	Water closet of dwelling, guest house, hospital, sanatorium, kindergarten, old age pension	Public toilet and closet of dormitory, hotel and public building
α value	1.5	2.0~2.5

Note: When the calculated flow is greater than the accumulated outflow of plumbing fixture of the pipe section, the value of accumulated outflow of plumbing fixture of this pipe section must be taken when calculating. [2]

5. The calculated domestic sewage design second flow of living area of industrial enterprises, public bath room, launch, kitchen of public dinning hall or canteen, laboratory, cinema, stadium, waiting room (air plane, ship) etc. should be calculated according to the following Eq.(22-2):

$$q_p = \sum q_0 N_0 H_b \qquad (22\text{-}2)$$

Where q_p-Calculated pipe section drainage second flow (L/s); q_0-Outflow of sanitary fixture (L/s); N_0-Number of similar plumbing fixtures; H_b-Simultaneous drainage percentage of plumbing fixtures which must be taken according to the present code. The simultaneous drainage capacity of closet bowl of wash tank should be calculated according to 12%.

Note: When the calculated drainage flow is less than the drainage flow of one closet bowl, it should be calculated according to the drainage flow of one closet bowl. [3]

6. The hydraulic calculation of horizontal drainage pipe should be according to the following Eq. (22-3):

$$D_v = R^{2/3} I^{1/2} / n \qquad (22\text{-}3)$$

Where D_v=Velocity (m/s); R=Hydraulic radius; I=Hydraulic slope taking the slope of drainage pipe; n=Roughness coefficient, 0.13 for cast iron pipe, 0.013-0.014 for concrete R.C. pipe, 0.012 for steel pipe, 0.009 for plastic pipe.

7. Building domestic sewage cast iron pipeline's minimum slope and maximum designed degree of fullness may be determined according to Table 22.2.

Table 22.2 Building domestic sewage cast iron pipeline's minimum slope and maximum designed degree of fullness

Pipe diameter(mm)	General slope	Minimum slope	Maximum designed degree of fullness
50	0.035	0.025	0.5
75	0.025	0.015	
100	0.020	0.012	
125	0.015	0.010	
150	0.010	0.007	0.6
200	0.008	0.005	

8. Building plastic drainage horizontal branch pipe standard slope should be 0.26. Drainage horizontal main pipe may be used according to Table 22.3.

Table 22.3 Building drainage plastic horizontal main pipe minimum slope and maximum designed degree of fullness

Exterior diameter	Minimum slope	Maximum designed degree of fullness
110	0.004	0.5
125	0.0035	0.5
160	0.003	0.6
200	0.003	0.6

9. Domestic drainage vertical pipe's maximum outflow capacity should be determined according to Table 22.4. Diameter of vertical pipe must not be less than the connected horizontal branch pipe diameter.

Table 22.4 Domestic sewage vertical pipe's maximum outflow capacity without vent

Working height of vertical pipe (m)	Outflow capacity (L/s)				
	Vertical pipe diameter (mm)				
	50	75	100	125	150
≤2	1.00	1.70	3.80	5.00	7.00
3	0.64	1.35	2.40	3.40	5.00
4	0.50	0.92	1.76	2.70	3.50
5	0.40	0.70	1.36	1.90	2.80
6	0.40	0.50	1.00	1.50	2.20
7	0.40	0.50	0.76	1.20	2.00
≥8	0.40	0.50	0.64	1.00	1.40

10. Closet bowl drainage minimum pipe diameter must not less than 100 mm.

11. Minimum outflow pipe diameter from building must not less than 50 mm.

12. Multiple floor kitchen vertical pipe diameter must not be less than 75 mm.

13. Drainage horizontal pipe of following places, pipe diameter should be determined according to following demands:

(1) When drainage pipe of building base floor individually discharges, horizontal branch pipe

diameter may be determined according to Table 4 working height ≤2 m.

(2) Public dinning hall kitchen sewage, the pipe diameter is one grade greater than calculated diameter, the main must not be less than 100 mm, the branch less than 75 mm.

(3) Hospital washing tub drainage pipe diameter must not be less than 75 mm.

(4) Urinal through or connected with 3 or more 3 urinals, sewage branch pipe diameter may not be less than 75 mm.

(5) Both pools outflow pipe diameter may be 100 mm.

Notes

[1] 住宅小区的生活污水的设计流量应根据住宅生活污水最大时流量和公共建筑生活污水最大时流量确定。

[2] 当计算流量大于管段的累积流量时，该管段的累积流量必须计算。

[3] 当计算流量小于坐便器的额定流量时，应按坐便器的额定流量计算。

Unit 23　Fire-Fighting Systems

The history of organized fire-fighting dates back to the ancient Romans, who introduced the first public water supply system and organized "Vigiles" (watchmen of the city) to combat fires using methods such as bucket-brigades.[1] Since that time, the planning and design of water systems for fire suppression has evolved significantly to limit loss of life and property. While advanced fire suppression systems in buildings and brave firefighters are responsible for directly combating today's fires, water system utilities must have the necessary water main and hydrant infrastructure in place to deliver adequate fire flows throughout their systems.

Determining if a water distribution system can provide adequate fire flow throughout a service area can require significant data collection, and thousands of hydraulic calculations to account for the numerous possible fire flow scenarios that could occur. Performing this type of analysis may seem like a daunting endeavor; however, there are modern computer software and analysis tools that can be leveraged to make this a very manageable effort. This paper provides an overview of how current hydraulic modeling and GIS technologies can be used to help utilities effectively and efficiently evaluate the fire suppression capabilities of their water systems. A case study that illustrates how a Florida water utility has recently utilized these technologies to analyze and improve their fire suppression capabilities is also provided.

Overview of Fire Suppression Planning for Water Utilities

Fire suppression planning for a water utility should include the following steps：

(1) Define fire suppression requirements and goals;

(2) Evaluate water distribution system infrastructure and operations to determine any current or projected future fire flow delivery issues;

(3) Evaluate system improvement options to address fire flow delivery issues; and

(4) Develop recommended system improvements and/or operational modifications.

Defining Fire Suppression Requirements and Goals

The first step in fire suppression planning for a water distribution system is to define the fire suppression requirements and goals for the service area. The fire suppression goals that are selected can have a significant impact on the water system infrastructure requirements and operating protocol for the system. [2]

Defining these goals should be a collaborative effort between the water utility department and the fire department. City managers and key staff from other municipal departments such as land-use planning and building and development should also be included. It is common for a municipality to develop a Fire Prevention and Protection Code by adopting guidelines from water industry reference manuals such as AWWA manuals M31 (Distribution System Requirements for Fire Protection) and M32 (Computer Modeling of Water Distribution Systems). These AWWA manuals reference information published by the Insurance Services Office (ISO), which is an advisory organization that provides guidelines for property and casualty insurance companies to rate a community's local fire protection capabilities.

Examples of the type of distribution system requirements for fire suppression that should be defined include:

Minimum fire flow delivery requirements: The flowrate required for fire suppression in an area will vary significantly based on the type of structure being served. A single family residential property will have a significantly lower fire flow requirement than a high-rise condominium building or commercial building. For example, the fire flow needed for a residential area may be 750 gallons per minute (gpm) for a duration of 2 hours, whereas the fire flow required for a highrise building may be 3,500 gpm for a 3 hour duration.

Minimum system pressures to be maintained during a fire flow event: A typical requirement for fire suppression planning is to be able to maintain a minimum of 20 psi pressure throughout the distribution system while operating under maximum day demand conditions and also meeting the demand requirements of a fire flow event anywhere in the system where fire service is provided by the utility.

Fire hydrant spacing: The number of fire hydrants that must be located within a specified distance from a structure should be defined. The number of hydrants required and the proximity of the hydrants to the structure can vary depending on the type of structure served. For example, a low density residential area may only require a single hydrant to be located within 500 feet (ft) of each property. Whereas a high-rise condominium or a commercial property may require multiple hydrants to be located within specified distances from the property. Also, a hydrant that is located closer to a property may be given more fire flow credit than a hydrant located further from a property.

Minimum water storage capacity maintained for fire flow events: The amount of storage capacity that should be reserved for fire protection is typically defined by multiplying the maximum fire flow needed in the system by a specified maximum duration. For example, a municipality may have a maximum fire flow of 3,500 gpm for a duration of 3 hours. This would result in a total fire flow volume requirement of 630,000 gallons. The average daily minimum water storage capacity for the system should be greater than the calculated maximum fire flow volume requirement.

Evaluating System Infrastructure and Operations

The water distribution system infrastructure must be adequately sized to accommodate the potable water supply needs (including fire protection) for the customers throughout the service area.[3] The system must have the capacity to accommodate a sudden high fire flow water demand anywhere in the service area where fire service is provided. Simply over-sizing system infrastructure (storage tanks, pumping stations, pipelines, and fire hydrants) to conservatively plan for meeting the defined fire flow requirements is not a cost-effective solution, and could also result in water quality/water age issues due to extended detention times in over-sized storage and piping infrastructure. A detailed evaluation and analysis is required to make appropriate plans for water system infrastructure improvements that will allow the water utility to meet current and projected future system demand conditions.

Determining if a water distribution system can provide adequate fire flows throughout a service area can require a significant amount of data collection and analysis, and thousands of hydraulic calculations to account for the numerous possible fire flow scenarios. A description of how water utilities can leverage the data storage and analysis capabilities of modern GIS and hydraulic modeling software to make this seemingly arduous task a very manageable effort is provided below.

Using GIS for A Fire Hydrant Spacing Analysis

A geographic information system (GIS) is any system that captures, stores, analyzes, manages and presents data that are linked to a location. Today it is common for municipalities and water utilities to use GIS software as a system mapping and data management tool. [4]There are many ways that GIS can be leveraged to support fire suppression planning. The spatial data storage provided by GIS is one key benefit. Data that a utility may already have in its GIS database include: a detailed mapping of the water distribution system network (pipeline layout, lengths, diameter material, etc), fire hydrant locations, information on the type of property/structure on each parcel, and future land use information. Having this information in a GIS database provides a great starting point for evaluating a water system's fire suppression capabilities.

If the GIS database includes a mapping of the distribution system, fire hydrant locations, and property tax parcel information, a user can run interactive queries to identify any properties that are not located within a specified maximum distance from the closest fire hydrant. GIS software can also generate useful maps that clearly illustrate hydrant spacing deficiencies and proposed improvements.

Once a plan is developed to ensure that there is adequate fire hydrant coverage throughout the system, an analysis should be completed to verify that adequate fire flows can be delivered to the hydrants throughout the system. [5]

Important Words and Expressions

bucket-brigades 水桶旅
hydrant ['haidrənt] n. 消防栓；水龙头；给水栓
fire flow 消防流量；消防水耗
daunt [dɔ:nt] vt. 使气馁，使畏缩；威吓
leverage ['li:vəridʒ] n. 手段，影响力；杠杆作用；杠杆效率
fire suppression 消防队；灭火；火灾扑救
land-use planning 土地利用规划
condominium [,kɔndə'mini:əm] n. 共同统治；财产共有权
proximity [prɔk'simiti] n. 亲近，接近；[数]邻近

conservatively [kən'sə:vətivli]   adv. 谨慎地；保存地；适当地
arduous ['ɑ:dʒu:əs]   adj. 努力的；费力的；险峻的

Notes

[1] 有关有组织的灭火行为的历史可以追溯到古罗马时期，他们最早引入了公共供水系统并组织了 Vigiles（城市的监管者）利用诸如传递水桶的方法来灭火。

[2] 在一个水处理系统中消防规划的第一步是确定服务地区的消防用水量和消防人员数，这些消防员都是经过精心挑选的，他们对水系统的基础设施和消防系统的操作有着深刻的了解。

[3] 水处理分配系统中所需的设施必须有足够大的尺寸用来满足各个用水地区中用户的饮用水需求（包括消防）。

[4] 地理信息系统（GIS）是这样一个系统，它通过获取、储存、分析，并提供数据管理和显示来链接到一个位置。现在市政单位和供水单位通常利用 GIS 作为一种系统绘测和数据管理的工具。

[5] 确定了消火栓能够覆盖整个系统的计划后，就要做分析验证，看是否有足够的消防流量提供给整个消防系统的消火栓。

Exercises

1. Answering the following questions in English according to the text：

(1) What is the first step in fire suppression planning for a water distribution system?

(2) How a general procedure for performing a fire flow analysis with a hydraulic modeling software?

2. Using the following each word to make up the sentences, respectively：

(1) fire hydrant
(2) fire suppression planning
(3) adopt
(4) account for
(5) illustrate

3. Put the following English into Chinese：

(1) The maintenance of water and sewer lines, as well as fire hydrants, is vital for a city to survive. If water cannot be properly disposed of once it has been used, serious health problems can occur. Not only is it important to drain the wastewater, it is equally important to have a potable water supply. Without a reliable water supply and a system to deliver the water, city life would be impossible.

(2) The City maintains a hydraulic model of its water system that was recently updated and calibrated. The updated model included maximum day demand scenarios for existing conditions as well as projected future conditions. Fire flow values consistent with the City's fire flow goals and minimum residual pressure requirements were entered into the model for the fire flow analysis runs. The model was run for existing conditions as well as projected future conditions. The model predicted that adequate fire flows could be provided to most locations throughout the system through the future projected conditions. However there were some potential fire flow deficiencies identified.

4. Put the following Chinese into English:

(1) 消防系统

(2) 消防队

(3) 消防设备

(4) 供水部门和消防部门应当共同努力制定这些目标。

(5) 住宅区需要的火流可能是 750gal/min，每次持续 2h。

5. Put the following abbr.into full phrases:

GIS；AWWA；gpm；ISO

Reading Material A
Fire-Fighting Equipment
Evolution of Fire Apparatus and Equipment

Today's fire apparatus and equipment have evolved over a number of centuries as new inventions have emerged and been adapted to the needs of the fire service. Colonial-era fire fighters had only buckets, ladders, and fire books at their disposal. Because early American settlements featured buildings with thatchroofs and wooden chimneys, firefighting with these limited tools posed a serious challenge. Fire protection was limited to the use of water relays with leather buckets passed from person to person, a system called a bucket brigade. These buckets were made from leather, which was either secured by rivers or sewn together. In many communities, residents were required to place a bucket filled with water on their front steps at night in case of a fire in the community. Any fire would require all residents to help stop the progress of the fire and save the settlement.[1] Water would be dipped from a well and passed from one person to another until the bucket reached the fire. A second line would return the bucket to the water supply. Compared to today's fire suppression capabilities, this method of firefighting seems archaic and time-consuming.

Some towns also required that ladders be available so that fire fighters could access the roof to extinguish small fires. If all else failed, the fire book would be used to pull down a burning building and prevent the fire from spreading to nearby structures. The "hook-and-ladder truck" evolved from this early equipment.

Triple-Combination Pumper

The real breakthrough for today's modern fire apparatus came in 1906, when the triple-combination pumper was introduced.[2] This truck carried water in a tank generally used for the booster line and commonly called the booster tank. The triple-combination pumper also had a pump capacity of 250 gallons (946 liters) per minute (GPM) or greater. Additionally 2½" (6.35 cm) hose was carried for water supply purposes, as well as firefighting hose, commonly 1½" (3.81 cm) in diameter. A driver/operator and a fire officer rode in the cab, and others members of the company rode on the tailboard.

Diesel-Powered Fire Apparatus

Today's fire apparatus may be equipped with an anti-lock braking system (ABS) which monitors all wheels on the vehicle to determine if one or more wheels are starting to skid or actually skidding during braking. Many of today's transmissions are also equipped with an automatic gear shifter. Another device commonly found on modern-day fire apparatus is the automatic traction control system (ATC), an electronic sensor that controls wheel slippage. Regardless of which system is used, it is the driver/operator's responsibility to be familiar with the driving and braking functionality on the apparatus.

Modern Fire Apparatus

The fire apparatus being used by many fire departments today is larger, heavier, taller with a higher center of gravity, and generally more difficult to maneuver through traffic than the devices used by earlier-era fire fighters. Essential Fire Fighting Gear includes Fire Shelters, Hot Shield Protection, Radio Harness and Hydration Packs. Drip Torch burners, fire hose supplies and the finest quality fiberglass handle tools assure fire brigade is well equipped in all conditions.[3] Effective fire fighting depends on good training and quality equipment. Additionally, traffic continues to increase, cars are better insulated and often have stereos blaring, and drivers are generally less patient and often distracted by devices such as cell phones. This provides an ever-increasing challenge for you to maneuver the fire apparatus safely through traffic.

In addition, the capacities of fire apparatus continue to increase. Only a few years ago, a 750 GPM (2838 liters) pump was common. Today, however, the water delivery rate of many pumps exceeds 1500 GPM (5677 liters). Water capacities have also increased from 100 gallons on a pumper to 1000 gallons (3785 liters) or more today. This increased water capacity, along with enclosed cabs, makes the fire apparatus heavier, larger, and more challenging to drive.

Finally, the computer age has made its way into the fire apparatus. Today's fire apparatus have computer systems to prevent the vehicle from skidding (antilocking brake system), electrical load management systems to make sure the electrical load does not exceed the ability of the fire apparatus to produce electricity, and computer systems that monitor the engine's performance. In addition on the fire apparatus's speed and engine performance (rpm) to the fire officer's monitors.

Notes

[1] 任何火灾都需要所有居民帮忙才能阻止火势的蔓延，解救受灾的人。

[2] 对于消防设备而言，真正的突破是从1906年水罐泵浦车的引进而开始的。

[3] 基本的消防设备包括防火保护、热屏蔽保护、无线电背带、水袋包。滴液点火器、消防水带供应和优质的玻璃纤维柄工具保证了消防队在任何情况下的优良配备。

Reading Material B

Design of Automatic Fire Sprinkler System

Automatic Sprinklers

In the past fifteen years the variety of sprinklers available has grown tremendously. Years ago an engineer would simply specify an upright, pendent or sidewall sprinkler, a sprinkler temperature classification and thread and outlet size. Today, sprinkler specification is a much more difficult task. Characteristics such as the Response Time Index, water spray pattern, operating component type and appearance must be addressed.[1] While there have been numerous advances in sprinkler technology, sprinklers still work in the same manner as they did 100 years ago. Sprinklers are heat sensitive devices, which open to flow water at a preset temperature. More specifically, a sprinkler operating component releases at a specified temperature. Upon release of the operating component, the sprinkler plug falls from the sprinkler orifice and water flows through the orifice, hitting the sprinkler deflector and spraying into a predetermined spray pattern and onto the fuel below.

Of sprinkler components the most interesting is the operating component. There are two basic types of operating components, the fusible-style operating component, which is a soldered type element that melts when subjected to sufficient heat, and the glass bulb operating components, which is an oil containing glass bulb that become pressurized and fails under sufficient heat. For either type of sprinkler operating components, sufficient heat must be provided over a sufficient period of time to cause the solder to melt or bulb to fail. Neither the fusible or glass bulb operating component are better than the other; however, specification of a quick response operating component, available in either fusible or glass bulb style, will result in faster operating times than a standard response operating component. This is a result of the low mass surface area ratio of the quick response operating component as opposed to that of a standard response operating component. In offices and other light hazard applications quick response sprinklers have proven superior to standard response sprinklers. As a result, it is a current code requirement that all light hazard occupancies be protected with quick response sprinklers.

Wet-Pipe Systems

In the United States the wet-pipe sprinkler system is the most common and affordable sprinkler system available. In consideration of the approximately $1.50/sqft installation cost, minimal maintenance costs, and the impressive record for reliability, wet-pipe sprinkler system is clearly established as the workhorse of the fire protection industry.

Unless out of service, wet-pipe sprinkler systems are always water filled. Consequently, building temperature must be maintained above 40°F to prevent freezing. [2] Other than a gate valve and an alarm valve or "shot-gun" riser assembly, there are no devices between the water supply and sprinklers.

Sprinkler System Layout

A sprinkler system is generally laid out as a "Tree", "Loop" or "Grid" type system. Whatever the case, sprinkler are attached directly to pipes called branch lines. [3] Branch lines, normally the smallest of sprinkler pipes, are supplied water from cross mains or feed mains which are directly connected to the system riser.

The riser, configured to control the water supply and monitor water flow and valve position, may support a single sprinkler system or if manifolded, many system. In any case, the maximum area per floor to be protected by a single riser is 52,000-2 for light and ordinary hazard area and 40,000-2 for extra hazard areas.

In high-rise buildings where standpipes and sprinklers are required a combined standpipe/sprinkler system is normally used. In these situations there may be no true system riser; rather, each floor is provided with a floor control valve consisting of a control valve, drain, test connection and flow switch. In this configuration the individual floor control valves accomplish the function of the system riser. An inherent advantage of using floor control valves is that individual floor can be isolated so sprinkler system repairs on one floor do not reduce the level of protection on another floor.

As a practical matter, when lying sprinkler piping out it is advantageous to consider the pipe hanging arrangement. Where construction consists of joist construction, mains should be run parallel to the joist channels. This accommodates pipe hanging since the branch lines, which out number the mains, can be hung directly off the joists. Where construction is concrete pipe hanging is an easier task but one should give consideration to arrangement of beams and bays such that unnecessary fittings and pipe lengths can be avoided.

Notes

[1] 响应时间系数、喷水模式、操作组件类型和外观等一些特性方面的问题必须加以解决。

[2] 除非湿式自动喷水灭火系统总是充满水,否则无法运行。所以,为了防止水冻结,楼内温度必须保持在40°F以上。

[3] 自动喷水灭火系统通常以"树状"、"环状"、或者"网状"布局的。无论在什么情况下,喷头都直接连接到被称为支线的管线上。

References

[1] James L. Sipes. Sustainable Solutions for Water Resources. Hoboken:John Wiley &Sons, Inc., 2009.

[2] World Health Organization. Guidelines for Drinking-water Quality.Geneva :WHO Press, 2008.

[3] Patricia Wouters. National and International Water Law: Achieving Equitable and Sustainable Use of Water Resources. Water International, 2000,25(4):499~512.

[4] Mackenzie L. Davis. Water and wastewater engineering-design principles and practice. New York:McGraw-Hill, 2010.

[5] Prabhata K. Swamee and Ashok K. Sharma. Design of Water Supply Pipe Networks. Hoboken:John Wiley & Sons, 2008.

[6] Water Resources Planning - Manual of Water Supply Practices, M50 (2nd Edition). American Water Works Association (AWWA), 2007.

[7] Tebbutt THY. Principles of Water Quality Control. 5th Edition. Elsevier Science, 1998.

[8] Andrew Chadwick, John Morfett, Martin Borthwick, Hydraulics in Civil and Environmental Engineering. London:Spon Press,2004.

[9] Design Specifications and Requirements Manual. Environmental and Engineering Services Department, the Corporation of the City of London, Updated: December 2005.

[10] Smita S. Borchate et al. Application of Coagulation-Flocculation for Vegetable Tannery Wastewater, International Journal of Engineering Science and Technology (IJEST), 2012,4(5).

[11] Yan Jin. Use of A High Resolution Photographic Technique for Studying Coagulation/Flocculation in Water Treatment. Saskatoon: University of Saskatchewan, 2005.

[12] George Tchobanoglous, Franklin L.Burton, H.David Stensel.Wastewater Engineering Treatment and Reuse. 4th ed.New York: McGraw-Hill,2003.

[13] Joanne E.Drinan and Frank E.Spellman.Water and Wastewater Treatment: A Guide for the Nonengineering Professional. Boca Raton CRC Press, 2012.

[14] Akbar Baghvand, Ali Daryabeigi Zand, Nasser Mehrdadi and Abdolreza Karbassi. Optimizing Coagulation Process for Low to High Turbidity Waters Using Aluminum and Iron Salts. American Journal of Environmental Sciences, 2010, 6 (5) 442-448.

[15] Alan C.Twort, Don D.Ratnayaka, Malcolm J.Brandt.Water Supply.Oxford:Elsevier Ltd., 2000.

[16] Syed R.Qasim. Wastewater Treatment Plants: Planning, Design, and Operation. Lancaster, PA:Technomic Publishing Company, 1999.

[17] BSI (British Standards Institution), Robert H. Garrett. Hot and cold water supply [M]. 3rd Edition. London: Wiley-Blackwell, 2008.

[18] 上海市建设和管理委员会. 建筑给水排水设计规范 GB 50015—2003（英文版）[M]. 北京：中国建筑工业出版社, 2007.

[19] Greeno BA(Hons.) FCIOB FIPHE FRSA Roger. Building Services Handbook. Sixth Edition: Incorporating Current Building & Construction Regulations, Butterworth-Heinemann, 2011.

[20] Fire Service Pump Operator: Principles and Practice.Mississauga,Ontario: Jones & Bartlett Publishers,2009.

[21] Frederick S.Merritt and Jonathan T. Ricketts.Building Design and Construction Handbook.Sixth edition.New York:McGraw-Hill,2001.

[22] N. F. Gray. Drinking Water Quality: Problems and Solutions, Second editions. Cambridge: Cambridge University Press, 2008.